Better Money

The recent rise of dollar, pound, and euro inflation rates has rekindled the debate over potential alternative monies, particularly gold and Bitcoin. Though Bitcoin has been much discussed in recent years, a basic understanding of how it and gold would work as monetary standards is rare. Accessibly written by a pioneering economist, *Better Money* explains and evaluates gold, fiat, and Bitcoin standards without hype. White uses simple supply-and-demand analysis to explain how these standards work, evaluating their relative merits and explaining their response to shocks, allowing for informed comparisons between them. This book addresses common misunderstandings of the gold standard and Bitcoin, using historical evidence to review the history of money with emphasis on the contest between market and government provision. Known for his work on alternative monetary institutions, White offers a reasoned discussion of which standard is most likely to provide a better money.

Lawrence H. White is Professor of Economics at George Mason University. He has pioneered research on private monetary systems since before Bitcoin, authoring *Free Banking in Britain* (1984), *Competition and Currency* (1989), and *The Theory of Monetary Institutions* (1999). He is also author of *The Clash of Economic Ideas* (2012).

Better Money

Gold, Fiat, or Bitcoin?

LAWRENCE H. WHITE
George Mason University, Virginia

CAMBRIDGE
UNIVERSITY PRESS

Shaftesbury Road, Cambridge CB2 8EA, United Kingdom

One Liberty Plaza, 20th Floor, New York, NY 10006, USA

477 Williamstown Road, Port Melbourne, VIC 3207, Australia

314–321, 3rd Floor, Plot 3, Splendor Forum, Jasola District Centre, New Delhi – 110025, India

103 Penang Road, #05–06/07, Visioncrest Commercial, Singapore 238467

Cambridge University Press is part of Cambridge University Press & Assessment, a department of the University of Cambridge.

We share the University's mission to contribute to society through the pursuit of education, learning and research at the highest international levels of excellence.

www.cambridge.org
Information on this title: www.cambridge.org/9781009327473

DOI: 10.1017/9781009327466

First published 2023

A catalogue record for this publication is available from the British Library

A Cataloging-in-Publication data record for this book is available from the Library of Congress

ISBN 978-1-009-32747-3 Hardback
ISBN 978-1-009-32745-9 Paperback

To Neera, meri jaan

Contents

Contents

Figures

Acknowledgments

I thank the Eudaimonia Institute at Wake Forest University and particularly Professor James Otteson for a visiting fellowship that enabled this project to get underway. I thank the Mercatus Center at George Mason University for ongoing support. For constructive criticism I am grateful to: Neera Badhwar, Jim Epstein, Virgil Storr, Peter Boettke, and other participants in the Philosophy, Politics, and Economics workshop of the Mercatus Center; and participants in a manuscript workshop organized by the American Institute for Economic Research (AIER): Carola Binder, Nicolas Cachanosky, Nic Carter, Nick Curott, Bryan Cutsinger, Jerry Dwyer, Cameron Harwick, Thomas Hogan, Jerry Jordan, Lydia Mashburn, Allison Reichel, George Selgin, Scott Sumner, and Craig Warmke. I thank the AIER's Reagan Sobel and Brad DeVos for organizing the workshop. Juan Carlos Ortega helped to prepare the index. All of the above are blameless for errors and infelicities that remain.

Introduction

In the mining town of Tumeremo, Venezuela, according to 2021 news story, grocery shops accept payment in flakes of uncoined gold. The shops post prices in gold grams as well as in US dollars and have scales for weighing gold on the checkout counter. A local hotel-keeper estimates that two-thirds of retail transactions in the town are made in gold (Vasquez and Fieser 2021). Meanwhile, some urban Venezuelans have switched in recent years to earning (often by working online for international clients) and spending in Bitcoin (Hernandez 2019). Bitcoin can reportedly be spent at "fast food chains Pizza Hut and Church's Chicken as well as some supermarkets" and shopping malls (Ellsworth 2021).

Venezuelans who choose to transact in gold or Bitcoin are choosing better money. The inflation rate in the national fiat money, the bolívar, was 2959.8 percent in 2020 and 686.4 percent in 2021, according to the Central Bank of Venezuela (Armas 2022). At 2000 percent inflation per year, a currency loses half of its purchasing power every five weeks. Triple-digit inflation has led Venezuelan businesses and families to switch most of their transactions into US dollars. Popular dollarization has been observed elsewhere in Latin America with high inflation in recent decades. The use of gold and Bitcoin is something new.

In countries with bad official money – like present-day Venezuela, Lebanon, Zimbabwe, Turkey, and Argentina – workers and shoppers have to think daily about how to get hold of a better money. Very high inflation brings an eventual switch to better money only at a high cost, deranging the economy in the process of destroying the official currency (Heymann and Leijonhufvud 1995, ch. 5). The inflation rate can rise with surprising speed: Argentina had 9.8 percent inflation rate in 2006 but 25.7 percent the following year (Cachanosky 2022). A reasoned public discussion of alternative monies *before* high inflation occurs may facilitate a lower-cost switch to a better money. This book aims to contribute to the discussion. And to do so now, while dollar and euro inflation rates are higher than before but still below double digits.

What does it mean to call one money "better" than another? My approach is *non-paternalistic*, meaning: We rank monies according to the preferences of money-users. We do not consult only the criteria of macroeconomic policymakers, as in the standard approach to "optimal currency areas." Ideally, we can imagine a representative potential money-user in an abstract setting without an incumbent money, informed by local and global monetary history, ranking candidate monetary standards according to their likely performance. The performance that most money-holders seem to care about is some combination of (a) serving them individually as a convenient and low-cost medium of exchange, which favors non-declining and predictable purchasing power, and (b) the monetary system as a whole having desired properties like avoiding depressions associated with severe monetary disequilibria.

The questions motivating this book are straightforward: Given that our inherited discretionary fiat monetary regimes have performed imperfectly, and lately seem to be getting worse, might an alternative system – a commodity money or a cryptocurrency – do better? If so, which alternative is the most promising? To make useful comparisons and contrasts we need to spell out not only how each standard operates in theory, but what their historical track records tell us. Too often defenders of one monetary standard compare an *ideal* version of it to the *actual* performance of another standard. It is fair to contrast an ideal version of one standard to the ideal version of another, but for real-world relevance, we also need to compare actual historical experiences across standards, warts and all.

To discuss fiat, gold, and Bitcoin as alternative monetary *standards* is to emphasize the behavior of the purchasing power of the monetary unit, which includes considering the institutional structure of money production insofar as that matters for stability. A monetary standard is defined by the good in which prices are expressed (the "medium of account") and contracts are ultimately settled (the "medium of redemption").[1] In a fiat US dollar standard, prices are expressed in USD and settled in base

---

[1] These two roles are normally played by the same good (White 1984a).

dollars (Federal Reserve Notes or bank reserves on the books of the Fed). Production of base dollars by a central bank is implied, while a competitive banking system may issue dollar-redeemable transaction deposits. In a gold coin standard, prices are expressed in units of coined gold mass and settled in gold coins. The model in Chapter 2 assumes a competitive global gold mining industry, production of full-weight coins at negligible cost, and a competitive banking system that issues gold-redeemable banknotes and transaction deposits. In a Bitcoin standard, prices are expressed in BTC and settled in Bitcoin. Growth in the stock of Bitcoin proceeds according to a release schedule programmed into the original source code. "Second-layer" payment systems that settle on the Bitcoin blockchain, a recent development, can be assumed.

In the two decades before 2007, all seemed well in the world of fiat monetary institutions. A common view among economists was that central banks in developed economies had conquered inflation and tamed the business cycle. It was the period of the Great Moderation. Research on alternative systems, having flourished after the high-inflation years of the 1970s and early 1980s, no longer attracted as much attention.

Then came the global financial crisis of 2007–2009, followed by sovereign debt crises among several members of the Eurozone. In 2009, objecting to bank bailouts and a history of bad monetary policy, a pseudonymous programmer named "Satoshi Nakamoto" launched Bitcoin. Other cryptocurrency projects soon followed. Although so far used more often as an investment than as a transaction medium, Bitcoin today has established itself around the world as a niche medium of exchange for payments that need to be routed around censorship by central banks. It has the *potential* to serve as a global monetary standard. Meanwhile, new enterprises are adopting the blockchain technology that Bitcoin introduced to make gold more readily spendable, either in circulating token form (gold stablecoins) or in online-transferable deposit form (gold account balances), lowering one barrier to re-emergence of a private gold standard. Now is a good time to think about whether one of these alternative monetary standards would be better than the status quo fiat standard.

Our focus here is on the choice among alternative standards – gold versus fiat versus Bitcoin – rather than on ways to reform monetary policy under existing fiat money standards.[2] Gold will here stand in for

---

[2] Discussions of fiat policy reform can be found in many other books, including Boettke, Salter, and Smith (2021); Taylor (2019); Guttman (2016); and White, Vanburg, and Köhler (2015).

commodity standards generally and Bitcoin for cryptocurrencies generally. For reasons explored in the following text, they are the leading candidates in their categories to become more widely adopted as money in the future.

My interest in monetary alternatives goes back to the earliest stages of my career (White 1984a, 1984b). My interest was piqued by F. A. Hayek's thought-provoking monograph *The Denationalisation of Money* (1976). Responding to the double-digit inflation of the 1970s, Hayek proposed that we should not expect good money from fiat-issuing central banks with national monopolies in the provision of basic money, just as we do not expect high-quality goods or services from other government-chartered monopolies like the Post Office. My earliest research studied the historical choice between central banking and free banking but did not directly consider the choice among alternative standards. More recently, I have written on the contrast between gold and fiat standards (White 2015). The present book considers the choice among three alternative standards, synthesizing earlier work and adding Bitcoin to the contest.

The approach taken here is analytical, not alarmist. Inflation has risen, but most countries are not on the verge of a hyperinflationary collapse of their fiat monies. Understanding how a gold standard or a bitcoin standard would work is nonetheless relevant for contingency planning at the very least. The potential alternative monies have been in the news, but they are seldom discussed by academic economists in journals or books. They are little understood outside "goldbug" and "Bitcoiner" communities. Gold-standard advocates too seldom understand Bitcoin, and Bitcoin advocates too seldom understand the gold standard. If nothing else, thinking about alternative monies can give us a better understanding of the status quo fiat monetary regime. But perhaps the main reason to critically evaluate alternative monies is prudential. It will help to understand their advantages and disadvantages in the event, however unlikely, that inflation gets out of hand in more than just a few fiat currencies. Should the unfortunate day arrive when we find that the status quo is failing, we will need to choose which monetary regime is the best option going forward.

I.I THE CHAPTERS AHEAD

Chapter 1 summarizes the broad sweep of monetary history, from barter to commodity money to the switch from the classical international gold standard to national fiat standards. It emphasizes the contrast between market provision and government provision of money, arguing from historical evidence that the "state theory of money" is false: Market institutions gave rise to money and have successfully provided it in many forms.

Chapter 2 uses supply-and-demand diagrams to examine the operation of gold standard. It explains what determines the purchasing power and quantity of monetary gold, and how market forces stabilize the purchasing power of gold in response to demand disturbances and certain supply disturbances. The chapter also discusses the "resource costs" of a gold standard, the expenditure of labor and capital to extract and coin gold.

Chapter 3 debunks academic and popular misconceptions about the gold standard, both by its critics and by its defenders. Misconceptions include: "The Gold Standard caused the Great Depression" and "The volatility of the price of gold in recent years shows that gold would be an unstable monetary standard" and "A gold standard provides a perfectly stable measure of value, like a yardstick provides a stable measure of length, because it fixes the definition of the monetary unit."

Chapter 4 describes the historical origins of fiat money and analyzes the determination of its quantity and purchasing power using supply-and-demand analysis. It emphasizes theoretical and historical contrasts with the gold standard. The chapter also discusses the resource cost of a fiat standard, especially the expenditure of labor and capital to hedge against inflation and uncertainty.

Chapter 5 examines the operation of Bitcoin, by far the leading cryptocurrency. After sketching its history and operating features, it discusses Bitcoin's pros and cons as a potential monetary standard. It uses supply-and-demand analysis to explain the volatility of Bitcoin's purchasing power and who bears the cost of the Bitcoin system.

Chapter 6 compares and contrasts gold and Bitcoin as potential monetary standards. Gold and Bitcoin supply-and-demand diagrams from earlier chapters are brought side by side to explain the greater purchasing-power volatility of Bitcoin in the short run and especially in the long run. Legal obstacles facing gold and Bitcoin as media of exchange are compared and contrasted. The differences between the two standards in censorship resistance are also considered, in relation to the question of which standard is more likely to be adopted should fiat monies break down. The policy conclusion is not a blueprint for top-down monetary reform but a plea to let potential monies compete freely on a legally level playing field.

I

Markets and Governments in the History of Money

Some commentators and policymakers, apparently innocent of monetary history, have declared that better money and finance has always, and can only, come from greater government control. Consider the statement made in July 2021 by Congressman Jim Himes (Democrat, Connecticut), a member of a newly formed House Financial Services Committee working group on regulating digital finance: "There is not a single shred of evidence over many centuries that new financial systems or new systems of currency grow organically in an unregulated way and lead to good outcomes" (quoted by Michaels and Ackerman 2021). There is, in fact, a mountain of evidence. This chapter documents beneficial organic monetary evolution in history, providing the very sort of evidence that the Congressman says does not exist.

The prominent Princeton financial historian Harold James (2018), in a commentary on "The Bitcoin Threat," errs almost as badly when he writes that money "has almost always been an expression of sovereignty as well, and private currencies have been very rare." In fact, the historical development of silver- and gold-based payment systems was driven largely by private initiative. While sovereign rulers have historically commandeered the coinage, private currencies in the form of banknotes were the most popular form of payment in the nineteenth century, and their introduction preceded government paper currencies. Today, private banknotes survive in a few places (Scotland, Northern Ireland, Hong Kong, and Macau) where their issue has not been monopolized, and cryptocurrency payment systems operate without government participation. While *fiat* money (non-commodity money issued by government) represents an expression of sovereignty, gold and Bitcoin do not require the imprimatur of the state to serve as money.

To provide a foundation for discussing whether a future private gold or Bitcoin standard may be better than a fiat standard, we first establish that a private monetary system is viable. This chapter offers historical evidence that the origins of money and the development of better monetary institutions have stemmed from private initiative rather than from government.

1.1 THE ORIGINS OF MONEY: MARKET VERSUS STATE THEORIES

A long tradition of economic thought recognizes money as a market-born institution. The Scottish moral philosopher and economist Adam Smith proposed in his justly celebrated work *The Wealth of Nations* (1982 [1776]) that money arose from the initiative of traders in markets. He hypothesized that as people became increasingly specialized in production, and began to trade for (rather than make at home) most of the goods they wanted to consume, they found it advantageous to offer in payment not only whatever commodities they produced (which might have relatively few consumers) but commodities that other traders would more readily take:

[E]very prudent man in every period of society, after the first establishment of the division of labour, must naturally have endeavoured to manage his affairs in such a manner as to have at all times by him, besides the peculiar produce of his own industry, a certain quantity of some one commodity or other, such as he imagined few people would be likely to refuse in exchange for the produce of their industry.

In other words, traders discovered the advantages of *indirect* exchange using popular commodities as *media of exchange*. Smith listed oxen, salt, shells, dried fish, tobacco, sugar, animal hides, leather, and "rude bars" of metal as media of exchange used at various times and places.

The market-born theory was spelled out more systematically by the Austrian economist Carl Menger (2002 [1909]). Menger noted that it pays a trader, once he or she grasps the advantage of using more widely accepted commodities in trade, to learn which commodities were the *most* widely accepted at that time and place. When offered a choice, the alert trader prefers to be paid in the more widely accepted medium. Traders who are not so alert to wider market conditions can simply observe what commodities their successful neighbors accept and imitate their practice. Each trader (whether alertly or imitatively) who joins the set of people accepting salt (say) in payment enlarges the set of salt accepters and thereby attracts still more joiners. Popularity as a medium of exchange is self-reinforcing. When a trading network converges on a particular commodity, that commodity becomes a *commonly accepted medium of exchange*, which is the standard definition of money. No participant, no chamber of commerce, no committee of experts, and no government bureau has to organize the convergence or aim at the result. In this way, the social convention of treating a particular commodity as money emerged without top-down direction.

The market-born or Mengerian view of money has lately been challenged by a resurgence of the "state theory of money," also known as Chartalism, which maintains that governments played an essential role in the historical establishment of money. Randall Wray (2009) puts it bluntly: "The monetary system, itself, was invented to mobilize resources to serve what government perceived to be the public purpose."

Chartalists have made the valid point that *extensive* specialization in production could not have preceded the development of media of exchange. It would be foolish for a farmer to specialize in growing a single crop that few neighbors want to consume while direct exchange still prevails, because it would be very difficult to trade that crop directly for all the other things that the farmer wants. Greater specialization and wider acceptance of media of exchange must have developed together. This is a useful qualification but not a refutation of the Mengerian theory. A classroom lecturer spelling out the Mengerian theory may (and I have done this myself) ask the listener to imagine an asparagus farmer entering a moneyless market and meeting frustration in attempts to trade the asparagus directly for a plaid shirt. But this way of dramatizing the difficulty of direct barter should not be taken for the claim that, historically, societies developed extensive specialization and trade before the emergence of money. Indeed, because it starts from the premise that it is very difficult to find a trading partner who has what you want *and* wants what you have, Menger's theory suggests the opposite. As Adam Smith emphasized, the division of labor (specialization) is limited by the extent of the market. The extent of the market is limited by the ease of trade.[1]

The classic source of the Chartalist view is *The State Theory of Money* (1973 [1924]) by the German economist George Friedrich Knapp.[2] But Knapp's rejection of a market-evolutionary account, it appears on closer

---

[1] Selgin (2016) defends Smith and Menger against a Chartalist critic, anthropologist David Graeber (2011a).

[2] For a survey of "major figures whose work was important in building a modern version of Chartalism," see Wray (2014).

inspection, is more a matter of wordplay than of substance. Rather than regarding "money" in the conventional way as any medium of exchange commonly accepted in the market, and so viewing the explanatory challenge as how to account for a particular commodity coming to play that role, Knapp focused his attention on what he calls *public* money. The test of a *public* money, in his words, is that "the money is accepted in payments made to the State's offices," namely in fines and tax payments. Knapp (1973, p. 95) declared: "State acceptance delimits the monetary system." While Knapp (1973, p. 134) recognized that privately issued banknotes were widely used, he classified them as falling outside the system of *public* money and then proceeded to treat them as unimportant. A note-issuing private bank and its customers "form, so to speak, a private pay community; the public pay community is the State."

In other words, a purely market process cannot endow a payment medium with state acceptance. Only the state can do that. True enough, a Mengerian would reply, but this does nothing to contradict Menger's account of how a commonly accepted means of payment arises in a market economy without state action. In a classic money and banking textbook, the economist Charles A. Conant (1905, vol. 1, p. 128) points to the Old Testament (Genesis 23:16), where Abraham is said to make a payment in "current money with the merchant," and observes that this language "shows that it was the mercantile community, and not the government, which determined the standard."

In his best-selling book *Debt: The First 5000 Years*, the late anthropologist David Graeber criticizes Menger's theory of the origin of money for promoting what Graeber calls "the myth of barter." The economists' talk about money being preceded by barter, Graeber (2011a, p. 213) writes, is "absurd when applied to transactions between neighbors in the same small rural community" or to transfers mediated by religious temples. Transactions there were conducted with credit or record-keeping systems, not by hand-to-hand spot exchanges. But Menger's theory need not deny a role to credit or other record-keeping systems in communities where one knew and could trust one's trading partners to repay or return favors in kind.[3] Credit with repayment in kind is intertemporal barter, so including its role in pre-monetary exchange broadens rather than

---

[3] Indeed, as Selgin (2016) notes, Menger explicitly recognized that before individual property and spot exchange there were "tribal and family no-exchange economies" characterized by "[v]oluntary as well as compulsory unilateral transfers of assets ... occasionally based on tacitly recognized reciprocity."

refutes Menger's scenario of barter preceding money (Watson 2022, p. 9). Money emerges rather where familiarity and trust are absent, where credit is not feasible, that is, where one trades with strangers. Graeber (2011a, p. 213) himself granted the point. The full sentence, of which a fragment was quoted above, reads: "The economists' barter scenario might be absurd when applied to transactions between neighbors in the same small rural community, but when dealing with strangers it suddenly begins to make sense." He continues:

For much of human history, then, an ingot of gold or silver, stamped or not, has served the same role as the contemporary drug dealer's suitcase full of unmarked bills: an object without a history, valuable because one knows it will be accepted in exchange for other goods just about anywhere, no questions asked.

Some Chartalists focus not on the origin of the earliest money but on the origin of *standardized currency*. In the words of sympathetic economist Charles Goodhart (1998), Chartalists "argue that the use of currency was based essentially on the *power of the issuing authority* ... – i.e., that currency becomes money primarily because the coins or monetary instruments more widely are struck with the insignia of sovereignty." The claim that state power or sovereignty is an *essential* or *primary* condition for any currency to become a commonly accepted medium of exchange is, however, plainly at odds with the historical fact that privately issued banknotes without sovereign guarantees were the dominant media of exchange in the eighteenth and nineteenth centuries where they were allowed. It is also inconsistent with the fact that privately minted silver and gold coins were widely accepted when and where they were allowed (which was rarer), as in gold-rush California (White 2022) and apparently in ancient Lydia where some of the earliest coins were struck. More on these episodes follows. And, tellingly, an account of moneyness founded on insignias of sovereignty is plainly at odds with early non-manufactured monies like shells and salt, which bore no insignias.

Besides its defining function of serving as a commonly accepted medium of exchange, money characteristically also serves as the medium in which prices are posted and account books are kept. A unit of money (ounce, pound, or dollar) serves as the economy's "unit of account." Wray (2004), a modern Chartalist, writes: "Denominating payments in a unit of account would simplify matters—but would require a central authority"; and "Orthodoxy has never been able to explain how individual utility maximizers settled on a single numeraire." But decentralized private initiative also drives the use of a common unit of account (White 1984a). A seller of goods, say a donut maker, will ordinarily want to be paid in the commodity that she finds most useful as a medium of exchange, rather than something less widely accepted or less convenient to carry, so that she can most readily buy the donut shop's inputs and (with the income that remains) the bundle of goods that she wants to consume. For her customers' convenience and her own, she will denominate her shop's prices in units of silver if silver is the preferred medium of exchange. She could conceivably post prices in bushels of wheat, while wanting to be paid in silver, but that would drive away customers by imposing on them the burden of knowing today's exchange rate between silver and wheat. She will likewise want to keep her account books in units of silver when silver is the medium in which her income is received and expenditures are made. Although using bushels of wheat is again conceivable, it would impose additional information and computation costs. As they converge on a common medium of exchange, individual traders thus converge on a common pricing and accounting unit. The practice of using the medium of exchange as a unit of account arises as a social convention, without requiring a central authority.

1.2 WHY SILVER AND GOLD BECAME THE DOMINANT COMMODITY MONIES

In ancient Europe and Asia, silver and gold became the most popular commodity monies, out of a large set of contenders that included salt, cowrie shells, copper beads, and oxen.[4] Menger's approach offers a satisfying explanation of why silver and gold emerged as the most commonly accepted media of exchange, pushing other candidate commodities to the margins. Put yourself in the position of a trader in a market where there are a variety of commodity exchange media available (the market has not yet converged). You swap your produce for some other commodity that you then carry around with you until you spend away parts of it making purchases. In this situation, it pays you not only to consider which commodities are popular with many other traders but also which ones are easy to store and carry, divide, and trade away. As Menger (1892, p. 248) put it, a trader seeking a medium of exchange with "a wide range of saleableness both in time and place" would prefer commodities characterized by "costliness, easy transportability, and fitness for preservation."

Textbooks a century ago emphasized that the precious metals have a number of properties that make them better hand-to-hand media of

---

[4] Szabo (2002) provides a valuable account of the early monies and proto-monies.

exchange than other commodities. Silver and gold score high on (1) portability or preciousness, allowing you to carry around high purchasing power with little bulk or weight; (2) durability, not spoiling or eroding away between the date of acquisition and the date of spending; (3) divisibility and fusibility, allowing pieces to be made in a range of sizes to suit a range of transaction values, and allowing change to be given; (4) stability in purchasing power across the seasons, unlike foodstuffs that are cheap right after the harvest but dear six months later; and (5) uniformity or readily recognizable quality, once trustworthy coinage has been introduced. These properties enhanced their widespread acceptance.

Menger's theory assures us that some monetary standard will spontaneously emerge from the market through the process of self-reinforcing popularity, but some economists have worried that the theory does not assure us that the commodity on which the market converges will be the best of the available candidates. They worry that the process could converge on any commodity that accidentally got a head start in popularity, even if less suitable than others.[5] Once we take into account the physical properties that people want in a hand-to-hand medium of exchange, however, we have some assurance that the money chosen will be among the best candidates from the typical user's perspective. In choosing among potential exchange media that have widespread popularity, an alert trader will prefer to accept, and keep on hand to offer to other traders, commodities that have the physical properties (portability, divisibility, and so on) that serve not just his or her personal preferences but also provide the properties that *other traders* are likely to want in their exchange media. Even if I personally like salt and don't mind the extra bulk, I won't try to use salt as a medium of exchange if other traders prefer the lesser bulk of silver or gold. The trader's aim is to have a medium that will be most readily taken by other traders, after all.

When an isolated economy that uses a bulkier or less durable money (e.g., medieval Sweden had a copper standard) begins to trade with foreigners who use a better money, those involved in external trade have reason to adopt the better money. From them it can spread to the rest of the economy. In this way, convergence on a commodity money involves a social winnowing process. Commodities that are found more suitable to use will tend to prevail over those found less suitable. And "what people

[5] Kirzner (1992); for counterpoint, see White (2002).

prefer to use" is the only non-paternalistic criterion we have for being the most suitable.

1.3 THE INTRODUCTION OF COINAGE[6]

An important technical advance came with the introduction of coinage. Some of the earliest known coins appeared in the ancient civilization of Lydia, located in what is now Turkey, during the seventh-century BCE. By contrast to raw nuggets straight from the mine or river, or even variously refined precious metal bars, coined silver and gold pieces from reputable mints enjoyed a major advantage: They were manufactured to be uniform in weight and fineness (percentage of pure precious metal). When coins were reliably up to standard, traders did not need to be expert assayers of precious metals or incur the cost of hiring an expert to test the pieces offered (because the risk from not testing was negligible). At most they needed to weigh visibly worn coins.

The evidence is not definitive (there is debate among numismatic historians about this), but it indicates that many of the earliest Lydian coiners were private individuals. Perhaps they were precious metal merchants or other rich businessmen, who could more easily spend their own metals after converting irregular pieces into uniform pieces, or perhaps they were metalsmiths, who had the know-how and could charge others for the service. Since they serve the convenience of traders, it is likely that coins were already in use before political authorities established their own mints (or commandeered existing mints). Why then would ancient monarchs operate their own mints and outlaw private competitors? The historical record suggests that they did so mostly to have a lucrative source of revenue from monopoly minting fees and from debasement. As a bonus, some took advantage of the opportunity to stamp their own faces on the coins.

The online *Ancient History Encyclopedia* (van der Crabben 2011) states: "It appears that many early Lydian coins were minted by merchants as tokens to be used in trade transactions. The Lydian state also minted coins." Regarding Lydian coins inscribed with the names Walwel and Kalil, the British Museum (n.d.) website remarks: "It is unclear whether these are names of kings or just rich men who produced the earliest coins." Numismatic historian David Schaps (2006) points out that

---

[6] This section draws on White (2018b).

there are "some twenty" types of markings on Lydian coins, and twenty is "many more than the two or three kings who reigned from the time coins were invented until the end of the Lydian empire." He considers it "the prevailing opinion" among experts that the markings "identify not the king under whom they were struck, but the producer of the coin—perhaps a royal functionary, more likely an independent gold merchant."[7]

The French numismatic historian Ernest Babelon (1897, pp. 91–92) remarks that "the individual and private guarantee" on pieces of precious metal everywhere preceded the guarantee of the State, "in the historical and natural evolution of monetary invention."[8] He continues:

But if, in the social state that was that of all peoples before the appearance of the currency of State, no legislative measure prevents anybody from having his monetary stamp, neither does the law intervene to give forced currency to the ingots thus punched. Merchants, bankers, goldsmiths, private individuals, may have their mark, just as well as a provincial governor, a head of state. It is the good reputation of a wealthy merchant that will give, on the market, credit to ingots bearing his name or emblem.

Coinage appears to have been independently invented around the same time in India, where coins were cut from sheets of silver and certified by punch marks, like old-fashioned train tickets. In additional to Imperial coins, Schaps (2006, p. 16) points to local Indian coins in the third-century BCE that "may have been issued either by local magnates or by merchants." He cites a contemporary written work indicating that "a private person could make coins as long as he took them to the [official] mint to be checked for weight and fineness, and to have the proper marks placed upon them. The survival of this practice in a period of radical centralization strongly suggests that the earliest coins were also made by merchants or silversmiths." Further written evidence that coins were privately issued comes from a monk named Buddhaghosa (quoted by Schaps 2006, p. 17), who wrote in the fifth-century CE that the typical Indian banker "knows all the varieties" of coins so well that he can identify which particular coins were made by which artisans in which locations.

With the spread of coinage throughout the ancient world, traders found silver and gold payments easier to make and to accept. The use of bulkier commodity monies like shells and salt dwindled when the areas

---

[7] For a complementary defense of the market origins of coinage by an economist against a Chartalist critic, see Selgin www.alt-m.org/2017/08/30/lord-keynes-contra-white-on-the-beginnings-of-coinage/.

[8] All quotations from Babelon are my own Google-aided translations.

where they circulated came into contact with traders offering silver and gold coins. Market convergence on the precious metals in coined form reflected a "survival of the fittest," a rise to dominance by the most suitable media for hand-to-hand exchange.

The top-down Chartalist approach is at a loss to explain how silver and gold became the dominant commodity monies.[9] In the Chartalist view, the sovereigns of various lands must have chosen to produce and promote coins made of silver and gold. But why would they? A Mengerian would reasonably suppose that ancient rulers adopted the precious metals because they, like other transactors, were aware that coined pieces of silver and gold were already popular, and embodied better than other commodities the useful properties of portability, divisibility, durability, and so on. If so, then rulers did not originate or alter the choice of precious metallic standards but merely *reinforced the market* in the standardization process already underway.

Chartalists, by contrast, suggest that ancient rulers *invented* coinage. For example, Wray (2000, p. 46) has written: "Coins appear to have originated as government 'pay tokens' (in Knapp's colourful phrase), as nothing more than evidence of debt." The late anthropologist David Graeber, author of *Debt: The First 5000 Years*, stated in an interview (Graeber 2011b) that

... coinage seems to be invented or at least widely popularized to pay soldiers – more or less simultaneously in China, India, and the Mediterranean, where governments find the easiest way to provision the troops is to issue them standard-issue bits of gold or silver and then demand everyone else in the kingdom give them one of those coins back again.

Graeber and Wray see early silver and gold coins as state-issued taxanticipation tokens, their value resting on the state's requiring that subjects to pay them back to the state in taxes.

It doesn't make sense for governments to use bits of gold or silver as the material for their pay tokens, however, rather than something cheaper, say bits of iron or copper or even paper impressed with sovereign emblems. Use as "government pay tokens" therefore doesn't provide an economically logical account for the emergence of silver and gold coins. In the Mengerian market-evolutionary account, preciousness is an advantage in a medium of exchange because it lowers the costs of transporting any given sum of purchasing power. In a Chartalist pay-token account, preciousness is a *dis*advantage – it raises the costs of the material used to

---

[9] Here I draw on White (2018c).

pay the troops – and so is not a sensible choice. Remember that the value of the tokens is supposed to come from the sovereign imprint, not from the material that is imprinted. Issuing tokens made of something cheaper would accomplish the same purpose at lower cost to the sovereign.

Graeber uses the equivocal phrase "invented or at least widely popularized." Proposing that governments *promoted* the acceptance of coins, after the market economy had already begun using them, is very different from saying that governments *invented* coinage. Menger himself had no problem with the former proposition, but he rejected the latter as an unfounded prejudice.

Wray (2000, p. 46) suggests that kings likely minted coins "in the form of precious metal to reduce counterfeiting." But a sovereign imprint on silver or gold coins is not in any obvious way harder to counterfeit than the same imprint on iron or copper coins, or even on pieces of rawhide (as the general Frederick Augustus is said to have used temporarily as tokens in an emergency, later redeeming them in gold).[10] So Chartalism does not plausibly explain how silver and gold coins began or how they achieved dominance over other monies.

1.4 EARLY MEDIEVAL PRIVATE COINAGE

Private coinage proliferated in western Europe with the decentralization and weakening of political authority after the decline of the western Roman Empire. Babelon (1897, pp. 124, 127) comments on the period of the Merovingian dynasty (476 to 750 AD) in what is now France and western Germany:

No period of history has furnished, better than the Merovingian period, a striking application of our theory of private coinage. After the fall of the Roman Empire, in the midst of the great upheaval provoked in the West by the invasions of the barbarians, the sovereign right to coin money, which was exercised in Gaul in three imperial workshops, ceased to be respected. Whoever had gold in his possession arrogated to himself the right to convert it into money, imitating ... the types of the imperial currency, but substituting, as a guarantee to the public, his own name for that of the emperor.

By the end of the period, Gaul had:

three categories of coins: the royal coins, the coins of the churches, and finally the coins of the gold handlers and the goldsmiths who take the name of *monetarii* [coiners]. The last generally bear, on one side, the name of the locality where they were struck, and on the other side the name of the coiner. Such is their abundance that we know the names of twelve hundred Merovingian coiners, striking

---

[10] Juan de Mariana (2018 [1605], p. 19), citing Collentius, *History of Naples*, Book Four.

in more than eight hundred different localities. Royal and ecclesiastical coins are relatively rare.

Post-Roman dynasties were unable to reinstate a government monopoly on coinage for many centuries. Private entrepreneurs resumed the business of making coins. "Everyone can strike money, without control and at their personal initiative," in Babelon's (1897, pp. 126, 127) account of the era. Coiners put their own names on their products "to attest to the public the excellence of the weight and fineness of the gold and silver coin."[11]

1.5 VALUATION BY METALLIC CONTENT

The notion that full-weight silver and gold coins served mainly as tokens, deriving their value from the tax liabilities they could discharge, is contradicted by a raft of historical evidence.

In the Middle Ages, large-value silver and gold coins issued by a national mint often circulated well outside the set of the nation's taxpayers. For example, Spanish gold coins circulated well outside of Spain (Motomura 1994). These coins were valued as media of exchange by holders who had no tax obligations to the government of the issuing mint.

In both international and domestic markets, coins issued by various mints were routinely valued against one another in proportion to their precious metal content. The Spanish Jesuit scholar Juan de Mariana (2018, p. 19) observed in 1605 that "people do not value a currency any more than the quality and amount of metal allows—not even if there are strict laws against doing this." Medieval bankers were experts at assessing (by weighing and assaying) the silver and gold content of variously worn and debased coins. Doing so was such a large part of their business that the symbol bankers hung outside their doors was the balance scale. After weighing the silver coins that a customer brought in to deposit, the banker's common practice was to record the customer's new account balance in "ghost money" units: pure silver mass units not embodied in (and thus unaltered by the debasement of) any existing coin (Cipolla 1956, ch. 4).

Valuation by bullion weight continued the archaic Greek practice of using weighed bullion as money before the introduction of coinage (Kroll 2011). Schaps (2006, p. 6) notes that ancient "Greek and Indian coins certainly" derived their value "from the weight of metal they contained," while in China "the names and nominal values of the later coins are often those of weights," such as the *banliang* or "half-ouncer." The Chinese *tael* was also a weight unit. Many of the names of western monetary

---

[11] For a modern account of Merovingian coinage, see Grierson and Blackburn (1986).

units originally designated a mass of precious metal, such as the *pound sterling*, where the "pound" was the weight unit conventionally used in medieval trade fairs and "sterling" denotes an alloy that is 92.5 percent silver mixed with 7.5 percent copper or other metals to make it harder than pure silver. Charlemagne's *livre* (from the Latin weight unit *librum*) was a monetary unit designating one pound of silver. The German *mark* and the Spanish *peso* (from the Latin *pensum* or weight) were likewise measures of mass used for precious metals. Thomas Jefferson in his *Plan for Establishing Uniformity in the Coinage, Weights, and Measures of the United States* (Jefferson 1790) understandably proposed "that the quantity of pure silver in the money unit be expressed in parts of the weights so defined."

Non-debasing mints conformed to the market's valuation by mass, denominating silver coins in proportion to their unworn silver content. In other words, they put proportionally more silver into higher-denomination coins. There is no reason to observe such correspondence of precious metal content to face value in tax-anticipation tokens.

The practice of denomination by mass began with the very earliest coiners in ancient Lydia, who made coins of electrum, a silver–gold alloy. The British Museum (n.d.) comments: "Although irregular in size and shape, these early electrum coins were minted according to a strict weight-standard. The denominations ranged from one stater (weighing about 14.1 grams) down through half-staters, thirds, sixths, twelfths, 1/24ths and 1/48ths to 1/96th stater (about 0.15gm)." In 1351, a standard English silver penny contained double the silver (18 grains) of a standard halfpenny (9 grains), and one-fourth the silver of a standard four-pence groat (72 grains) (Kelleher et al., n.d.). In the years before the Royal Mint, mint began producing farthings (quarter-pennies) and half-pennies, change for a penny was made by cutting it into quarter pieces or half pieces. All of these practices point to a market-based source of acceptance and a metallic-mass-based valuation of silver and gold coins, not a state-based or tax-discharging source of valuation.

The idea that a gold or silver coin had market purchasing power in proportion to its bullion content is consistent with the idea that the original purpose of coining silver and gold was to certify the mass of pure metal in a piece (rather than to produce government pay-tokens). Following the terminology used by Joseph A. Schumpeter in his *History of Economic Analysis*, the view that precious metal coins were valued according to their metallic content is sometimes called *Theoretical*

Metallism. Schumpeter (1954, p. 288) wrote: "By Theoretical Metallism we denote the theory that it is logically essential for money to consist of, or to be 'covered' by, some commodity so that the logical source of the exchange value or purchasing power of money is the exchange value or purchasing power of that commodity, considered independently of its monetary role." But Schumpeter's statement carries two pieces of excess baggage. That pieces of precious metallic money are valued by content (in a metallic monetary system) does not imply that non-commodity money with positive value (in a fiat money or Bitcoin system) is impossible. The "logically essential" part of Theoretical Metallism as defined by Schumpeter is obviously false in light of our practical experience in recent decades with fiat monies and cryptocurrencies. Nor does it make sense to imply that global monetary demand is irrelevant to determining silver's or gold's purchasing power.

To be more precise about valuation by weight, the purchasing power of a gold coin was equal to its pure gold mass in grams, multiplied by the purchasing power of gold bullion per gram, plus a premium over the bullion value corresponding to the value of the greater spendability that coinage provides. In a competitive minting industry equilibrium, the premium corresponds to the marginal cost of minting. The existence of a premium is not evidence for the state theory of money, because privately minted coins exhibit a premium in the same way that state-minted coins do. The purchasing power in goods and services of one gram of gold bullion was determined by the total supply and demand for gold (encompassing both its monetary and its nonmonetary uses), as explained in detail in Chapter 2. For silver coins, replace "gold" with "silver" in the previous sentences of the present paragraph.

What explains the valuation of paper banknotes that contained no gold or silver? Banknotes were redeemable *claims* to gold or silver coins. In cities where a bank's notes could easily and surely be redeemed at face value, and in towns where they were in sufficient demand by people heading to such cities, they traded at values equal to those of the silver or gold coins to which they were claims. In countries like Canada where issuing banks were allowed to establish a wide-ranging branch network for par acceptance and redemption, the area of par circulation in the nineteenth century was wide. In the antebellum United States, by contrast, legal restrictions against establishing branch banking networks made redemption difficult and unsure away from the home city of an issuing bank. Its notes then naturally fell below par away from home.

They did not commonly *circulate* below par, which would have been a computational hassle for users, but could be sold at a discount to specialist note dealers.[12]

Underweight and worn coins can also trade at par, above the market value of their metallic content plus an ordinary mint premium, like banknotes stamped on metal, if they are redeemable claims to full-bodied standard coins. Redeemability thus explains what seem to be exceptions to valuation by metallic content. In the United States, for example, silver alloy coins (dollars, quarters, dimes) circulated at par with gold coins (5, 10, and 20 dollars) even as the market value of silver fell relative to gold, and even when worn. Nickel-alloy 5-cent coins and copper cents continuously circulated at face value despite variations in the market price of nickel and copper. The key is that 5 dollars' worth of worn silver coins, nickels, or cents could be redeemed for a 5-dollar gold coin. Political forces – such as the desire to subsidize silver producers – help to explain why the US Mint continued to put any silver at all into dollar, quarter-dollar, and ten-cent coins after the Gold Standard Act of 1900 officially ended the "bimetallic" era.

Under "bimetallism," two different metals were simultaneously and often inconsistently used to define the monetary unit. Bimetallism was never a market-evolved system, but always a system imposed by a government that monopolized the mints. The US government (for example) defined the "dollar" as 23.22 grains of gold *and*, at the same time, as 371.25 grains of silver. It produced both full-bodied gold coins and full-bodied silver coins. Market evolution, by contrast, yields either mono-metallism, under which a single metal serves as the standard and the exclusive material for full-bodied coins, or parallel metallic standards with a freely floating market exchange rate between the metals. The next chapter will consider bimetallism in more detail.

Valuation by metallic content or metallic redemption value cannot, of course, explain the positive purchasing power of money that has no metallic basis, namely fiat money or cryptocurrency. The purchasing power of fiat money or cryptocurrency depends on supply and demand, in ways to be examined in Chapters 4 and 5 on fiat and cryptocurrency standards. Chartalism suggests that money's value generally rests on its acceptance in tax payments by the state. While state acceptance no doubt adds to the demand for any money, it does not follow that demand is zero without it, or that the money's market value does not fall as its supply expands.

[12] Gorton (1999) describes the non-par pricing of antebellum banknotes by distance and risk.

The case of Bitcoin, which as of 2022 only El Salvador accepts in taxes, shows us that the demand for irredeemable non-metallic money need not rest on the collection of taxes or the enforcement of legal tender status.

1.6 GOVERNMENTS MONOPOLIZED THE MINTS – AND DEBASED THE COINAGE[13]

Ancient rulers seeking a source of revenue granted themselves a legal monopoly on the minting business (Burns 1965), a policy followed by most (but not all) governments since. We consider below some exceptional cases of private mints. As ancient and medieval governments extended their territories from city-states to regions to modern nation-states, so grew the scope of mint monopolies. The fiscal importance of the mint monopoly is shown by estimates that, in times of war, some medieval rulers derived more than half (and even as much as 92 percent during emergencies) of their revenue from the mint (Spufford 1988).

A national mint monopolist can earn an above-normal profit while producing full-weight coins by charging a service fee greater than the cost of turning bullion into coins. The net profit from money production is called *seigniorage*. A monopoly is necessary to maintain a high fee because competition would drive the fee down to average cost. Because the fee is higher than the competitive level, the volume of metal brought to be coined is less than the competitive level. The national economy suffers from under-provision of coins as it incurs the higher transaction costs of using second-best exchange methods where it would otherwise use coins.

Foreign coins produced and imported at lower cost could help to satisfy the national demand for coins. In so doing they would take business away from the national mint. To keep profits high, then, a national government would ban imports of foreign coins. It would also compel all gold and silver miners within its territory to sell their metals to the national mint. Following this monopoly-profit logic, the Spanish monarchy insisted that all silver and gold from its New World territories go into the Spanish royal mint (Motomura 1994). The national mint is then the only buyer (a *monopsonist*) in the national market for uncoined gold and silver as inputs to coinage. As the only buyer facing captive sellers, it can purchase gold and silver at prices below those in the international market. Because the price is paid in the coins that the mint itself produces,

---

[13] This section draws in part on Selgin and White (1999).

this is a high minting fee in another guise. Legal monopsony enlarges the volume of metal on which the mint can impose a high markup, as miners would ship the gold and silver elsewhere for a better deal if they were allowed to do so. Of course, it is difficult to enforce the restriction against taking the metal elsewhere. It is more difficult the farther the national mint's buying price is below the international market price, and thus the greater is the reward to smuggling the metal out. The Spanish crown avoided dealing with independent miners by imposing state control on the entire supply chain. It claimed ownership of all subsurface minerals, and thus the state owned the rich silver mines in its colonies of Mexico and Peru.[14] It also required that all silver and gold bound for Spain be loaded onto Spanish-owned ships.

State mints produced gold and silver coins in a variety of denominations. Like any alert profit-maximizing monopolist, a state mint maximized its profit by placing higher markups on its products that faced less competition than on its products that faced more competition (such that sales volumes would shrink more rapidly as markups rose). In the Middle Ages, a national mint faced relatively little competition for its medium- and small-denomination silver coins, which circulated exclusively in the domestic market that it had to itself, but faced substantial competition for its gold and high-valued silver coins, which circulated among international traders who could readily use coins from other national mints (Cipolla 1956). Accordingly, minting fees were more reasonable, and seigniorage profits were less, on gold coins than on silver coins, and on high-valued than on low-valued silver coins.

In addition to monopoly minting fees, *debasement* provide a second and more notorious way to exploit the profit potential of a mint monopoly where the public can be compelled to accept underweight coins at face value. A mint debases the coinage when it replaces full-weight coins with underweight coins of the same denomination, for example, mints new shillings containing half as much silver (replaced by base metal) while using the familiar coin dies. Because coins are valued by their precious-metal content, once the debased status of the new shillings is discovered they will purchase half the basket of goods that old shillings purchased. The purchasing power of pure silver remaining the same, shilling prices will double.

---

[14] The colony of Peru included present-day Bolivia, site of the abundant Potosí silver mine. Taylor (2002, p. 63) states that Spain shipped "about 181 tons of gold and 16,000 tons of silver" from the New World to Spain during 1500–1650.

But if the debased coin buys proportionately less in goods, where is the profit? There is a transitory profit until the debasement is discovered. More importantly, in the presence of legal tender laws that declare new shillings the legal equivalent of old shillings in the discharge of pre-existing shilling-denominated debts, an indebted state makes a profit by discharging its debts to bondholders and other creditors with half the silver. Commentators from the French bishop Nicholas Oresme circa 1355 to Adam Smith in 1776 denounced as frauds such pretended repayments that were really partial debt repudiations. Despite the considerable personal risk that came from calling the monarch a criminal fraudster, a tyrant, and a sinner, Oresme (1355) wrote "that to take or augment profit by alteration of the coinage is fraudulent, tyrannical, and unjust, and moreover it cannot be persisted in without the kingdom being, in many other respects also, changed to a tyrany." Here, he referred to the many restrictions imposed on citizens to prevent them from diminishing the king's profit by switching to foreign money. "Wherefore, it not only brings disadvantages of its own, but involves many other evils either as either its conditions or its consequences."

Many late medieval rulers tried to extend the profit beyond debt repayments by prohibiting traders from discriminating against the new lightweight shillings even in spot transactions. They made the new coins not only a *legal tender* in repayment of existing debts, but a *forced tender*. Then the state could more cheaply pay wages to its employees and buy its supplies in lightweight coins (until shilling prices rose accordingly). "Until the sixteenth century," write Boyer-Xambeu et al. (1994, pp. 49–59), "princes in most countries prohibited the weighing of coins and made people accept them all, even when used up, simply in view of their imprints and inscriptions." It was "expressly forbidden" to value coins by bullion weight. Princes outlawed domestic payments in foreign coin, and banned contracts that specified payment by bullion weight, rather than in nominal units of variable weight. In some jurisdictions the practice of "culling," keeping heavy coins and passing on lightweight coins, "carried the death sentence."

The sad historical pattern of debasements in Europe is shown clearly in Figure 1.1, courtesy of researchers Karaman et al. (2018). The chart tracks the various paths sovereigns in eleven leading European economies followed, 1500–1914, in reducing the silver or gold content of their standard coins. Every sovereign debased between 1500 and 1600, although one country – England – finally stopped debasing its currency around 1550. The Dutch Republic stopped around 1600. Not until around 1850

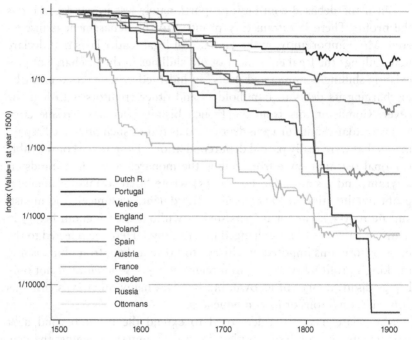

FIGURE I.I Index of the value of monetary unit, 1500–1914 (in silver/gold). Source: Karaman et al. (2018).

can we observe that most national governments have stopped relying on debasements and have for the time being turned to other taxes for revenue. Supposing that popular discontent with debasements was constant over time, the timing of the reforms can perhaps be explained by the development of modern tax systems for bringing in revenue from other sources. Just after the chart ends, the First World War saw widespread debasement and suspension or abandonment of the gold standard for the sake of the seigniorage available from issuing paper money. We will discuss that episode in Chapter 4.

1.7 COMPETING PRIVATE MINTS[15]

Alongside the lighthouse, famously scrutinized by Ronald Coase (1974), the precious metallic mint has played the role of what Coase called "an example of something which has to be provided by government rather

---

[15] This section draws heavily on White (2022). See that article for detailed citation of the evidence from contemporary newspaper accounts and from numismatic historians.

than by private enterprise." This despite governments' poor historical record at preserving coin quality. Prominent economists who have characterized the mint this way include Carl Menger (surprisingly), William Stanley Jevons, Henry Sidgwick, and more recently Charles Goodhart. Sidgwick offered *both* the lighthouse and the mint as examples.

Their leading argument: The public's inability to detect and discount low-quality coins makes it profitable for private mints to issue coins containing less precious metal than they are supposed to. Learning that they can't avoid being swindled, the public will shun all private coins and the market will break down from lack of trust. A trustworthy government mint solves the problem. Sidgwick and Jevons argued in purely theoretical fashion, without discussing any evidence on the historical performance of private mints. On the other side of the debate, Herbert Spencer defended competitive private enterprise in coinage, but he too argued his case deductively without reference to actual mints.

The basic function of a mint, under a silver or gold standard, is to fashion and certify pieces of precious metal that are uniform in weight and fineness and thus suitable to circulate as currency. Today under fiat standards we no longer have circulating gold coins, publicly or privately minted, but investors buy collectible gold coins from both government and private mints. The public buys gold bars and biscuits, with weight and brand name prominently displayed, almost exclusively from private firms like Credit Suisse, the Perth Mint, Johnson Matthey, and Engelhard. These firms have not found it profitable to issue coins or bullion bars containing less precious metal than their markings indicate.

Privately minted silver and gold coins were known in medieval India (Mukherjee 2012, pp. 422–3) and Merovingian Europe (circa 450–750), but the best documented cases are the most recent, those of private mints during nineteenth-century American gold rushes. In the American gold rushes, the record of the earliest mints was not unblemished, but mints producing low-quality coins were soon driven out of the market by those producing high-quality coins.[16] Problems that the above-mentioned economists imagined to be chronic – fraud, lack of standardization – were transitory.

The numismatic historian Ernest Babelon (1897, p. 127) indicates that in Merovingian Gaul the competition among private coiners favored the honest and well reputed:

---

[16] Here we focus on private gold coinage, but private coinage of copper for small change has also been important. Selgin (2008) provides an engaging account of British copper coin producers in the late eighteenth to early nineteenth century.

Anyone who possesses gold and silver and who, instead of trading it in the state of ingot, finds it more convenient or advantageous to exchange it in the form of a coin, carries it to the forge of the nearest coiner, or the one whose name has the best reputation of honesty. It is even noted that there were itinerant goldsmiths or coiners: they traveled to various localities to strike, with the gold that private individuals confided to them, coins that circulated under the guarantee of their name in a more or less extended geographical radius.

Nonetheless the Merovingian system suffered (pp. 131–32) "serious imperfections" and "the most glaring abuses" because the public often lacked timely information about the fineness of coins they were offered in the course of trade, information that they would have needed to appropriately discount substandard coins. (This problem of ignorance and abuse arose with royal and ecclesiastical coins as well as with privately minted coins.) Given the limited reach of communications in the fifth to eighth centuries, even the best of the "coins stamped by merchants, goldsmiths or bankers, could necessarily be received, with their fiduciary character, only in a rather restricted geographical area," namely where "these merchants traded and where they were honorably known." In the case of nineteenth-century American private gold mints, newspapers played an important role by rapidly spreading information about the quality of various private coins.

There were three distinct regional gold rushes with private mints in the United States: the southern Appalachians in 1830–1851, California in 1849–1854, and Colorado in 1860–1862 (Adams 1913, Kagin 1981).

Templeton Reid of Gainesville, Georgia opened the first private gold mint in the United States. Reid unfortunately over-estimated the purity of the gold he used. A letter to the local newspaper soon reported that his coins contained too little gold. He had to shut down operations within three months. The Bechtler family mint in Rutherfordton, North Carolina, by contrast, gained a reputation for competence and honesty that kept it in business for twenty years, 1831–1851. It produced more than $3 million in gold coins, in denominations of $1, $2.5, and $5, marked with weight in grains and fineness in carats.[17] Even after the US Mint opened a branch office in Charlotte, North Carolina, in 1835, miners continued to bring gold to the Bechtler mint (located about 70 miles west of Charlotte), a testimony to the widespread acceptance of its coins. The Bechtler mint closed when the local mines began to play out.

---

[17] Mint output figures are unadjusted, as of the dates minted. To convert to 2022 values using changes in the dollar–gold exchange rate since 1831, multiply by approximately 90. To adjust by the Consumer Price Index (CPI), multiply by approximately 30.

An 1837 visitor described a scene at the Bechtler mint where "country people" brought in "rough gold" that Christopher Bechtler weighed and recorded in his book, while "to others he delivered the coin he had struck," net of fees, from the gold that they had previously brought. The mint's operations were like "those at a country grist mill, where the miller deducts the toll for the grist he has manufactured." A mint's revenue consisted of fees deducted from the metal it "fluxed" (cleaned), assayed to determine fineness, and stamped into coins. The Bechtler mint charged 2.5 percent for assaying and coining. A miner who brought gold dust enough to make $102.50 would receive $100 in new coins. Their certified weight and fineness made the coins more valuable in trade than the dust, which might fetch only $90 worth of goods in barter due to uncertainty about its fineness.

A private gold mint accordingly did not need to produce substandard coins to make a profit. Deliberately issuing substandard coins would earn a greater profit per coin, but only until the ruse was discovered. As in the case of Templeton Reid, incompetence or fraud by some the first private mints in San Francisco was initially a problem. But the publication of independent assay results in local newspapers made honesty soon dominate as a strategy for profit maximization.

In California, private mints produced an estimated $36 million in gold coins during 1849–1854. Four of the six most prominent private mints established in 1849 produced substandard coins. Coins from the Mormon Mint (made of California gold but struck in Salt Lake City) were discovered to be far underweight, and those from the Miners' Bank to be slightly so. What happened next is not that the entire market collapsed, but merely that the underweight coins "speedily fell into disrepute," while the Mormon coins "were refused by all, when their spuriousness was once revealed" (Adams 1913). Coins from the Miners' Bank, which were about 1.5 percent underweight, were "only accepted at twenty per cent. discount. Both issues were soon driven from circulation." Holders of the discredited coins "were forced to sell them at their bullion value and pocket the loss."

Once newspapers reported substandard assay results, merchants refused or heavily discounted the underweight coins, and their holders had them melted and recoined elsewhere. The bad mints did not survive into 1850, while two good mints (Moffat & Co., which likely outproduced all the others combined, and the Oregon Exchange Company) did. Of the five major private mints established in 1850 and later, only one (Baldwin & Co.) produced underweight coins, and it quickly exited.

The other four were competent and honest, and three of them (Dubosq & Co.; Wass, Molitor, & Co.; and Kellogg & Co.) minted large quantities.

In Colorado, Clark, Gruber & Co. minted about $3 million in coins dated 1860 and 1861. Their coins were quite popular, known to contain a quantity of gold slightly above the US Mint's standard (Lee and Frajola 2008).

Because entry into the minting trade was open, substandard coins could be introduced into circulation. But such coins did not persist. Because money users were free to discount or reject bad money, and soon learned from news accounts which coins were underweight, the bad (underweight) money did not drive out the good (full weight) money. The legally fixed exchange rate required for Gresham's Law was absent. On the contrary, the good money drove out the bad because of the greater convenience of money that trades at par.

In 1855, the US Mint opened a branch office in San Francisco where miners could take their gold dust to be officially coined for a zero charge. The Branch Mint succeeded a US Assay Office, run by Moffat & Co. under contract from the US Treasury, which was supervised by a federally appointed United States Assayer. The Assay Office purchased gold dust and issued ingots only of $50 and higher, too large for ordinary domestic transactions. The Branch Mint purchased its building and machinery from the firm of Curtis & Perry, the successor firm to Moffat & Co. after Moffat retired (Adams 1913, pp. 13, 52).[18] In addition to their subsidized production, official US Mint coins also had the privilege of being the exclusive medium accepted at the US Customs House in San Francisco for payment of import duties. Kellogg & Co., the last of the private issuers, ceased issuing gold coins shortly after the establishment of the Branch Mint.

Apparently innocent of the American experience, the Cambridge University philosopher and political economist Sidgwick (1883) predicted chronic market failure from private coinage in his classic textbook *Principles of Political Economy*:

It is in the interest of the community that coins should be as far as possible hard to imitate, hard to tamper with, and qualified to resist wear and tear; but the person who procured the coin from the manufacturer—who would want, of course, to pass the money, and not to keep it—would be prompted by no motive of self-interest to aim at securing excellence in these points.

[18] The companies is question were partnerships, not corporations, and so had to be reconstituted on the death or retirement of a partner.

Other economists have predicted trouble from the temptation to profit by fraudulent debasement, made possible by the information asymmetry between mintmaster and coin-user. But in the American experience these problems were transitory rather than chronic. Precisely because the miners who procured coins wanted to pass them on without difficulty, it was in their self-interest to procure coins known to be excellent. The interest of the community in high-quality full-weight coins was thus brought to bear on private mints.[19] Private mints that did not produce high-quality coins did not stay in business.

Sidgwick's logic implies that nobody will reject or discount low-quality or substandard coin. Any person will readily take it at face value because she assumes that the *next* person to whom she offers it will do the same. No matter the coin's quality, the probability that the next person will reject or discount it is treated as negligible. But the historical evidence shows that people in California did in fact reject or discount substandard coins. Mints that produced substandard coins saw acceptance dry up and they failed. Successful private mints, by contrast, produced coins at least as resistant to imitation, tampering, or wear as government-minted coins. Clark, Gruber, & Co., for example, hardened their coins when they found that the early issues were too prone to wear. Issuing trustworthy up-to-standard coins was the only way to survive in a competitive minting business.

1.8 PRIVATE DEPOSIT TRANSFER AND BANKNOTES DEVELOPED TO REMEDY THE SHORTCOMINGS OF GOVERNMENT-DEBASED COINS

A mint with a government-granted monopoly, by contrast to a mint in a competitive setting, need not worry about losing its customers to a rival mint should it issue debased coins. Medieval Europe was a crazy quilt of principalities, city-states, and bishoprics, each typically with a local monopoly government mint. Common silver coins were debased to different degrees in different principalities, and degrees of debasement varied over time. Conant (1905 v. 1, p. 136) noted that "In 1636, a French Royal edict fixing the official ratio between French standard and foreign money named not less than thirty-eight foreign coins having circulation in law and in fact in France, and these were only a fraction of those in

---

[19] In economics jargon, what Sidgwick thought of as external benefits were actually internalized.

actual use." In earlier centuries "there had been still greater variety," with "the coinages of petty European princes, almost infinite in the variations of their weight and fineness."

Out of the coin-changing business, modern banking arose to provide a way for merchants to cope with the confusing welter of coins. As an alternative to the merchant having to carry variously debased coins, and keep track of exchange rates among them, money-changing bankers offered a ledger-based payment system of transferable account balances denominated in units of constant silver content. A merchant would occasionally take the various coins he had accumulated to a money-changing banker, who would weigh them, assess their fineness, and give the merchant a corresponding number of silver reference units (such as Flemish pounds, *livres de vieux gros tournois* [old full-weight pounds of Tours], or undebased pounds sterling) in account credit. Historians later called these stable silver accounting units "ghost monies" because they were not embodied in any of the debased contemporary coins. In this way private money (bank account balances), but not publicly produced money (debased coins), faithfully conformed to a fixed metallic standard.

Inter-regional medieval trade centered on a series of trade fairs, including the famous fairs of Champagne in the twelfth and thirteenth centuries, where merchants from across western Europe would meet to exchange wares.[20] Lugging bags of gold and silver coins along while traveling from fair to fair would have been cumbersome and risky. Merchants traveled and transacted more easily by instead keeping account balances on the books of money-changing bankers who also attended the fairs. A merchant from Genoa could establish an account balance in his home city by depositing local Genoese coins and receiving a balance denominated in silver units. At the fair, he could then conveniently make and receive payments, perhaps denominated in the coins of Provence (whose silver content was known), as book entries. The merchant would build up or draw down his account balance depending on the net of sales over purchases. Or he might run a negative balance, borrowing from his banker to cover purchases at one fair, repaying out of sales proceeds at a later fair. The bankers would clear inter-bank payments (compute the net balances owed) and settle up among themselves at the end of the fair. By offsetting incoming and outgoing payments, settlement took place with a minimum of metallic money.

[20] For details see De Roover (1963).

Around 1700, very few households had bank accounts even in the most prosperous parts of Europe or North America. Accounts were worth having mostly for business firms and wealthy individuals who spent and received large sums. After banknotes and interest-bearing checking accounts became available, both popularized by London goldsmith bankers in the late 1600s,[21] eighteenth-century England and Scotland were among the first places to see private bank money become an increasingly popular alternative to the use of coins for retail transactions and for wage payments. (For the details of how competitive systems of note-issue worked, see Selgin 1988, White 1995, 2015.) Private checking deposits and banknotes came to dominate the payment system. Banknotes largely displaced coins where their denominations overlapped. (Governments sometimes banned private banknotes below a certain sum.)

The adoption of banknotes and checking accounts spread with the branching out of the retail commercial banks that the public trusted. As Milton Friedman and Anna J. Schwartz (1986, p. 45) noted: "Historically, producers of money have established confidence by promising convertibility into some dominant money, generally, specie. Many examples can be cited of fairly long-continued and successful producers of private moneys convertible into specie."[22]

Commercial banking and bank-issued money spread through various economies during different decades of the eighteenth and nineteenth centuries. In the American colonies that were to become the United States, there were no commercial banknotes in circulation (although some colonial governments had occasionally issued circulating tax-anticipation notes) before the Bank of North America opened in 1782. But there were 29 commercial banks by 1800, and 382 by 1830 (Wright 2008, Table 2). By 1832, the value of commercial banknotes in circulation was three times the estimated value of specie in circulation (Annual Report of the Comptroller of the Currency 1903, Table 43, p. 98).[23]

---

[21] On the goldsmith bankers, see Quinn (1997) and Selgin (2012).

[22] This statement, informed by then-recent studies of competitive private note-issuing systems, corrected a much earlier statement by Friedman (1960, p. 6): "A fiduciary currency ostensibly convertible into the monetary commodity is therefore likely to become overissued from time to time and convertibility is likely to become impossible. Historically, this is what happened under so-called 'free banking' in the United States and under similar circumstances in other countries."

[23] The second Bank of the United States (80 percent privately owned) is included here among the commercial banks. The notes-to-specie ratio declined in subsequent decades for a variety of reasons including the federal government insisting on specie (the Independent Treasury System) and quantitative restrictions on note issue by the National Banking Acts of 1863, 1864, and 1865–1866.

In the colonies that would become Canada, between 1817 (the opening of the Bank of Montreal) and 1850, writes James Powell (2005, p. 18), "Bank notes were well received by the public and became the principal means of payment in British North America. The general acceptance of bank notes in transactions helped to mitigate the problems associated with having a wide range of foreign coins in circulation with different ratings."

In Switzerland, coins were still about 87 percent of the money held by the public (M1) in 1850, but declined to around 7 percent by 1906 under a free banking regime. (A government central bank, the Swiss National Bank, was established in 1907.) Checking deposits rose to around 74 percent of M1 from around 7 percent, while banknotes in circulation rose to around 19 percent from 6 percent. Total bank balance sheets grew sixfold over the period (Gerlach and Kugler 2018).

The development of bank-issued money was the most significant advance in payment technology since coinage. Banknotes and checks were able to become more commonly used than full-bodied coins by matching or surpassing precious metallic coins in the traditional virtues of hand-to-hand media (portability, durability, divisibility, and recognizability). The key contrasts between gold and fiat standards were not along the lines of those virtues, but would become the resource costs of the system and the stability of money's purchasing power, contrasts to be discussed in Chapter 4.

1.9 GOVERNMENT CENTRAL BANKS MONOPOLIZED BANKNOTES AND CLEARING SYSTEMS, AND OBSTRUCTED THE AUTOMATIC WORKING OF THE INTERNATIONAL GOLD STANDARD

Legislation, not market forces, created central banks. Although the institutions that would become central banks were first created during the era of silver and gold standards, their original mission was not to remedy any problem with metallic monetary standards. Their original mission in most cases was to help finance national governments. The English Parliament chartered the Bank of England in 1694 to provide its government with loans at low interest rates. Similar arrangements gave birth to the Swedish Riksbank, the Bank of France, and many others (Schuler 1992). In the United States, the Federal Reserve System was created in 1913, not so much to lend to the contemporary government (although it soon did so copiously when the US military entered the First World War) as to remedy problems in the financial system (banking panics) caused by Civil-War-era federal banking legislation. The National Banking Acts had made the banking system inflexible as an unintended consequence of requiring the banks to back their banknotes with a limited stock of federal Civil War bonds (Noyes 1910). Canada, likewise a mostly agricultural economy on the gold standard but without such bond-collateral restrictions on its banks, had no financial panics during the era.

A national legislature could increase the lending capacity of its client bank by giving it a monopoly in the issue of banknotes, which in some countries were the largest category of bank liabilities in the nineteenth century. Such legislation restricted ordinary commercial banks to deposit-taking. Note monopoly and an implicit government guarantee against the central bank's default fostered the centralization of gold reserves in the central bank's vault (Smith 1936).

Looking back on how the Bank of England had become the banker to ordinary banks and the sole holder of England's gold reserves, the great Victorian-era financial writer Walter Bagehot (1873) observed that these developments were not the result of market forces, but due to the Bank's having the exclusive right to issue notes in London and having the government's implicit guarantee to repay its note-holders and depositors should the Bank run into trouble (or if not to repay, to declare its notes legal tender, as the government did when the Bank suspended payments in 1797). By contrast, Bagehot saw the free banking system in Scotland as an example of "the natural system" in which each bank holds its own metallic reserves. In a free banking system, it might be noted, the gold standard is safer from suspension because no one bank's default suspends the contractual obligations of other banks to redeem in gold. All the eggs are not in one basket.

Under the classical gold standard before the First World War, a loss of gold reserves to the rest of the world would soon correct any over-expansion of the banking system's liabilities (or reduction in the demand to hold them) in an economy without a central bank like the United States or Canada. Gold flows operated automatically and continuously to stop domestic prices for traded goods from moving far above or below world prices, thereby avoiding the need for a belated and painful correction.

In the United States, the creation of the Federal Reserve System nationalized the functions of the commercial banks' cooperative clearinghouse associations. The banks switched from holding gold reserves in their own clearinghouse vaults to holding reserves in the form of Federal Reserve notes and deposit balances at the regional Federal Reserve Banks. Interbank settlement moved to the balance sheet of the Fed. The commercial banks (outside of those involved in international payments) no longer needed any gold on hand once the American public in March 1933 was prohibited from holding gold coins.

Central banks became convenient to national governments in other ways, allowing them even during the classical gold standard era (1879–1913) to over-ride automatic gold standard mechanisms with discretionary monetary policy, at least in the short run. During the First World War, European governments and their central banks left the gold standard to pursue inflationary finance for war expenditures, printing more central bank liabilities than could be redeemed at par after the war. Soon after the war, curiously, the Princeton economist Edwin W. Kemmerer led missions to Latin America to establish central banks on the grounds that central banks would help nations return to and stay on a gold or gold-exchange standard. He persuaded a number of governments (Bolivia, Chile, Colombia, Ecuador, Guatemala, Mexico, Peru) to create central banks, but they did not stay on the gold standard for more than a few years.

Central banks in Europe and elsewhere during the interwar period neither freely floated nor returned to full gold redeemability. As economist Leland Yeager (1966, p. 290) observed, "Gold standard methods of balance-of-payments equilibrium were largely destroyed and were not replaced by any alternative." Instability followed. Chapter 2 will discuss how gold-standard equilibrating mechanisms normally worked.

The American economist Lionel D. Edie (1932) warned in 1932 that the pre-war process of automatic regulation by gold flows had been disabled by the Federal Reserve System:

The Federal Reserve Act cut the tie which binds the gold reserve directly to the credit volume, and by so doing automatically cut off the basic function of the gold standard. ... [I]t is time to recognize that the Federal Reserve mechanism does not constitute an automatic self-corrective device for perpetuating a gold standard.

The same argument applied equally to other interwar central banks supposed to be managing a gold-exchange standard. A central bank that did not play by "the rules of the game" could slow or even reverse equilibrating gold flows. Its sovereign status meant that it could suspend gold redemption of the domestic currency without legal penalty, and its monopoly status meant that its concern to preserve its reputation was a rather weak constraint (see Selgin and White 2005). By comparison to the automaticity of a competitive free banking system, the discretionary power of a central bank existentially threatened (rather than safeguarded, as central banking evangelists sometimes claimed) a monetary system's commitment to gold redemption.

The monetary chaos of the 1920s and 1930s was thus not due to "golden fetters" imposed by the gold redeemability of currencies (no such chaos prevailed before the First World War, when central banks were absent or freely redeemed without question), but rather to the inconsistent policies of central banks that now ruled the roost. (A more detailed discussion of the claim that "the gold standard" failed during the interwar period will be found in Chapter 3.)

A central bank like the Bank of England or Bank of France, having gone off the gold standard during the First World War and printed so much domestic money for war finance that its purchasing power was well below its pre-war value, had two alternative paths to return to the international gold standard: either restrict the quantity of money until the purchasing power of the currency returned to that of its gold content at the old parity (as the United States had done before returning to gold redemption fourteen years after the Civil War) or devalue. Devaluation would cut the gold content of the currency unit by enough to restore purchasing-power parity between a paper currency note and the reduced amount of gold for which it could now be redeemed.

Interwar international agreements among central banks to economize on the use of gold, sometimes described as substituting a *gold-exchange standard* for the classical gold standard, did a little but not enough to reduce gold's purchasing power in the world market to match the reduced purchasing power of the major national currencies. Returning to gold redeemability for the pound sterling at the pre-war parity, as the Bank of England tried to do in 1925, when the holder of a pound note could still purchase much less with it than with the gold that it could be redeemed for, was a recipe for chaos. Predictably heavy redemptions created an unsustainable outflow of gold from the Bank's vaults, no matter the legal restrictions placed on gold exports.

1.10 THE INTERNAL INCONSISTENCIES OF THE POSTWAR BRETTON WOODS SYSTEM[24]

Under the Bretton Woods system, created during the Second World War, participating central banks pegged their national currencies to the US dollar, and settled international payments with US dollar balances rather than gold. Unlike the American public, foreign central banks could redeem their dollar claims at $35 per ounce for gold held by the US Treasury.

[24] This section draws on White (2021).

But the US government discouraged them from doing so. By contrast with the classical gold standard, the Bretton Woods system allowed national central banks more scope to adopt short-run expansionary monetary policies. When a relatively expansionary country began to lose its dollar reserves to the rest of the system, it could buy time by applying to the International Monetary Fund (IMF) for a loan, or it could ask permission to devalue against the dollar. The internally inconsistent system – promising both rules and discretion – operated much less automatically than the classical international gold standard had. Once international money and capital flows were liberalized, the Bretton Woods system was repeatedly marked by devaluations of currencies whose central banks had chosen expansionary monetary policies inconsistent with keeping their dollar pegs.

The same inconsistency undid the US dollar's peg to gold, and brought down the system. As the issuer of the world's reserve currency, the United States had what a French Finance Minister famously called an "exorbitant privilege." The United States could acquire goods and services from the rest of the world merely by expanding the supply of dollars, with the bill coming due only in the indefinite future. The temptation proved irresistible. The Bretton Woods set-up was not incentive-compatible: it enabled the US government to profitably issue the world's reserve currency, with immediate benefit but little immediate cost to pursuing a monetary policy too expansionary to maintain its peg in the long run. The Federal Reserve also had an important domestic motive for expansionary monetary policy: It was apparently trying to take advantage of the "Phillips Curve," that is, its seeming power to reduce the unemployment rate through an expansionary monetary policy that also increased the inflation rate.

Foreign central banks held dollar assets as reserves and therefore would gladly accept them – up to a point. (The foreign central banks did not hold Federal Reserve Notes or dollar checking account balances; they swapped those for interest-earning safe dollar assets.) The flow of dollars overseas meant that foreign monetary systems gained reserves and also could nominally expand, while (in contrast to the classical gold standard under which the United States would lose gold to settle its balance of payments) the United States did not need to contract. Thus the gold-exchange system, in Rueff's words, "substantially impaired the sensitivity and efficacy of the gold-standard mechanism" at self-regulation.

Notice the qualifier in the previous paragraph: up to a point. The immediate postwar period was characterized by complaints of a "dollar shortage" in Europe as central banks tried to build up the dollar reserves that they need to peg their national currencies to the US dollar. Over time, with the US government happily printing dollars to export to Europe in exchange for goods and services, talk turned to the problem of a "dollar glut." European central banks accumulated more dollar-denominated bonds than they wanted. As Rueff later noted, the United States could even go somewhat beyond the willing-accumulation point to the extent that it could successfully use political or diplomatic leverage to discourage foreign central banks from redeeming its currency. But such diplomatic talk could not be effective forever as ongoing US monetary expansion caused ever more unwanted dollars to pile up in Europe.

1.11 THE ARRIVAL OF FIAT MONEY AND CRYPTOCURRENCY

The Bretton Woods system ended in August 1971 with President Richard Nixon reneging on the US government's commitment to redeem foreign central banks' dollars for gold. Fiat monetary systems have prevailed around the world since then. Even economies without their own central banks to issue national fiat currency, like Panama where US dollars circulate or Bulgaria with its currency board tied to the euro, use another economy's fiat currency directly or as the medium of redemption.

In the belief that fiat money is prone to over-expansion and inflation by political authorities, but gold and silver are not, some entrepreneurs have tried to offer private alternatives in the form of transferable claims to gold ("e-gold") or private silver coins ("the Liberty Dollar"). Their efforts have been suppressed by governments through regulatory and legal restrictions (Dowd 2014, White 2014).

In 2009 a remarkable alternative was introduced, a stateless non-commodity and internet-resident asset called Bitcoin. Secured from digital counterfeiting ("double-spending") by cryptography, Bitcoin's remarkable growth in market value has inspired literally thousands of other "cryptocurrency" projects. The introduction of Bitcoin has re-opened public debate over what features make for better money. (Chapters 5 and 6 will discuss the features of Bitcoin in detail.) While much has been written in recent years on the contrast between Bitcoin and fiat money, just like much was written in an earlier era contrasting gold to fiat money, relatively little has been written to address the question: Does a Bitcoin standard provide a better money than a gold standard? In the following chapters we consider the three-way contest between gold (representing commodity monies in general), fiat, and Bitcoin (representing cryptocurrencies in general).

Chapter 2 walks through the market mechanisms that steer a gold standard, assuming that a central bank is passive or absent. Chapter 3 addresses common misconceptions about gold-standard systems. An exposition of the mechanisms of a fiat standard comes in Chapter 4, including a discussion of its contrasts to a gold standard. Finally, in Chapter 5, we examine the workings of Bitcoin and in Chapter 6 its contrasts to commodity and to fiat monies.

2

How a Gold Standard Works

A simple model of the market supply and demand for monetary gold allows us to examine in a very general way how a gold or silver standard works. We will explicitly talk about a gold standard here, but the same theory equally explains how a silver or other metallic standard works.

2.1 TYPES OF GOLD STANDARDS

Following common usage by monetary historians, "a gold standard" here means any monetary system – whatever the details of its banking system – in which a defined mass of gold coin or bullion is the *unit of account* in which prices are posted and accounts kept, and gold coins or bullion are the *medium of redemption* that ordinary currency and bank accounts promise to pay. Defining a gold standard in this generic way contrasts with describing "the gold standard" by reference to the policies of central banks (e.g., Bordo 2007). From ancient times South Asian, Mediterranean, and European economies operated on silver standards, before modern commercial banking let alone central banking began. Many countries (including the United States, Canada, Switzerland, and Australia) operated on gold standards before their governments created central banks.

Economic historians identify the heyday or "classical" period of the international gold standard as beginning with the post–Civil War return of the United States (except California, which never left the gold standard) to gold redemption in 1879. Most of Western Europe had adopted the gold standard during the previous six years. The era ended when European governments departed from gold redeemability with the

39

outbreak of the First World War in 1914. During the classical period, there were few central banks in the gold-standard countries outside of Europe, so a central bank policy cannot generically define what it meant for an economy to operate on the classical gold standard.

Under a gold standard, gold is the basic or definitive money. The gold definition of the monetary unit is made tangible when embodied in a gold coin. For example, if a "dollar" were defined as 0.5 gram of pure gold, then a full-weight "ten dollar" coin would contain 5 grams of pure gold. A gold standard does *not* require that gold coins are most common type of money that people use, much less the only type. As far back as the mid-1600s, people living in silver- and gold-standard economies with modern banking systems often found it more convenient to make payments with paper notes and account transfers (using checks and other methods) than with precious-metal coins.

Currency notes and bank balances are tied to gold by being *denominated in* and *redeemable for* the gold-defined monetary unit. To continue the example, people can cash a "10 dollar" banknote or check at the banking institution that issued it and get a coin containing 5 grams of gold. The continual interchange keeps currency and account dollars equal in purchasing power to coined gold dollars. A gold standard does not imply nineteenth-century payment technology. Gold redeemability of bank accounts is perfectly compatible with the most modern methods for making account transfers easy, including debit cards, online bill payment, and mobile banking apps, and with continuing innovation in payments.

We can distinguish among types of gold standards based on the physical form of gold that is paid out in redemptions. The normal case is a *gold coin standard*. The classical economist David Ricardo proposed a *gold bullion standard*, with redemption only available in large bars of gold. Ricardo offered his proposal as a way to reduce the system's use of physical gold, compelling the public to give up gold coins entirely in favor of paper notes and tokens. Ricardo failed to recognize that in the eyes of those members of the public who preferred gold coins to banknotes the cost was worth bearing. An even more indirect system, where the domestic currency is redeemable only for another (foreign) currency that can in turn be redeemed for gold in some form, is called a *gold-exchange standard*.

Gold-standard payment systems differ according to whether competing commercial banks are allowed to issue gold-redeemable common currency, or instead legislation has restricted currency issue to a public institution like a Treasury or a central bank. Additionally, the rules for reserve-holding may vary across systems. Under proposals for a "100 percent reserve gold standard," which have had their advocates, the law would require every paper dollar and every checking-account dollar to be backed at all times by one gold dollar in the issuer's vault. This means that issuing currency and checking accounts is a warehousing operation, not a banking operation. It is loaded terminology to say that only under such a restriction do we have a "genuine" or "real" or "honest-to-God" gold standard.[1]

Although a silver or gold standard does not require government to play an active role in producing money, governments have involved themselves extensively since the ancient emergence of silver and gold as means of payment. They created government mints, often banning private mints. They later created national central banks while restricting private firms from issuing silver- or gold-redeemable notes. Nothing in a metallic standard makes such intervention inevitable. As noted in Chapter 1, history has known competing private mints, just as we today see private minting of coin-like commemoratives and private certification of gold bars and biscuits by firms like Engelhard and the Perth Mint. Private commercial banks were the routine currency issuers before legislation created government banks and gave them national monopolies of currency issue. Private note-issue still survives in a few places today, namely Scotland, Northern Ireland, Hong Kong, and Macau, though it is no longer redeemable for gold.

Institutions for issuing and redeeming monetary claims for gold, and methods for determining the system's volume of gold reserve holdings, have run the gamut from operating entirely by market forces (or "automatically") to operating entirely at the discretion of government authorities. During the nineteenth and early twentieth centuries, many national governments empowered central banks as institutions for deliberate management of gold standards. As noted in Chapter 1, the Bank of England was a leader in this development. By contrast, a gold standard is automatic when no central bank or Treasury intervenes. No central bank existed in the United States before 1914, or in Canada before 1935, leaving market mechanisms to regulate the flows of monetary gold from region to region and bank to bank.

---

[1] These modifiers were used by, for example, Rothbard (1985, p. 1) and Friedman (1976, pp. 34–41).

2.2 DIFFICULTIES OF TRANSACTING WITH COINS ONLY

Even after the development of coinage, silver and gold pieces had a number of shortcomings as hand-to-hand media of exchange, which we can enumerate in terms of the five desirable properties listed in Chapter 1.[2]

(1) Silver and gold coins had *limited durability.* Coins in circulation experienced cumulative physical wear and tear as they passed from purse to purse, reducing their metallic content over time. Changing the alloy to harden the coins (e.g., a "sterling" silver alloy is 92.5 percent pure silver with 7.5 percent copper for greater hardness) reduced but did not eliminate the problem.

Honest wear and tear was not the only source of shrinkage. Silver and gold coins attracted sharp operators who found it profitable to filch some of the precious metal so long as the probability that the next recipient would weigh the coin was sufficiently low. Filching techniques included shaving, filing, and sweating (shaking coins together in a bag to knock flakes of metal loose). Deliberate shrinkage could be made unprofitable by weighing coins in a high share of transfers, but when you need to weigh you have lost one of the two main advantages of coining. (The other advantage is no need to test fineness.) Bankers and money-changers who culled the heaviest coins from circulation were not themselves filchers, but they contributed to the progressive lightening of the average coin remaining in circulation.

Debasement by sovereign mints, which sometimes recalled and reissued coins with less precious metallic content, can be seen as large-scale filching in its effects (and in its moral character, when the profit went to the sovereign's personal benefit). Coins were thus vulnerable to loss in precious metallic content from both private and public actors. Debasement, unlike wear or other shrinkage, could not be detected by weight or displacement when artfully done. Its detection required an assay, a costly test of a coin's metallic composition. With rampant debasement, using coins became little more convenient than using raw metal pieces.

(2) Variously worn or lightened or debased coins *lacked uniformity.* People who took in sizable numbers of coins (merchants, money-changers, bankers) found it practically necessary to weigh and assay coins to avoid overvaluing them. It was for good reason that the symbol of the medieval banker was a balance scale. A traveling merchant who bought and sold in coin across Europe's patchwork

---

[2] Here I draw on White (2000, pp. viii–ix).

of jurisdictions, each with its own silver coins in different stages of debasement, would have to pay fees to expert money-changers in order to swap unfamiliar foreign coins for better known and more spendable local coins when buying, and swap in the other direction to take home sales proceeds. Open competition among mints might have lessened the problem of debasement by enhancing the return to honesty, as we will argue in the following text, but – in large part because of the profits available to a monopoly mint that debased – governments that had the power to do so liked to monopolize minting services in their jurisdictions.

(3) Silver standards dominated the ancient and medieval worlds, but using silver coins alone was attended with inconveniences. They *lacked portability* (were bulky) for large-value payments. This became an increasingly important problem as the volume of world trade revived after the ninth century AD.[3] An economy using silver coins for small-value payments also needed a concurrent gold coinage (historically some 10 to 16 times more valuable per ounce) or some other suitable method for large-value payments. On the other hand, using gold coins alone would not do. Gold coins *lacked divisibility* in the sense that they could not practically be made tiny enough for small purchases. In the United States circa 1840, for example, a $1 gold coin was only about one-third the size of the smallest modern US coin, the dime. An economy with gold coins therefore needed a concurrent silver or token coinage, or some substitute, for small-value payments. This complication has been called the "big problem of small change" (Sargent and Velde 2003).

In many historical economies, even small silver coins were too large for *very* small payments, and copper coins (pennies) were used. I will skip that complication here, as all the relevant issues arise with two metals.

What is the big problem? Why not just have both silver and gold coins in circulation to cover the spectrum of payments? There are basically two ways to circulate full-bodied coins of both metals. The historically less common option is to have *parallel standards*, which means independence between the silver coins and the gold coins. The exchange rate between silver coins and gold coins moves from day to day, in tandem with the market exchange rate between silver and gold bullion. The drawback is

---

[3] On the revival of trade, see Henri Pirenne (1925).

obvious: When lower-value silver coins do not have a fixed value in terms of larger-valued gold coins, there are serious hassles in making change and keeping books. Imagine the inconvenience of living in an economy where US dollar notes circulate in denominations of US$10 and up, but Canadian coins (from C$ 0.05 to C$5) provide the low-valued currency, with the exchange rate between the two sets of currency varying as the US$-to-C$ exchange rate currently varies. At its high point in 2020, the US$10 note was worth C$14.49 in exchange; at its low point in 2021, it was worth $12.08.

2.3 BIMETALLISM

The more common practice was *bimetallism*, where silver and gold coins are denominated in a common unit. At a bimetallic dollar mint, ten silver "one-dollar" coins can always be exchanged for a "ten-dollar" gold coin, and vice versa. The "dollar" is defined as X grains of gold and simultaneously defined as Y grains of silver. When it works well, so that both silver and gold coins circulate, bimetallism has an advantage that we take for granted every time we make change, namely that larger-value currency pieces are worth a fixed multiple of smaller-value pieces.

As a result of the dual definitions of the monetary unit, bimetallism fixed an official domestic exchange rate between gold and silver, which rarely coincided with the variable world market exchange rate. Consider what happened when the world market gold–silver exchange rate moved against silver. Five silver dollars that were full weight when issued became underweight in the sense that the silver in them was now worth less on the market than the gold in a five-dollar gold coin. The silver dollars could retain their market value, provided that no more were issued, if the mint or other parties stood ready to accept every silver dollar as the equivalent of one-fifth of a five-dollar gold coin. In such a situation, the silver dollar functioned like a banknote stamped on metal, valued for the gold that it could be used to claim, rather than for the mass of silver that it contained.

A fixed mint ratio with free and unlimited conversion between silver and gold coins is unsustainable, however, when the world market price ratio wanders too far from the mint ratio. Suppose the market sells 1 oz. of gold for 20 oz. of silver, but the mint considers 1 oz. of gold equivalent to 15 oz. of silver. Suppose also that the mint allows anyone who brings in 15 oz. of silver to get a 1 oz. gold coin. An arbitrage opportunity is created: Buy 15 oz. silver in the world market, swap it at the mint for 1 oz.

in gold coins, swap the gold coins in the market for 20 oz. of silver, and pocket 5 oz. of silver as a profit at the mint's expense. Repeat many times, and the mint will be drained of gold and swamped with silver. If the mint replaces its lost gold, it has to pay 20 for what it then sells for 15. Its losses approach infinity. The mint ratio cannot be maintained. The coinage of silver at the fixed official ratio has to stop.

If the market price ratio moves away from the mint ratio in the other direction, arbitrageurs will profit against the mint in the other direction and drain it of silver.

Because running a bimetallic mint is a loss-making proposition whenever the market price of gold to silver varies beyond a narrow range, there are no known examples of free-market bimetallic standards. Bimetallism requires a monetary authority (a tax-subsidized government mint) ready to coin both gold and silver in a fixed value ratio despite the prospective losses. But even a government mint cannot withstand losses beyond some magnitude.

Building on the first example in which the mint undervalues gold, if the mint values are also the "legal tender" values for discharging debts, nobody will repay a debt in 1 oz. of gold when they can get 20 oz. of silver for it in the market, discharge the debt with 15 oz. of silver, and keep the difference. They will hoard the gold, or melt it down for non-monetary uses, or trade it on the world market where it buys more. In the limit, gold will disappear from domestic circulation. The legally overvalued money (here silver) drives out the legally undervalued money (here gold), a phenomenon known as "Gresham's Law." Bimetallism in theory becomes monometallism in practice.

Respectable economists such as Henry Sidgwick (1883, pp. 449–454) nonetheless made a sophisticated case for bimetallism in the late nineteenth century. A century later, Milton Friedman (1992, chs. 3–6) found much merit in their case. Ultimately, however, bimetallism became irrelevant because a payment system relying on physical transfer of coins became obsolete.

The sophisticated case for bimetallism begins by reconsidering the operation of Gresham's Law. Gresham's Law is really a special case of the general proposition that a binding price ceiling causes a shortage. A legally fixed gold–silver ratio acts as a price ceiling that tries to hold the domestic purchasing power of coins of one metal below their purchasing power in the rest of the world (this is what is meant by calling it the "legally undervalued" metal at the mint ratio). A domestic shortage of the undervalued coins arises: The quantity in circulation shrinks as arbitrageurs send them abroad to get more for in exchange for them. Because only a small difference in purchasing power will send coins abroad, the shrinkage can be dramatic, often amounting to complete disappearance of full-weight coins. For example, when the US government revised its official mint ratio in 1834 so as to legally overvalue gold and undervalue silver (adopting 16:1 as the mint ratio when the world market price ratio was lower), full-weight silver coins disappeared and gold became the de facto standard. In a simplified picture of the process, Gresham's Law creates a knife's edge: A small move in the mint ratio to either side of the world market price ratio will banish one of the metals.

Friedman argued that the knife-edge version of Gresham's Law is too severe. In historical experience, arbitrage was limited by significant costs of melting coins and exporting the metal. These costs create a range of world price ratios around the mint ratio in which both metals can circulate together. Friedman pointed to the remarkable fact that France managed to maintain a mint ratio of 15.5 to 1, with coins of both metals in circulation and the mint open to both, for seventy years (1803–1873), while the world market price ratio wandered between 15.2 and 15.7.

Furthermore, he noted, a policy of bimetallism in a country or set of countries that coins a large share of the world's precious metals (as France did) can actually help keep the world price ratio from wandering away from the mint ratio, making the system stable within an even wider range. In France, when 1 ounce of gold became cheaper than 15.5 ounces of silver in the world market, more gold came to the mint to be coined (and less silver). The mint's absorption of gold moderated gold's fall in relative price. When silver became cheaper, conversely, more silver came to the mint. Gold coins went from 30 percent of France's specie in circulation to over 80 percent in the years after 1850 when the California and Australia gold rushes reduced gold's market value relative to silver's, according to the economic historian Marc Flandreau (1995). By absorbing gold or silver in this way, Friedman argued, the French mint helped to stabilize the world market ratio. It was not just a lucky accident that the world market ratio stayed near to 15.5 for so many years.

For bimetallism to have this effect, however, there must be coin denominations that can be produced either in gold or in silver, and these coins must be held in large amounts to provide a large potential volume of gold–silver substitution. In mid-nineteenth-century France, 5-franc coins were issued in both silver and gold versions. (In the United States, $1 was issued in both metals between 1849 and 1889.) France provided a surprisingly large potential volume of substitution because, lagging behind other countries in the use of bank-issued money, its people held large shares of the world's monetary gold and silver.

But after 1873, France's luck ran out. The number of silver ounces equivalent to one gold ounce at the world price ratio rose so far above 15.5 that the French mint had to stop coining silver. This event convinced sophisticated bimetallists that one country could not maintain a fixed ratio alone, and they argued for an international bimetallic treaty, under which all participating countries would coin both metals in the same ratio, precisely to increase the potential volume of substitution.

The bimetallists were ultimately fighting a rearguard action. Modern banking provided a better solution than bimetallism to the problem of keeping currency pieces of small and large values at par. In a monometallic standard with the widespread use of bank-issued money, both small and large payments are typically made in banknotes and checks, all kept at par by redeemability for the standard metal. This became the standard solution as bank-issued money gained popularity with the public. By the late nineteenth century, in financially sophisticated countries, large-value silver and gold coins had been largely relegated to bank vaults, displaced from circulation by the popularity of banknotes. In countries where the law imposed a lower bound on the permitted denomination of banknotes, very small payments were mostly made in non-precious ("token") coins made of copper or low-grade silver alloy, kept at par by redeemability at the government mint. These developments meant that the potential volume of silver–gold substitution had shrunk dramatically, narrowing dramatically the range within which bimetallism could stabilize the gold–silver market ratio. But they simultaneously rendered bimetallism unnecessary. Now a banking system on a monometallic gold standard could provide currency in all desired denominations without shortages of small or large denominations.

2.4 HOW MARKET FORCES DETERMINE THE QUANTITY AND PURCHASING POWER OF GOLD IN A SMALL OPEN ECONOMY

A single region, say a city or even a small country, can be regarded as practically a "price taker" for gold when it is one corner of a much larger gold-standard world. That is, the region can obtain all the gold it wants from the rest of the world at the prevailing world price of gold measured in tradable goods and services, with changes in its demand having negligible impact on the world price. It can likewise sell any unwanted gold to the rest of the world at the prevailing price. A shorter expression for "the price

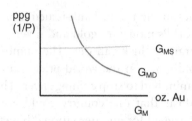

FIGURE 2.1 Supply and demand for monetary gold in a small open economy

of gold in terms of goods and services," is "the purchasing power of gold," or ppg for short, meaning how many bundles of goods trade for one ounce of gold. The ppg (bundles per ounce) is the inverse of an index of goods prices in gold (ounces per bundle).

The situation of the small open economy is represented in Figure 2.1 by the textbook device of a supply-and-demand diagram. In the market for monetary gold stocks, the demand curve G_{MD} illustrates the proposition that at a lower purchasing power per ounce of gold, households and firms would want to hold more ounces to accomplish the same transactions.[4] The nearly flat supply curve G_{MS} illustrates the proposition that even a slightly higher purchasing power of gold in the region would bring ample gold from the rest of the world seeking more goods per ounce.

Suppose that the local economy experiences an increase in real output of goods and services while in the rest of the world real output is flat. The local demand curve for monetary gold G_{MD} would shift to the right. (Drawing in the new curve is left as an exercise for the reader.) To acquire additional gold, the local economy exports some goods to the rest of the world and adds to its money balances (rather than spending on imports) some of the gold paid for its exports. In the new equilibrium, the local stock of gold is higher, with no appreciable change in the purchasing power of gold. Additions to the region's stock of monetary gold made in this way may be more or less rapid depending on the speed of the arbitrage process.[5]

---

[4] In fact they would want to hold *proportionally* more ounces, because what they care about is the size of transactions balances in purchasing power terms. This gives the demand curve a specific bowed-in shape known as a rectangular hyperbola. At any point along the monetary demand curve, the product of the horizontal coordinate and the vertical coordinate is a constant figure.

[5] McCloskey and Zecher (1984) argue that attainment of the new equilibrium position should be regarded as effectively instantaneous. David Hume (1752) in his classic description of the "price-specie-flow mechanism" assumed that it would be rapid but not instantaneous. His thought-experiment began by supposing "four-fifths of all the

The implication of this analysis is that the local quantity of money adjusts to satisfy changes in local demand, while the local price level sticks with the world price level measured in gold (or equivalently, the local purchasing power of gold sticks with the world ppg). Shifts in the local demand for money do not lastingly disturb the local price level.

The world purchasing power of gold, treated as given from the perspective of the small country, is the level that equates the global quantity of monetary gold demanded to the quantity supplied. We analyze its determination in Section 2.6.

2.5 WHY INFLATION WAS LOW UNDER THE CLASSICAL GOLD STANDARD

In what ways might a gold standard provide better money than today's fiat monetary standards? By contrast to the fiat standards that have prevailed since 1971, the classical international gold standard that operated before 1914 had at least five virtues: (1) lower inflation rates (and expected inflation rates), (2) lower price level uncertainty at medium to long horizons, (3) lower resource costs of gold mining for monetary or financial purposes, (4) greater global trade with a common currency between countries, and (5) greater fiscal discipline.[6] The present section discusses the first of these virtues; Chapters 3 and 4 discuss the others.

The inflation rate means the rate of increase of a general level of prices, or equivalently the rate at which the purchasing power of the monetary unit shrinks. A higher average inflation rate imposes a higher tax, or more negative return, on holding currency.

Average inflation rates were notably low under gold and silver standards. Over the United Kingdom's continuous time on the gold standard, 1821–1914, the overall inflation rate was very close to zero. The measured composite price index fell a bit less than 5 percent over the entire 93 years between the resumption of the gold standard in 1821, following the Napoleonic Wars, and the departure from gold at the start of the First World War in 1914 (O'Donoghue, Goulding, and Allen 2004). The

---

money in GREAT BRITAIN to be annihilated in one night." Local prices first drop below world prices, which prompts gold inflows, which then extinguish the discrepancy. For a secondary account of Hume's monetary thought, see Schabas and Wennerlind (2020, ch. 5).

[6] This summary rests on evidence in Selgin, Lastrapes, and White (2012) and White (2015).

corresponding compound annual inflation rate over the entire period rounds to -0.05 percent. In the United States' experience, the inflation rate was even closer to zero. Over the thirty-five years between the resumption of the gold standard in 1879, following a long suspension that began during the Civil War, and the start of the First World War in 1914 (also the year the Federal Reserve System first opened its doors), the measured Consumer Price Index rose only 2 tenths of 1 percent, for a compound annual inflation rate of 0.006 percent (Johnston and Williamson 2014a).[7]

Ongoing inflation is almost always due to ongoing expansion in the quantity of basic money: Dollar prices rise when more dollars chase each bundle of goods. Under a gold standard, the quantity of money does not expand much each year: Gold is costly to mine and refine, and the rising marginal cost of gold extraction limits profitable volume of gold output during any year. Under historical gold standards, the world quantity of monetary gold grew relatively slowly, and price inflation rates were correspondingly low. Gold held its purchasing power. In the next section, we examine the economic factors – including the costs of gold mining – that determine the rate at which the stock of monetary gold expands and so govern the global purchasing power of gold.

2.6 HOW MARKET FORCES GOVERN THE GLOBAL QUANTITY AND PURCHASING POWER OF GOLD

Between 1807 and 1869, according to credible estimates (Rockoff 1984), the world's monetary gold stock grew at an average compound rate of 1.95 percent per year. The real output of final goods and services that traded against gold grew at a similar rate: In the Western world (Western Europe and its offshoots) between 1820 and 1870 real output grew at an estimated 2.05 percent per year. During the next fifty years (1869–1919), roughly corresponding to the classical gold standard era, the world's gold stock grew slightly faster at 2.52 percent per year. Real output of goods in the West also grew slightly faster than before, at 2.67 percent per year between 1870 and 1913.[8] Figure 2.2 charts these numbers to show how the growth rates of monetary gold and real output moved together. The result of gold

---

[7] As measured by the gross domestic product (GDP) deflator, rather than the CPI, the compound annual inflation rate was 0.6 percent (Johnston and Williamson 2014b). All compound rates calculated by the present author.

[8] Gold figures have been taken from Rockoff (1984, p. 621, Table 14.1). Rockoff reports annualized growth rates by decades. Using those figures I have computed the compound

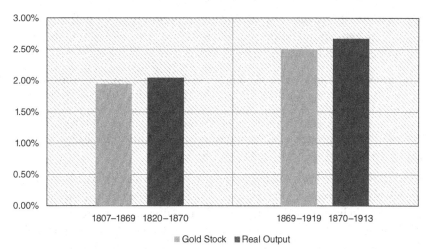

FIGURE 2.2 World gold stock and Western real output growth rates, 1807–1919

growth matching goods growth over the long term was near-zero long-term inflation, and price-level predictability over the medium to long term.

The similarity of the goods and monetary gold growth rates over these two long periods was not accidental good luck, but the reliable result of automatic adjustments in the supply of monetary gold that made its growth conform to growth in the demand for monetary gold, which corresponded to growth in real output of goods and services. It was the automatic outcome of market forces that with faster real output growth after 1870 would come faster growth in the stock of monetary gold. Profit-seeking gold miners and refiners, together with largely passive mints, acted to meet growing money demand and thereby pushed the purchasing power of gold back toward its nearly flat long-run trend. The system similarly corrected for other supply or demand disturbances that bumped the purchasing power of gold off its trend.

Economists writing about the gold standard have not always recognized the self-stabilizing character of the purchasing power of gold in response to variations in money demand. For example, one of the most famous economists of his day, Sweden's Gustav Cassel (1920, p. 42), observed the lowered purchasing power of gold and reduced gold mine production that accompanied lower demand for monetary gold as countries left the gold standard during the war years 1916–1919.

growth over the two sub-periods and backed out a corresponding annualized rate that is a geometric average of the decade averages. Real output growth rates over the specified periods have been taken from Maddison (2007, p. 71, Table 2.2.).

He erroneously warned that an indefinite period of price deflation was coming as growth in real output of goods and correspondingly demand for monetary gold resumed after the war:

This deficiency [of mine production] must result in a progressive scarcity of gold and a consequent continued rise in its value. This result could only be avoided if new goldfields were discovered and developed in the proportion necessary for a normal supply of gold. But leaving such a possibility out of consideration and assuming the production of gold to remain about constant, we have to face a growing scarcity of gold and a continued depression of prices.

Here Cassel failed to acknowledge that market forces would prevent an insufficient gold supply and consequent price deflation from persisting indefinitely. (He called for policy measures by central banks and Treasuries to fight deflation by keeping the demand for monetary gold from rising back to the prewar trend path.) Because the suppliers of any good will increase its output in response to a higher price driven by higher demand, it is contrary to economic logic to assume both "the production of gold to remain about constant" and simultaneously a "continued rise" in the purchasing power of gold due to faster growth in demand for gold.[9]

To make a first approach to understanding how the self-correcting forces work, we can walk through a scenario like Cassel's.[10] Specifically, let us consider what happens if the growth in the economy's real output, and correspondingly growth in the demand to hold monetary gold, outpaces the production of monetary gold for a number of years. With more bundles of goods chasing each ounce of gold, the purchasing power of gold indeed rises (the price of goods in gold units falls), as Cassel said. But the story does not end there. The higher purchasing power of gold stimulates a greater annual volume of gold output even without lucky discovery of new goldfields. Owners of existing gold mines who observe a higher purchasing power per ounce (holding constant the cost of extracting any given number of ounces per year, as we assume in order to isolate the effect of the monetary demand growth) find it profitable to increase annual gold production. It pays them to dig deeper into the earth, increasing the volume extracted, until the real cost of the last ounce extracted and refined rises to the new purchasing power. Meanwhile,

---

[9] For more discussion of Cassel's views on the gold standard, see Irwin (2014) and Hogan and White (2021).

[10] It is not clear whether Cassel thought that gold mine production was low because reduced central bank demand for monetary gold had lowered the purchasing power of gold, or because something had increased the costs of gold production. Here we consider the former case. The latter case is analyzed below in connection with Figure 2.10.

so long as the purchasing power of gold remains higher than its initial level, industrial users of gold cut back on the quantity they demand. With the mines producing more ounces of gold per year, but industrial users absorbing fewer ounces, more gold flows into the mints to be coined, which adds to the stock of monetary gold at a faster rate than before. Over time, the faster-growing stock of monetary gold brings the deflation to an end and even reverses it, returning the purchasing power of gold to its flat long-run trend path.

2.7 THE DYNAMICS OF GOLD SUPPLY AND DEMAND IN DIAGRAMS

We can illustrate the stabilizing dynamics of this scenario by making more extensive use of supply-and-demand diagrams.[11] For the global economy, we have to modify the monetary gold supply curve from the one we used for the small open economy. The supply curve cannot be flat for the world as a whole, because a small increase in the world purchasing power of gold will not bring additional monetary gold to our planet from outside it.[12] We need an upward-sloping supply curve to represent the annual output flow of the gold mining industry that actually does add gold to the world as a whole, and a second upward-sloping supply curve to represent the allocation of existing gold stocks between monetary and non-monetary uses. We need a flow demand curve for industries that use up gold, and another for those who hold monetary gold stocks. Readers unfamiliar with diagrams of this type can read the text between them that explains the process being illustrated.

To explain why we now need two sets of curves, we begin with the simple distinction between "stocks" and "flows." The volume of water currently sitting in the bathtub is a stock; the rate at which warm water comes out of the faucet is a flow. Existing holdings of gold coins and bullion, and of non-monetary gold objects like jewelry and candlesticks, are stocks, measured simply in *ounces* at a point in time. Gold mining production and industrial uptake of gold are flows, measured in *ounces per year*. We have one diagram to illustrate the market for monetary gold stocks (Figure 2.3) and another to illustrate the market for gold flows (Figure 2.4).

---

[11] This section draws on and amplifies White (1999, pp. 28–35).

[12] Nor will higher interest rates. It reportedly used to be said in the City of London that when the Bank of England raised the interest rate it paid on deposits to 5 percent it would attract gold from the Continent, while a rate of 7 percent would "bring gold from the moon" (Mayhew 2000, p. 193).

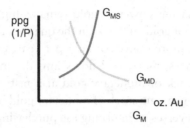

FIGURE 2.3 Global stock demand and supply of monetary gold

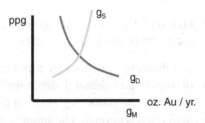

FIGURE 2.4 Global flow demand and supply of gold

The total stock of available above-ground gold can be divided between the part currently in non-monetary uses (primarily jewelry and industrial input inventories) and the part in monetary uses (coins and bullion).[13] In the market for monetary gold stocks, the demand curve G_{MD} again illustrates the proposition that at a lower purchasing power per ounce of gold, households and firms would want to hold proportionately more ounces to accomplish the same transactions. The supply curve G_{MS} illustrates the proposition that at a higher purchasing power of gold, because non-monetary gold objects are more expensive, some existing jewelry and candlesticks are melted down and coined into money.[14] The flatter is the supply curve (the greater the volume of jewelry that will be melted and coined in response to a small rise in the ppg), the more stable is the ppg in the face of any demand curve shift, as Milton Friedman (1951, p. 207) noted.

Additions to the world's stock of monetary gold made in this way are immediate and do not involve additional gold mining. The market-clearing price in the market for monetary gold stocks is the level of the

[13] For simplicity, we assume that the gold taken up by industry is "absorbed" in the sense that it cannot be profitably recovered at any purchasing power of gold within the relevant range.

[14] We assume here that the costs are negligible of converting (say) the 18K gold used in jewelry into the 22K gold used in coins.

purchasing power of gold that equates the quantity of monetary gold demanded to the quantity supplied.

The *flow supply curve* for gold, labeled g_S, illustrates the proposition that a higher relative price of gold (which means a higher purchasing power of monetary gold) brings forth a greater flow quantity (ounces per year) from mining firms as it pays them to exploit sources with higher extraction costs. The *demand curve* in the flow market g_D illustrates the proposition that industrial users will buy a smaller volume per year, because some will switch to substitutes, at a higher price of gold.

To take the simplest case first, consider a *no-growth economy* (unchanging population, unchanging income per person) where the demands to own monetary and non-monetary gold (coins and jewelry) are static. Assuming no wear and tear on existing gold stocks, there is zero annual flow of gold into mints or jewelry workshops. Then the *market clearing price* in the flow market is the purchasing power of gold that equates the flow quantity produced to the flow quantity purchased by industrial users. At any higher purchasing power, the quantity produced would exceed the quantity absorbed by industrial users, the difference would flow into the mints, and the stock of monetary gold would grow.

With this apparatus in hand, let's return to the scenario where economic growth has increased the transactions demand for monetary gold stocks. To show interactions between the markets for gold flows and stocks, we place them side by side. Assuming that gold producers or owners of non-monetary gold can always take their gold to the mint to be coined for a negligible fee, and can melt coins for non-monetary use, arbitrage insures that the same ppg prevails in both markets.

The initial impact of an increase in the demand to hold gold money due to economic growth is shown in Figure 2.5. The monetary gold demand curve shifts outward in the stock diagram, which raises the purchasing power of gold and triggers some conversion of non-monetary into monetary gold as we move northeast along the given stock monetary supply curve G_{MS}. (For simplicity we leave the stock supply curve unchanged. If we assumed instead that economic growth brought an increase in the demand to hold gold jewelry, the monetary stock supply curve would shift leftward, which would amplify the rise in the purchasing power of gold.) In the flow market, the higher ppg increases the quantity supplied by the mines and reduces the quantity demanded by industrial users. The difference between mine output and industrial uptake, labeled g_M, represents a now-positive flow of gold that will go into the mints.

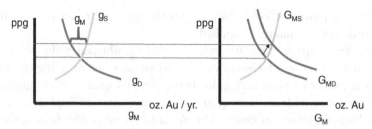

FIGURE 2.5 The initial impact of an increase in the demand to hold monetary gold is to raise the purchasing power of gold, expand mine output, and diminish industrial use

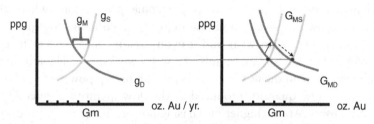

FIGURE 2.6 The long-run impact of an increase in the demand to hold monetary gold is to increase the stock of monetary gold but not the purchasing power of gold

The minting of coins expands the stock of monetary gold, which rebounds to the stock market as a gradual rightward shift in the stock supply curve for monetary gold, shown by the dashed arrow in Figure 2.6. As the stock supply curve moves rightward, the high ppg begins to decline, and the inflow to the mints begins to slow (g_M begins to shrink).

How far will the stock supply curve shift when all is said and done? The shift must stop when, but not before, the flow market returns to a zero gap between supply and industrial demand. This means: when the original ppg is re-established. The process thus eventually re-establishes a *stationary equilibrium* in the flow and stock markets, and returns the purchasing power of gold to the original level consistent with the initial flow market equilibrium. In the long run, an increased stock demand for monetary gold is met entirely by increased production of gold. Automatic market forces return the purchasing power of gold to normal after such a disturbance.

Perhaps the largest monetary gold demand shift in history occurred in the early 1870s when a number of European countries left silver or bimetallic standards to join the gold standard. Their governments sold silver and bought tons of gold to produce new coins, and banks traded silver for gold bullion reserves. The newly unified Germany went first in 1872, minting new gold Marks to replace a variety of regional silver coinages. Sweden, Denmark, and Norway immediately made the same switch, with the Netherlands, Finland, Belgium, France, and Switzerland following within the next few years (Meissner 2005). In response, the purchasing power of gold rose in the world market. By 1887 an index of the purchasing power of the gold British pound was 17 percent higher than it had been in 1872.

The high purchasing power of gold triggered a supply response: not only greater production from existing mines (as depicted by our basic supply-and-demand diagrams), but also greater prospecting, eventually leading to the Klondike gold field discovery of 1896, and even more intensive research into gold refining, leading to the 1887 discovery of the cyanide process for economically extracting gold from lower-grade ores. (We could show this in graphical terms by drawing a long-run gold flow supply curve that is flatter, because it allows new mines to be added, than the short-run curve mapping gold supply from existing mines.) The supply response drove the ppg back down. Between 1887 and 1913 the purchasing power of the gold pound declined by 13.5 percent. By 1913 it had returned to its 1875 value, and nearly back to its 1872 value.[15] The increased monetary gold demand was ultimately satisfied almost entirely by an enlarged stock of monetary gold rather than by a permanent rise in the purchasing power of gold.

Our stock-flow supply-and-demand apparatus can be applied in a similar manner to other cases. The result that the ppg is restored to its starting point also emerges from thought-experiments that begin with shifts in the stock supply curve. If James Bond (spoiler alert!) fails to stop villain Auric Goldfinger from detonating a dirty nuclear bomb in Fort Knox, where the bulk of the US Treasury's gold stock is stored, and if we assume that rendering the gold unapproachably radioactive is equivalent to making it disappear, the monetary stock supply curve initially shifts to

---

[15] O'Donoghue, Goulding, and Allen (2004), p. 45, Table 3. On the connection of the cyanide and Klondike discoveries to the high purchasing power of gold, see Rockoff (1984, pp. 628–30). Why might the ppg not have fully returned to its 1872 value? Note that the speed of convergence slows down, because the size of the gM flow into the mints gets smaller and smaller, as the current ppg gets closer to the long-run equilibrium ppg. Convergence is asymptotic, meaning that the gap becomes arbitrarily small but not zero in a finite number of periods.

the left.[16] The same monetary gold supply curve shift could alternatively happen due to a large increase in the popularity of high-carat gold jewelry. The ppg rises, enriching holders of large stocks of unimpaired gold like Mr. Goldfinger. But eventually (presumably Goldfinger plans to have sold his gold by then) comes a supply response to the high ppg. Mines increase their flow output, and industrial users cut back on their absorption, resulting in a flow of gold into monetary use.[17] The world stock of monetary gold grows, eventually reversing the initial rise in the ppg.

In the reverse case of a one-time *addition* to the stock of monetary gold – say a forgotten sunken ship full of gold coins is discovered, or a gold-rich meteorite lands on Earth – the initial impact of a rightward shift in the stock supply curve of monetary gold lowers the purchasing power of gold, which discourages mining and encourages greater industrial absorption, which in turn works off the extra gold, until the ppg again returns to its starting point.

2.8 SUPPLY AND DEMAND FOR GOLD IN A GROWING ECONOMY

We can analyze the effects of shifts in supply and demand in the more realistic case of a growing world economy adapting the supply-and-demand apparatus we have used in the simpler case of the no-growth economy. As a benchmark, Figure 2.7 shows one period in the life of an economy with steady growth in the demand to hold monetary gold (associated with steady growth in real output) in an equilibrium

---

[16] Goldfinger's assumption that radioactive gold would be valueless is dubious. Although irradiated gold could no longer be sold for industrial or jewelry use, the bullion in Fort Knox was never held for such uses. Ownership of numbered gold bars could continue to be transferred in settlements without anyone touching the bars, if the recipients are willing to leave their holdings in the Fort Knox vault. Foreign governments have in fact left their holdings in the Federal Reserve Bank of New York even when ownership changes. The gold in the FRBNY vault is a criminal's target in a different film, 1995's *Die Hard with a Vengeance*.

[17] When the film *Goldfinger* was released (1964), gold coins were no longer circulated or held in reserve by commercial banks. Under the Bretton Woods dollar–gold-exchange system of the time, however, the US government still held gold bullion reserves for redeeming, at $35 per ounce, the Federal Reserve liabilities held by foreign central banks. Goldfinger's plan assumed that, after his dirty bomb explodes, the US government would have to buy gold to replace the radioactive gold, driving up the purchasing power of gold. The US government might instead choose (a) to redeem in radioactive gold, (b) devalue its dollar obligations against gold, or (c) renege completely on gold redeemability, "closing the gold window" and floating the now-fiat dollar as President Nixon did only a few years later (1971).

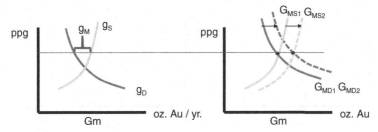

FIGURE 2.7 An economy with steady growth in the monetary demand for gold matched by equal growth in stock of gold

where growth in the stock of monetary gold matches the growth in monetary gold demand. The matching growth rates are shown by the stock supply curve and the stock demand curve for monetary gold in the right-hand diagram shifting rightward by identical horizontal distances. Due to the equal rightward shifts, and the assumption of no shifts in flow supply or demand, the ppg that clears the market for monetary gold stocks (equates quantity demanded to quantity supplied) at the end of the period is the same ppg that cleared the market at the beginning of the period.

As can be seen in the left-hand diagram of Figure 2.7, the growing economy produces a higher equilibrium level of ppg than a no-growth economy, given the same flow of gold supply and demand curves. In the no-growth economy, gold production is only great enough to meet industrial use with nothing left for adding to the stock of monetary gold or to the stock of gold jewelry. Nor is there any demand for additional monetary gold or jewelry. By contrast, the growing economy's equilibrium ppg is higher, inducing a greater volume of gold production. Specifically, the ppg is just enough higher so that the volume of gold that annually flows into the mints, shown by the horizontal difference g_M between flow quantity produced and flow quantity absorbed at that ppg, is just large enough to expand the monetary gold stock each period (shown by the rightward shift in G_{MS}) by just enough to match the growth in the monetary demand for gold. The equilibrium level of the ppg is such that any higher ppg would make the correspondingly larger gold flow into the mints exceed the growth in money demand, which would drive the ppg down. (Any lower ppg would make the flow so small as to drive the ppg up.)

To trace graphically the effects of an increase not in the *level* but in the ongoing *growth rate* of monetary gold demand would be quite messy if we started with Figure 2.7 and depicted the shift relative to the initial

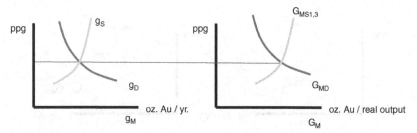

FIGURE 2.8 Alternative representation of an economy with steady growth in the monetary demand for gold matched by equal growth in stock of gold

end-of-period curves by drawing in yet another monetary gold demand curve. A less cluttered way to conduct the analysis is to repurpose the flow and stock diagrams we have been using, revising them to depict a growing economy. Measured in ounces of gold, as seen in Figure 2.7, the stock supply and demand curves are moving evenly rightward through time with growth in the economy's real output, so as to maintain an ongoing monetary equilibrium. (For simplicity we assume that the level of money demand is proportional to the level of real output.) If we measure the money stock relative to real output, however, the same steady-state-growth equilibrium can be shown with curves that remain in place. In Figure 2.8, the units on the horizontal axis of the stock diagram are no longer simply ounces of gold, but are now ounces of gold *per unit of the economy's real output*, where "the economy" encompasses all the gold-standard areas of the world.

The revised flow diagram continues to measure production in ounces of gold per year, but the demand curve now has a different interpretation. In the baseline, no-growth economy the flow demand for gold came only from industrial users. In a growing economy, the flow demand for gold is not only for industrial use but also for equilibrating additions to the stocks of monetary and non-monetary gold. We assume that as real income rises, people want to hold more gold jewelry and ornaments. They also want a greater stock of monetary gold: The real demand for money rises in proportion to income. The flow demand curve g_D is now the sum of these three annual demands for gold. The World Gold Council, which tracks current gold market statistics, in similar fashion divides annual sales of gold into four categories: technology (industrial uses), private investment (coins, medallions, bullion, and reserves backing exchange-traded gold funds), central banks, and jewelry. In 2019 Q2, gold production went 7.2 percent into technology, 25.4 percent into private investment, 20.0 percent into central banks, and 47.3 percent into jewelry.

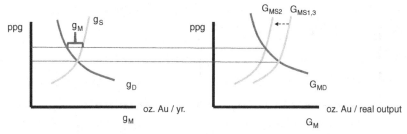

FIGURE 2.9 Faster growth in real output initially diminishes the monetary gold stock per unit of output, raises the ppg, and expands monetary gold production

If the real output of goods shifts from a lower to a higher growth rate, as we saw when comparing the 1820–1870 period to the succeeding 1870–1913 period, then the demand for monetary gold correspondingly grows faster, raising the equilibrium ppg until the supply catches up. The higher ppg induces faster growth in the monetary gold stock G_M and brings the monetary gold stock up to the higher level of demand for monetary gold in the faster-growing economy.

An initial growth equilibrium is shown in Figure 2.9 by the intersection of flow supply curve g_S and flow demand curve g_D in the flow diagram, and the intersection of stock demand curve G_{MD} with stock supply curve G_{MS1} in the stock diagram, both at the same ppg. Suppose the economy's real output now begins to grow more rapidly. For example, imagine that on a particular date the economy switches from growing at 2 percent per year to growing at 2.5 percent per year. The corresponding increase in the growth rate of monetary gold demand does not shift the monetary stock demand curve, which (recall) is now measured relative to real output. Rather, because the economy's real output initially outpaces the inherited growth rate of the monetary gold stock, in Figure 2.10 the monetary stock supply curve drifts to the left (gradual movement denoted by the dashed arrow), fewer and fewer ounces being available per unit of real output. The ppg rises relative to trend, which induces an expansion in the quantity of gold production and a reduction in industrial consumption, creating an excess of flow production (shown by the gap g_M) that goes to the mint, adding to the monetary stock each period.

In such a case the higher gold production allows the stock of monetary gold to catch up to higher monetary demand for gold, which returns the ppg to trend. In cases where the flow supply and demand curves do not shift, as we have so far been considering, the purchasing power of gold returns to a constant trend line. To consider economies with a rising or

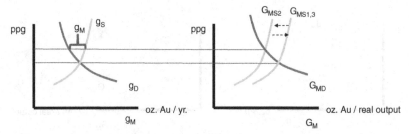

FIGURE 2.10 Following a positive shock to the economy's real growth rate, the induced faster growth of the monetary gold stock returns ppg to its steady-state equilibrium value

falling trend ppg, we will later turn our attention to cases involving shifts in flow supply or demand.

2.9 BANKING ON A GOLD STANDARD ECONOMIZES ON THE USE OF GOLD

Adam Smith (1982 [1776], pp. 303–304) praised the voluntary replacement of gold and silver coins by bank-issued money as a boost for the economy's production of goods and services:

> The gold and silver money which circulates in any country, and by means of which the produce of its land and labour is annually circulated and distributed to the proper consumers, is ... all dead stock. It is a very valuable part of the capital of the country, which produces nothing to the country. The judicious operations of banking, by substituting paper in the room of a great part of this gold and silver, enables the country to convert a great part of this dead stock into active and productive stock; into stock which produces something to the country.

The export of gold and silver coins, made redundant by banking, had enabled Scotland to import machines and materials that promoted its real economic growth.

In a similar vein, the Austrian economist Ludwig von Mises (1980 [1912], pp. 196–7) noted that the progressive development of fractional-reserve banking from the Middle Ages onward had historically spared the world much of the expense that would have been incurred if all the growth in money demand over the centuries had instead been met by gold mining:

> In fact, the development of the clearing system and of fiduciary media [banknotes and checking deposits in excess of gold reserves] has at least kept pace with the potential increase of the demand for money brought about by the extension of the money economy, so that the tremendous increase in the exchange value of money,

which otherwise would have occurred as a consequence of the extension of the use of money, has been completely avoided, together with its undesirable consequences. If it had not been for this the increase in the exchange value of money, and so also of the monetary metal, would have given an increased impetus to the production of the metal. Capital and labor would have been diverted from other branches of production to the production of the monetary metal. ... [A] smaller quantity of economic goods would have been available for the direct satisfaction of human wants if a part of the capital and labor power that otherwise would have been used for their production had been diverted to mining precious metals.

We will return to the question of the resource costs incurred by a gold standard in Section 2.12.

We can use our growth-adjusted supply-and-demand apparatus to illustrate Smith's and Mises' arguments about how the development of banking reduces the costs of a gold-based monetary system. Suppose that the banks develop payment methods that enable the public to switch from making many payments in gold coins to making them in fractionally backed banknotes or checking account transfers. Figures 2.11 and 2.12 illustrate the immediate and long-run effects of the introduction of new payment methods that enable the banks to operate safely with progressively lower gold reserve ratios over time. These developments shift the monetary gold demand curve in the stock diagram *inward*. (The same shift can also represent some large counties leaving the gold standard, for example, during the First World War, as discussed in Chapter 3.) Less monetary gold is demanded at any given level of the ppg. The initial impact lowers the ppg and prompts some conversion of monetary into non-monetary gold (shown by the southwest movement along the stock supply curve). In the flow market, the lower ppg reduces the quantity supplied by gold mines and increases the flow quantity demanded.

Flow production now falls short of flow quantity demanded by the amount g_M. The difference is met by reducing the volume annually added

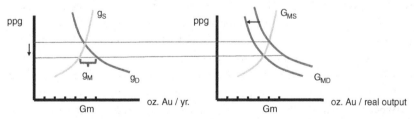

FIGURE 2.11 The development of bank-issued money (or alternatively the exit of some countries from the gold standard) reduces the demand for monetary gold relative to real output, lowering the ppg and shrinking the stock of monetary gold per unit of real output

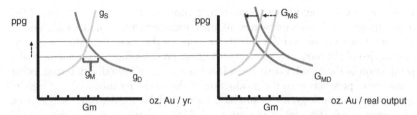

FIGURE 2.12 Reduced demand for monetary gold per unit of real output is ultimately met by shrinkage in the stock of monetary gold per unit of output, stabilizing long-run ppg

to the monetary gold stock below the volume necessary for the stock to keep up with growing real output. In the stock diagram, the reduction in new coinage volume begins to pull the stock supply curve leftward over time relative to real output. The relative reduction in the stock of monetary gold pushes the ppg back up. The process of shrinking monetary gold stock and rising ppg continues until the flow market gap disappears, as seen in Figure 2.12. The reduction in monetary gold demand is ultimately satisfied by less growth in the stock of monetary gold rather than a permanent change in the purchasing power of gold.

2.10 THE EFFECTS OF SHIFTS IN FLOW SUPPLY AND DEMAND

In January 1848, John Marshall was helping to build a sawmill for John Sutter on the bank of the South Fork American River in northern California. On January 24, Marshall was checking the tailrace, the channel where water exited the mill. He spotted something shining in the stream. He picked up a small gold nugget, the size of a pea, and several flakes. When Sutter learned of the discovery, he asked the sawmill's employees to keep it a secret (Hurtado 2006, pp. 216–17). Other millworkers also found gold bits scattered about the site, and word quickly got out. San Francisco newspapers reported on Marshall's and other nearby gold discoveries. Prospectors flocked to the gold-rich area from other parts of California and neighboring Oregon. The "gold rush" year of 1849 saw prospectors come from all over the world. By one account (Eifler 2016), more than a quarter-million people moved to California between 1848 and 1854. They mined an estimated $550 million worth of gold between 1848 and 1857 inclusive (Whaples 2008).

Using our supply-and-demand diagrams for a growing economy, this discovery of the California gold fields is represented in Figure 2.13 by a large rightward shift in the flow supply curve: At any level of the ppg,

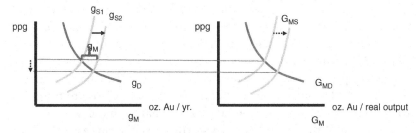

FIGURE 2.13 A major goldfield discovery shifts the flow supply curve to the right, permanently enlarging the stock supply of gold per unit of output and lowering the ppg

more gold ounces would henceforth be produced each year. (By treating it as a single supply curve shift, we abstract from the fact that the volume of California gold production grew until 1853, then declined as miners depleted the gold sources.) As the flow supply of gold increases above the previous equilibrium volume, which just matched flow demand at the prevailing ppg, additional gold g_M goes into the mints to be monetized. The accumulation of new coins and bullion at a higher rate pushes the monetary gold stock supply curve G_{MS} to right over time, lowering ppg. As ppg declines, production from pre-existing non-California gold mines shrinks, and flow demand from industrial users grows. (Flow quantity demanded for gold jewelry probably increases because of its lower relative price, but this is not certain because owners of existing jewelry suffer wealth losses and may reduce their demands for that reason.)

A new equilibrium ppg is eventually reached at which annual production is greater and just matches the increased annual flow demand. Not surprisingly, the stock of monetary gold is on a higher growth path (both in ounces and in relation to the economy's real output) than the path it would have reached without the discovery. The ppg is lower than before, and that change is not self-reversing because the flow supply curve's shift has lowered the equilibrium ppg in the flow market. Unlike our earlier cases that began with a curve shift in the market for monetary gold stocks, shifts in *flow* supply (or flow industrial demand) *can* permanently alter the ppg by altering the marginal cost of producing monetary gold. Our earlier cases left the flow curves unchanged, and thus left unchanged the flow market equilibrium ppg that governs the stock market ppg in the long run.

Curve-shifting exercises do not tell us how large, how frequent, or how long-lasting gold flow supply shocks have been historically. As it happens, the California Gold Rush, the largest supply shock in the historical record, together with the Australian gold rush that began in 1851, brought about a cumulative world price level rise of 26 percent (as measured by the United Kingdom's Retail Price Index) over a span of eighteen years (1849–1867), which works out to a compound annual inflation rate of 1.3 percent per annum. The swing in the monetary expansion rate was large for a gold standard regime, but modest by comparison to historical swings in the postwar expansion rates of national fiat monies.

The return of the ppg to its exact starting level in the case of a stock supply or demand curve shift, as analyzed in the section above on shifts in monetary stock supply or demand curves, depends on the marginal cost of gold extraction remaining constant within the relevant range, that is, on the flow supply and demand curves not shifting. If the marginal cost instead rises over time because remaining gold gets progressively harder to reach as the veins of existing gold mines are depleted, then the flow supply curve drifts leftward over time. The long-run trend value to which the market purchasing power of gold returns after a shift, instead of remaining unchanged, will be rising over time. Figure 2.14 shows the effect of depletion in making the ppg rise over time in a growing economy. The leftward shift in g_S means that flow quantity demanded (including annual additions to the stocks of monetary gold and gold jewelry) exceeds flow quantity supplied at the previous ppg. Monetary and nonmonetary gold stocks grow less slowly than real output (and implicitly stock monetary gold demand) as a result, so that the monetary stock supply curve migrates leftward over time, raising the ppg. This process does not reach a long-run ending point, but continues indefinitely.

Figure 2.14 considers depletion acting in isolation, holding constant the number of gold mines and the state of gold-mining technology. The long-run supply curve is flatter when we allow additional prospecting activity, induced by a higher ppg, to bring new mines online. This will reduce the magnitude of the depletion effect. Technological

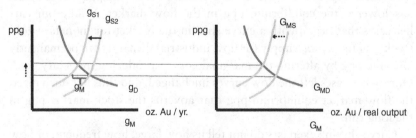

FIGURE 2.14 Progressive depletion of gold mines raises ppg over time by reducing the growth of monetary stock supply relative to real output

improvement in gold-mining and refining help to offset depletion by lowering the cost of extracting gold from previously uneconomical sources. Considered alone, technological progress shifts the flow gold supply curve to the right. In a growing economy, to the extent that the growth in real output of goods and services is driven by technical progress that lowers their costs of production, it is reasonable to assume that technological progress will similarly lower the costs of producing gold. The time trend in the ppg can then be nearly flat, as seen in the historical record over long periods.[18]

If a significant part of the monetary gold stock consists of coins in circulation, physical wear-and-tear will slowly shrink the monetary stock measured in ounces. If annual wear is (say) 0.5 percent of the existing stock of monetary gold, then as the monetary gold stock grows in a growing economy, a correspondingly growing volume of new gold ounces per year is required to replace the wear on existing coins. In the growing-economy diagrams, the flow demand curve migrates rightward over time. Like depletion, wear-and-tear taken by itself imparts a rising trend to the ppg. During ancient and medieval eras the physical circulation of silver and gold coins was important, and preserving or replenishing the coinage against wear-and-tear (and against the sharp operators mentioned above who deliberately filched precious metal from the coins that passed through their hands) was an important problem. By the time of the classical gold standard era beginning in the 1870s, however, wear-and-tear had become negligible because gold-redeemable paper banknotes and token coins had almost entirely displaced gold coins from physical circulation. Monetary gold was concentrated in clearinghouse and bank vaults, where wear-and-tear is negligible.

2.11 HOW MODERN BANKING STABILIZES THE PURCHASING POWER OF GOLD IN THE SHORT RUN

The accumulation of additional gold in response to a major increase in monetary demand, as shown in Figure 2.6, is a slow process, perhaps taking decades to bring the purchasing power of gold back to trend. Doesn't

---

[18] Bordo and Ellson (1985, p. 118) numerically calibrate and simulate models of the gold standard (based on Barro 1979) with and without depletion. They find that "introducing technological progress at the same rate as the underlying growth rate of the economy ... almost fully offsets the deflation [created by real output growth] in the Classical Model [without depletion] – restoring price stability." Introducing depletion to the model, however, creates "an inescapable tendency towards long-run deflation [a rising ppg], a tendency which is not overcome by technological change."

this mean that the purchasing power of money is unstable from month to month, varying with seasonal or other variations in money demand? Here the development of fractional-reserve banking provides another benefit. If the demand for a payment medium rises to a distinct seasonal peak (as in the late nineteenth century, when farmers paid their farm hands during "crop-moving season," bank-issued monies can provide a desirable flexibility. When the public wants to hold a larger volume of bank-issued money, banks will find it profitable to expand even without additional reserves (can safely lower their reserve ratios) to meet the additional quantity demanded by holders (see White 1999, pp. 64–67). A free banking system varies the quantity of bank-issued money promptly with demand to hold money, dampening movements in the purchasing power of money. Mises (1980 [1912], p. 347), using the term "fiduciary media" to refer to banknotes or deposits in excess of gold reserves, explained the result clearly:

A single bank carrying on its business in competition with numerous others ... will be able to circulate more fiduciary media only if there is a demand for them even when the rate of interest charged is not lower than that charged by the banks competing with it. Thus the banks may be seen to pay a certain amount of regard to the periodical fluctuations in the demand for money. They increase and decrease their circulation *pari passu* with the variations in the demand for money, so far as the lack of a uniform procedure makes it impossible for them to follow an independent interest policy. But in doing so, they help to stabilize the objective exchange value of money.

Competition among many issuing banks limits the danger of a large-scale *over*-expansion, that is, bank expansion in the absence of an increased demand to hold money. The interbank clearing system will discipline any one bank that issues more notes or deposits that its customers want to hold. If Bank A over-issues, spending will put more Bank A notes and checks in the hands of customers of other banks, who will deposit the excess. Other banks will receive more claims on Bank A, and will bring these claims to the clearinghouse, with the result that Bank A loses reserves. One can imagine all the banks conspiring to over-issue together, but it is an implausible scenario. (Firms that act as a cartel profit by restricting output to get higher prices, not by expanding output.) The danger of large-scale over-issue is greatest when a single issuer has a 100 percent share of the circulation, which is why the historical Free Banking School (White 1995, chs. 4–5) opposed the creation of central banks with national monopolies on note-issue.

Historical studies of free banking in Scotland, Canada, Sweden, Australia, New England, Chile, Colombia, and other places (see Dowd

1992 and Briones and Rockoff 2005) show that, with few exceptions, free banking on silver and gold standards was overwhelmingly successful at fostering efficiency, innovation, and growth. Episodes of antebellum American "wildcat banking" and non-par banknotes, though frequently cited by critics of stablecoins and other market-based monies, were fostered not by free competition but by state government restrictions on banking (Selgin 2021). Across the world, where banking was less restricted and less privileged, as a rule it was safer and sounder. Open competition in banking fostered prudence and standardization along with innovation and efficiency.

2.12 THE RESOURCE COST OF A GOLD STANDARD

The development of modern fractional-reserve banknotes and account balances provided inexpensive substitutes for ordinary gold coin payments. We quoted above Mises' observation that modern banking thereby enabled the world to release some labor and capital resources from gold mining, allowing those resources to enlarge the supply of other goods and services. Yet a fractional-reserve banking system on a gold standard still holds a non-zero stock of monetary gold in the form of bank reserves. How much do those reserves cost in foregone other output? The idea that we can realize still further resource cost savings by eliminating *all* gold reserves, and thus eliminating gold mining for monetary purposes altogether, is a common argument among economists for preferring a fiat standard over a gold standard. It might seem straightforward that demonetizing gold will allow the economy to devote zero worker-hours and machine-hours to digging up gold that will be formed into bars and coins, only to be buried in vaults. Historically, however, the demonetization of gold since 1971 has not accomplished this goal. More gold than before is being mined, and formed onto bars and coins, to be held in vaults. The hoped-for resource cost saving has not been realized.

Early in his career Milton Friedman (1951, 1960) provided influential back-of-the-envelope estimates of the size of the resource costs required to operate what he called a "strict" gold standard. Because his estimates continue to be cited, it is worthwhile to review them here.

Assuming an economy in the steady growth equilibrium depicted in Figure 2.7, Friedman in effect calculated the size of g_M, the annual production (or importation) of monetary gold consistent with meeting the growing stock demand for monetary gold at a stable ppg. A stable ppg follows from assuming a constant cost of gold production over time. Friedman (1951) assumed that the demand to hold money (currency and checking deposits; what the US Federal Reserve includes in the M1 measure of the money stock) grows at the same rate as the economy's real output growth. Extrapolating from contemporary US data, he assumed real output growth to be 3 percent per year, and the M1 money stock to be about half of the economy's real output. To meet growing money demand, annual growth in the M1 money stock must therefore be equal in value to half of annual real output growth, or 1.5 percent of real output. To calculate how many ounces of additional gold are needed to support 3 percent growth in the M1 money stock he assumed that all of the M1 money stock was gold coins or 100 percent backed by a gold reserves (this was what Friedman meant by a "strict" gold standard). He thus arrived at a large estimate: 1.5 percent of real output must be devoted to adding to the stock of monetary gold each year.

In a later revised version of the calculation (Friedman 1960, p. 5 and pp. 104–5 n. 6), Friedman switched to a broader measure of the money stock (M2) which gives a higher ratio of money to real output. Allowing for an observed US trend, he added 1 percentage point to the annual growth rate in the stock of broad money per unit of real output (he assumed that the "velocity" of money continues to fall by 1 percent per year), so that the money stock would need to grow at 4 percent per year to maintain a stable ppg. He thereby arrived at the even higher estimate that maintaining a strict gold standard would consume 2.5 percent of the economy's output per year.[19]

The higher estimate is the one more commonly cited. It implies a gold reserve cost of $550 billion per year when national product (or gross domestic product, GDP) is $22 trillion.

In the course of reaching these figures, Friedman made two key assumptions that in retrospect dramatically bias the figure upward if we regard it as an estimate of the cost savings available by switching from a gold standard to a fiat standard. First, he considered a gold standard not in its modern form with fractional reserve banking, but in a hypothetical form with 100 percent gold reserves against currency and deposits. In 1960 he even assumed a 100 percent reserve against time deposits, an inexplicable assumption because a time deposit needs no reserves at all to provide for

---

[19] Specifically, Friedman (1960, pp. 104–5) assumed that the US monetary gold stock was equal to the M2 money stock, and that the ratio of this all-gold M2 to real output was the same as the actual ratio of M2 to Net National Product in 1959.

its redemption until the day it matures. Because the M2 measure includes all bank deposits, assuming 100 percent gold reserves against M2 means assuming a curious world in which there is no lending by banks, only gold storage and checking services. What we actually observe in historical cases of well-developed banking systems on specie standards, without statutory reserve requirements but with prudential reserve holding, are reserve ratios around 2 percent of M2 bank liabilities rather than 100 percent. If we use Friedman's 1960 estimation procedure, but assume 2 percent rather than 100 percent reserves, the resulting estimate is 1/50th of his estimate. The estimated cost of operating a gold standard is only 0.05 percent (5 hundredths of 1 percent) of national income, or $11 billion rather than $550 billion in a $22 trillion economy.[20] When thinking about the resource costs implied by gold reserves theoretically, we should keep in mind that a modern gold standard with fractional-reserve banking uses relatively little gold.

To be fair, Friedman (1951, p. 210) certainly recognized that historical gold and silver standards were characterized by fractional rather 100 percent reserves. He noted that "gold (or other currency commodity) has been 'economized' through the use of fractional reserves for mediums of circulation in the form of hand-to-hand currency and, even more widely, in the form of demand deposits." Still, his exposition confused the distinction between monetary standards and banking systems when he labeled fractional-reserve banking systems "partial commodity standards," or "nominal gold and silver standards," and 100 percent reserve banking or money-warehousing systems "strict commodity standards." Partial bank reserves do not imply a partial commodity standard, much less a commodity standard in name only. Systems with different bank reserve ratios do not have different commodity standards when the unit of account and the medium of redemption are the same.

Friedman (1951, p. 210) sought to explain the development of fractional-reserve banking by reference to the sacrifice in the economy's real output of other goods and services required by 100 percent reserves in a growing economy:

As we have seen, in a world in which total output is growing in response to technological and other changes and in which the velocity of circulation is fairly constant, a strict commodity standard requires the regular use of a considerable volume of resources for additions to the monetary stock in order to keep

---

[20] For more details on Friedman's procedure and the results of alternative parameter values, see White (1999), pp. 42–48.

prices stable. To use the example given above, something like 1½ per cent of the resources of the United States would have had to be devoted to the production of currency commodities for monetary use.

It is not surprising, therefore, that the countries of the Western World have not used strict commodity standards. ... In the main, gold (or other currency commodity) has been "economized" through the use of fractional reserves for mediums of circulation in the form of hand-to-hand currency and, even more widely, in the form of demand deposits.

The disadvantage of 100 percent reserves that historically drove the development of fractional-reserve banking, however, was not felt at the aggregate level where economy-wide real output is determined but at the level of each bank and its customers. Once competitive fractional-reserve banks were available, paying competitive interest rates on deposits, few members of the public chose to store their money in 100-percent-reserve vaults. Warehousing one's gold, rather than placing it on account at (or lending it to) a competitive bank, meant the sacrifice of interest on account balances and the payment of storage fees. To prefer fractional-reserve banking, no individual or bank needed to consider the economy-wide cost of reduced real output. Note that even in a no-growth economy, with no production or importation of monetary gold necessary and thus zero annual resource cost of monetary gold acquisition, depositors who preferred interest and no storage fees on their accounts would still switch from warehousing to fractional-reserve banking.

The second way in which "2.5 percent of the economy's real output" is too high, as an estimate of the savings available by switching from a gold standard to a fiat standard, is that the estimate assumes that accumulation of monetary gold would be zero under a fiat money regime. That is, banking systems would stop accumulating gold reserves as broader money stocks grow, and the public would not start accumulating gold coins or bullion as hedges against inflation. Under those assumptions the stock and flow demand curves for gold in our growing-economy diagrams would both shift leftward, dramatically reducing the ppg and the volume of gold mining. In practice, while central banks did stop buying gold and some became net sellers in the first decades after 1971, since 2010 they have become net buyers again. More importantly the public, in response to unanchored and inflationary fiat monetary policies (Friedman's proposals for explicit rules constraining fiat money creation not having been adopted) since 1971 has demanded so much gold for hedging purposes that the demand curves for gold have actually shifted *rightward*, ironically *raising* the purchasing power of gold and the volume of gold production since the termination of the gold standard.

Friedman (1986, p. 644), to his credit, was alert to the gold-hedging resource cost of fiat money regimes as it emerged in practice. He observed in 1986 that inflation in western nations had become higher and more variable since 1971, and noted its result for gold coin and bullion accumulation:

Real resources are employed ... in the production of the gold and silver absorbed into the hoards accumulated by [individuals] who have come to regard gold or silver as a prudent component of their asset portfolios. Since the end of Bretton Woods, even the direct resource cost of the gold and silver accumulated in private hoards may have been as great as or greater than it would have been under an effective gold standard. That depends on whether gold production since 1971 has been greater or less than it would have been under an effective gold standard—a promising research topic whose conclusion is by no means obvious from casual empiricism.

Recent data on gold production from the World Gold Council (2019) point rather clearly to a conclusion: The production volume of gold coins and bullion is currently greater than it would have been under a gold standard with reasonable prudential reserve ratios.[21] Private stocks of gold coins, bullion, and exchange-traded funds have grown so much since 1971 that they now exceed official gold reserves. The Council reports that the planet's above-ground stocks of gold at the end of 2018 totaled 193,473 tonnes, divided in the following proportions: 47.6 percent jewelry (92,043 tonnes); 21.3 percent private investment holdings of coin, bullion, and exchange-traded funds or ETFs (41,279 tonnes); 17.2 percent official holdings by central banks, Treasuries, and the IMF (33,230 tonnes); and 13.9 percent "other" including mainly industrial inventories (26,921 tonnes). The Council does not provide a data series back to 1971, but if we contrast its 2018 figures with its 2006 figures, we find that of the estimated 35,473 tonnes of gold produced overall during the period, 15,479 tonnes or 43.6 percent went into private investment holdings. Meanwhile, the stock of jewelry grew 12.7 percent, and official holdings grew 16.6 percent. It is curious that some countries have chosen to add to their official gold holdings despite being on fiat standards.

The purchasing power of gold has risen substantially since the United States left the gold standard for the fiat dollar. When President Richard Nixon "closed the gold window" to end what remained of gold redemption of the US dollar on August 15, 1971, the official par value was $35 per ounce, while the market price had floated to $44.60. As of late 2022, with fiat standards prevailing around the world, the price of gold

---

[21] The remainder of this section draws on White (2019b).

was above $1750 per ounce. The ratio of $1750 to $44.60 means that
the dollar price of gold has multiplied 39-fold since August 1971. This
increase is much greater than the increase in the dollar prices of goods
and services in general, the GDP deflator index having multiplied less
than 6-fold between 1971-Q2 and 2022-Q2. Thus the purchasing power
of gold in terms of goods and services has risen considerably. The rise
is not principally due to higher gold mining costs (as shown by production volumes rising rather than falling), or growth in the non-monetary
demand for gold (coin and bullion stocks having grown much more than
jewelry stocks), but is principally due to increased demand for gold bars
and coins by people hedging against the uncertain future value of fiat
monies.

Combining the price and quantity numbers, we can make a back-of-
the-envelope estimate of the share of world real output that is currently
going to produce gold coins and bullion. We begin with the value of the
coins and bullion purchased 2006–2018. One metric tonne of gold is 1000
kilograms, which is equal in mass to 32,151 troy ounces, so 15,479 tonnes
meant 497,665,329 ounces added to private investment holdings of gold
coins, bullion bars, and bullion ETFs. The average gold price over the
period was $1224 per troy ounce.[22] Multiplying the ounces purchased by
the price per ounce, the total value of monetary gold purchased worldwide
was $609 billion over twelve years, or an average of $50.8 billion per year.
Average world GDP over the period, as measured by the World Bank's
website[23], was $77.15 trillion per year. Dividing $50.8 billion into $77.15
trillion, we find that monetary gold purchases were about 0.066 percent of
the world economy's annual output. This figure is 32 percent larger than
the estimate reported above (using Friedman's method but with a reasonable fractional reserve ratio) that under a gold standard some 0.05 percent
of national income would go to acquiring monetary gold. And so we conclude that going off the gold standard has not reduced the flow of resources
used in producing gold coins and bullion, but has increased it something
like 32 percent above what an effective modern gold standard requires.

Put another way, private gold acquisition under fiat standards over
recent years have been costing the world an estimated average of $12.3
billion per year ([.066 percent minus .050 percent] times $77.15 trillion)
more in production of coins and bullion than an international gold

[22] This price is the simple average of annual average gold prices, 2006–18 inclusive, in the
series reported by Garside (2019).
[23] https://data.worldbank.org/indicator/ny.gdp.mktp.cd.

standard would have cost, not even counting recent gold acquisitions by central banks (or acquisition of investment-grade gold jewelry to be stored in vaults, a common practice in India and elsewhere). In a \$96 trillion world economy (as projected for 2021), the excess annual cost of 0.016 percent comes to \$15.4 billion dollars per year.

These estimates indicate that the historical switch from gold to fiat standards, contrary to the sincere hopes of Milton Friedman and other advocates of the switch, has increased the resource costs associated with the production of gold coins and bullion. Perhaps this was avoidable. The establishment of trustworthy non-inflationary fiat money systems (as Friedman prominently advocated) might have given private citizens no reason to invest in gold coins and bars, and might have brought a resource cost saving over the gold standard. But that experiment has not been run.

3

Common Misconceptions about the Gold Standard

The mechanisms that govern how a gold standard works, and the historical performance of gold standards in practice, have often been misunderstood or inaccurately described – both by critics and by supporters. This chapter tries to correct some common misconceptions on both sides, starting with those of critics. The following subheads in quotation marks are not direct quotations, but paraphrases of common arguments.

3.1 "THE GOLD STANDARD CAUSED THE GREAT DEPRESSION"

The most prominent indictment of the gold standard among academic economists in recent decades charges it with creating the Great Depression in the United States and then spreading it internationally.[1] The indictment rests on a combination of at least three propositions: (1) The monetary system prevailing during the period between the two world wars is appropriately called "the gold standard," (2) the gold standard is inherently deflationary, and (3) deflation under the gold standard usually caused depression. All three propositions are mistaken, as explained in the following text.

Economist Douglas Irwin (2014, p. 200) has summarized the indictment and identified its most cited source:

Modern scholarship regards the Depression as an international phenomenon, rather than as something that affected different countries in isolation. The thread that bound countries together in the economic collapse was the gold standard.

---

[1] Here and elsewhere in the chapter, I draw on White (2008, 2013).

Barry Eichengreen's 1992 book *Golden Fetters* is most commonly associated with the view that the gold standard was the key factor in the origins and transmission of the Great Depression around the world ...

The stylized fact most often cited for the "Golden Fetters" hypothesis, in Irwin's words, is that "countries not on the gold standard managed to avoid the Great Depression, while countries on the gold standard did not begin to recover until they left it."

3.2 "THE GOLD STANDARD PREVAILED BETWEEN THE FIRST AND SECOND WORLD WARS"

The First World War began in August 1914. The governments of Austro-Hungary, France, Germany, and Russia soon left the gold standard, suspending redemption of their currencies and placing embargos on private exports of gold. Although the British government did not formally suspend or embargo, it effectively blocked redemption by the Bank of England and the export of gold by London dealers, and blunted the arbitrage motive for exporting gold by pegging the UK pound to the US dollar. Nonetheless, billions of dollars worth of gold flowed from the UK and Europe into the safe haven of the United States. The dollar remained gold-redeemable for the time being. Once the United States entered the war in 1917, it too effectively embargoed gold exports (Crabbe 1989, p. 426).

It is evident in Figures 3.1 and 3.2, showing the prewar and postwar paths of the US dollar Consumer Price Index (CPI) and the UK pound Retail Price Index (RPI), that the international monetary system during and after the First World War was quite unlike the classical gold standard that preceded the war. The US and UK price level paths (and the similar paths of price indices for other European currencies, not shown) dramatically changed their behavior after 1914, reflecting the scuttling of the classical international gold standard. If the prewar regime was "the gold standard," the wartime and interwar periods need a different label or labels. Reference is often made to a "gold exchange standard" during the interwar period, but that label properly applies only to some countries during some years. Other countries floated. No coherent international system prevailed between the Wars, certainly not a gold standard of the prewar sort.

Under a gold standard, as explained in Chapter 2, the purchasing power of gold does not move far from, before prompting a return to, a flat trend (absent a permanent shock to the costs of gold extraction that alters the trend). The US dollar CPI, measured in dollars per bundle of

US Consumer Price Index (average 1982-1984 = 100)

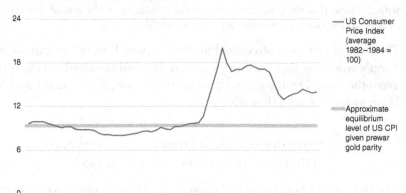

FIGURE 3.1 US Consumer Price Index, 1879–1940. Source for US CPI path: MeasuringWorth.com/graphs.

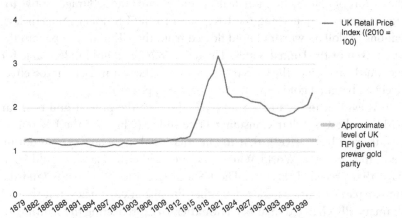

FIGURE 3.2 UK Retail Price Index, 1879–1940. Source for UK RPI path: MeasuringWorth.com/graphs

goods, plots the inverse of the purchasing power of the dollar, bundles of goods per dollar. The CPI indicates how many dollars it takes each year to buy a bundle of goods that represents a typical consumer's expenditures. A rise in the price of the CPI bundle, say from $100 to $125, can alternatively be described as a fall in the purchasing power of the dollar from 100 to 80 (where 100/125 = 0.80). When the number of dollars per ounce of gold is fixed, as it was under the US gold standard from 1879 to 1934, the international arbitrage that underlies the price-specie-flow mechanism (as discussed in Chapter 2) ensures that movements in the purchasing power of the dollar track movements in the world purchasing power of gold. Accordingly, the US and UK price levels followed very similar paths up to 1914. If the purchasing power of gold follows a flat long-run equilibrium trend, so does the CPI of a gold-redeemable US dollar and the RPI of a gold-redeemable UK pound. The dramatically changed paths of the US dollar CPI and the UK pound RPI after 1914 show the dramatically changed behavior in the global purchasing power of gold.

Figures 3.1 and 3.2 show that during the classical gold standard period of 1879–1914, the US dollar CPI and UK pound RPI followed flat equilibrium trends, but in the period after 1914 clearly broke from that pattern. Price levels in Europe soared during the First World War because they were no longer constrained by the automatic mechanisms of a gold standard. The major European combatant nations left the gold standard, suspending the redemption of national currencies into gold. Switching to wartime paper standards allowed them to finance some part of war expenditures by issuing copious amounts of central-bank money. National currencies were now "backed" merely by promises that they would again be redeemable *someday* at some rate. Voluminous expansion in the quantities of pounds, francs, lire, and so on resulted in doubling and tripling of price levels in those currencies. In the UK, according to the RPI, a basket of retail goods priced at £100 in 1914 was priced at £239 in 1920. Following the cessation of hostilities, the gold redeemability of the pound was not immediately restored – and could not be, without either dramatic cuts in prices and wages (returning the market price of the RPI basket to £100), or a dramatic cut in the gold content of the pound (raising the RPI basket's gold price to £239).

US dollar banknotes and deposits remained legally redeemable for gold throughout the War, although as Crabbe (1989, p. 426) remarks. "In practice, however, even the redemption of notes for gold became difficult until the end of the war." The United States experienced large inflows of gold from Europe during the War. The gold flow into the US, amplified by the new Federal Reserve System's creation of additional member bank reserves through purchases of Treasuries and commercial paper ("bills"), substantially expanded US bank reserves and the US money stock. With more dollars chasing each basket of goods, the US CPI slightly more than doubled during the war. A basket of consumer goods priced at $100 in 1914 would take $207 to buy in 1920.

Looked at in terms of the gold supply and demand model of Chapter 2, the end of gold redeemability and gold coinage by European governments was a large reduction in the stock demand for monetary gold (see Figure 2.8a and 2.8b for step-by-step analysis). It reduced the purchasing power of gold in the immediate run, depressing the annual volume of gold mining. At a ppg below the equilibrium level in the flow market, some monetary gold will be melted for jewelry and industrial purposes each period, gradually shrinking the stock of monetary gold and thereby pushing the ppg back up, until the original equilibrium ppg is restored with a lower volume of gold per capita.

The Shakespearean character Dogberry observes in *Much Ado About Nothing* (Act 3, Scene 5) that when two men ride the same horse, one must ride behind. Central banks held the reins of the international monetary system during the interwar period, while automatic gold-standard mechanisms rode behind. In 1920, only the United States among the leading economies operated a gold standard without exchange controls. At the 1922 Genoa Conference, notes Crabbe (1989, p. 425), European governments did not pledge to return to traditional gold redemption of currencies with each central bank holding its own gold reserve, but rather "resolved to adopt a gold exchange standard under which gold-based assets [meaning US-dollar-denominated assets] would serve as reserve assets." Redemptions of national currencies even for dollars, however, were seldom free from exchange controls.

Resumptions of direct gold redemption (returns to gold standards from gold-exchange standards) were sporadic and could not be trusted to last. Great Britain's resumption lasted only six years, 1925–1931. Italy resumed in 1927 and exited again in 1934. France resumed with an 80 percent devaluation in 1928, and devalued again in 1936.

Germany famously experienced a hyperinflation under the paper mark in 1922–1923. To stabilize, the government instituted a gold-exchange standard (fixed its exchange rate to the US dollar) in November 1923, supplemented by a gold reserve requirement for the central bank in 1924. The Hitler government's foreign exchange controls effectively ended the gold-exchange standard in 1933, allowing the Reichsbank to resume copious emissions of paper marks to cover the government's expenses (Hetzel 2002, pp. 4–9, 14, 20).

Professor Eichengreen is of course aware of these facts. He clearly distinguishes the poorly functioning and more discretionary interwar system from the well-functioning and more automatic prewar system. He notes (Eichengreen 1992, p. 9) that after the First World War, facing new political pressures, central banks became far more willing to override the gold standard's automatic mechanisms in pursuit of internal goals like high employment. "When employment and balance-of-payments goals clashed," he writes, "it was no longer clear which would dominate." This discretion and lack of clear commitment undermined the credibility of the central bank's fixed exchange rate with the dollar or gold, subjecting central banks to speculative attacks and thus subjecting banking systems to destabilizing reserve drains.

The economist Leland Yeager (1966, p. 290) observed that interwar central bank policies "involved the neutralization or offsetting of international influences on domestic money supplies, incomes, and prices. Gold standard methods of balance-of-payments equilibrium were largely destroyed and were not replaced by any alternative." Yeager's account, and to some extent Eichengreen's account when read judiciously, bear out the prediction that F. A. Hayek (2012 [1931], p. 280) made in the midst of the Great Depression: "a good deal of the harm which is just now generally ascribed to the gold standard will ... by a future and better informed generation of economists be recognized as a result of the different attempts of recent years to make the mechanism of the gold standard inoperative."

Interwar central banks, to put it mildly, failed to maintain stability as well as the prewar classical gold standard had. The prewar system had been more automatic in part because many countries (United States, Canada, Australia, and Switzerland before 1907) did not have central banks to interfere in the automatic working of the price-specie-flow mechanism.[2] Where central banks did exist before the First World War, they were less active in trying to manage gold flows.

3.3 "A GOLD STANDARD IS INHERENTLY DEFLATIONARY"

The gold standard was not deflationary on average in historical practice. Based on United Kingdom data (O'Donoghue, Goulding, and Allen 2004), the international gold standard before the First World War exhibited a period of (mild) price deflation 1873–1898 followed by a period of (mild) price inflation 1898–1914. The overall record was one of near-zero inflation, not one dominated by deflation. Slightly more

---

[2] As Hayek (1999 [1937]) emphasized, both prewar and interwar systems were subject to the destabilizing interference that commercial banks were not allowed to branch across national borders, so that gold outflows meant national credit contractions.

than half of the UK's ninety-three years between the resumption of the gold standard in 1821 and its suspension in 1914 were characterized by a rising price level. Over that period as a whole, the compound annual inflation rate was (barely) positive, 0.1 percent per year. Going back even further to 1717, when the UK first switched to the gold standard, the average annual inflation rate was positive 0.53 percent per year (Skidelsky 2018, p. 43). The United States, having suspended the gold standard during the Civil War, finally rejoined the international gold standard in 1879. Over the ensuing classical gold standard period in the United States (as seen in Figure 3.1), the compound average annual inflation rate was also positive 0.1 percent per year.

The only way to read the CPI path shown in Figure 3.2 as evidence that "the gold standard is deflationary" would be to ignore the classical gold standard period and take the 1920–1940 period out of context. It would be to mistakenly attribute the falling price level during the latter period to the operation of "the gold standard" rather than to European governments' wartime decisions that doubled and tripled the price levels in their currencies, followed by their postwar decisions to re-institute prewar parities, requiring deflation to return to prewar price levels.

The tendency of the price level to return to a nearly flat trend under the classical gold standard was not a lucky accident, but inherent in the economics of commodity money, to reiterate a key takeaway from Chapter 2. A downward price-level movement due to rapid growth in demand for monetary gold (rather than to a permanent increase in the cost of gold mining) increases the profitability of gold mining and thereby stimulates more gold production. More gold production raises the price level back to trend. And vice-versa for an upward price level movement due to slow growth in monetary demand for gold. Price level changes driven by changes in demand for monetary gold are self-reversing.

The experience of European nations after the First World War was foreshadowed by the experience of the United States after the Civil War. The Northern American states went off the gold standard at the end of 1861 (Selgin 2013, p. 5). Copious wartime printing of irredeemable greenback dollars drove the purchasing power of the paper dollar to about half that of the gold dollar. After the war, rather than devalue the dollar to half its previous weight in gold, the federal government decided to return to the gold standard at the prewar parity, which implied a need for deflation to raise the purchasing power of the paper dollar back to equality with the global purchasing power of the gold dollar. The government adopted a patient strategy, holding the stock of dollars roughly constant, and letting growth in the output of goods and services gradually bring their prices down. Thus, the period 1865–1879 was one of almost continuous deflation in the United States – not because of the operation of the gold standard (the United States was *off* the gold standard then), but because of the sequence of suspension, copious wartime money-printing, price inflation, and the decision to return to the prewar parity. Countries that were continuously *on* the gold standard during this period never had elevated price levels and thus did not experience any such continuous deflation.

The need for deflation in interwar Europe was similar to the need for deflation in the post–Civil War United States. At the First World War's end, price levels in national currencies stood much higher than before the war, and higher than postwar price levels measured in constant gold units. In the United Kingdom the RPI had more than doubled (the 1920 RPI was 245 percent of the 1913 RPI). In France, prices had more than quadrupled. Between February and October 1920, a French wholesale price index stood above 500 percent of its 1913 level (Williams 1922), while in the fourth quarter of 1920 a Paris RPI was 423 percent of its 1914 level.[3]

The postwar situation in the UK found the prevailing world purchasing power of the gold contained in the prewar pound sterling (ppg) well above the purchasing power of the current paper pound sterling (pp£). To make the pound redeemable at its prewar parity (and exportable without restriction) under these circumstances would provoke (and did provoke during 1925–1931) sizable redemptions of paper pounds and exports of gold, because gold would buy more goods than the paper pounds redeemed for them.[4]

To return to the prewar gold parity without draining the Bank of England required near-equality between the purchasing power of the Bank of England note and the purchasing power of the quantity of gold for which it was to be redeemable. Churchill, unfortunately, chose to reopen redemption in 1925 while the discrepancy, although reduced from

---

[3] Wholesale French prices from Federal Reserve Economic Data historical NBER series M04057FRM360NNBR. Retail Paris price series from series Q0473AFR00PARQ360NNBR.

[4] To be precise, Britain went off the gold standard in 1914 not by formally suspending redemption, but by replacing gold coins in circulation with Bank of England notes, by effectively blocking redemption of Bank of England notes, and by effectively embargoing exports of gold. The return to a gold standard in 1925 lifted the export embargo but did not reintroduce gold coins, so the 1925–1931 system was a gold bullion standard rather than a gold coin standard.

1920, was still large. To achieve near-equality required some combination of (a) deliberate deflation (increasing the purchasing power of the
paper pound by shrinking the stock of pounds relative to the output of
goods and services, so that fewer pounds chased each bundle of goods),
in other words raising the actual pp£, and (b) devaluation (reducing the
gold content of the pound), in other words lowering the equilibrium pp£
given the prevailing ppg. In the short run, the prevailing ppg had also
fallen (as shown by US prices) due to the reduction in monetary gold
demand by central banks, but not as much as the pp£.

The US dollar CPI in 1920, as noted, stood at 207 percent higher than
its 1914 value. The compound annual inflation rate over the span was 12.9
percent per year. The inflation followed an expansion of the dollar money
stock. The monetary expansion followed an influx of gold escaping the
war in Europe, and expansionary asset purchases by the Fed that created
additional commercial bank reserves. The Fed's gold holdings rose by $1.9
billion during the four years 1915–1918 inclusive, reaching $2.1 billion
at year-end 1918 from a starting point of only $0.2 billion at year-end
1914. During the same years, the Fed purchased $311 million in Treasury
bonds and nearly $2 billion in commercial bills. Gold stopped flowing in
after 1918, but the Fed kept buying financial assets for the next two years,
another $1.1 billion worth between year-end 1918 and November 1920.[5]

With the inflow of gold and additional expansion of bank reserves
from Fed asset purchases, the broad M2 measure of the money held by
the US public rose 112 percent in six years (1914–1920).[6] After a partial
correction in 1920–1921, the CPI remained 73 percent above its starting
level, what economist Robert Mundell (1999, p. 227) in his Nobel Prize
lecture termed "the prewar equilibrium," and stayed at or above that
elevated level until 1930.

The US price level thus remained above its long-run-sustainable equilibrium path after 1921 given the continuation of the prewar parity.
In Figure 3.1, this path is approximated by the 1913 CPI, shown as a
dashed line. Absent a devaluation of the dollar, the US price level would
sooner or later have to fall further – and it did fall, sharply, from 1929
to 1933. The price level began to rise following an increase in the Federal

---

[5] Federal Reserve balance-sheet figures from "Federal Reserve Weekly Balance Sheet
since 1914," available as an Excel file download from the Center for Financial Stability,
centerforfinancialstability/hfs.php.

[6] Anderson (2003), Table 3. The narrower M1 measure, for which the statistical series does
not begin until 1915, grew 82 percent in five years (1915–1920).

Reserve's gold reserves from the confiscation of privately held monetary gold in 1933. The devaluation of the dollar in early 1934, reducing the gold content of the US dollar from 1/20.67 ounce of gold to 1/35 ounce, in one stroke raised the dollar value of the Fed's gold reserves by 69.3 percent. It raised the equilibrium price level in the same proportion, bringing to an end the deflationary reversal of the First World War inflation.[7]

Mundell points out that some leading defenders of the gold standard in the postwar period, such as the French economist Charles Rist and the Austrian economist Ludwig von Mises, recommended devaluation as a more prudent policy than returning to the prewar parity through a painfully large deflation. Mises (1978 [1923]) argued that a deflationary policy "could not undo or reverse the 'unfair' changes in wealth and income brought about by the previous inflationary period and ... also brings other unwanted shifts of wealth and income." According to Greaves (1978, p. xxxiii), Mises later offered the analogy that once you have run a man over with your car, you do not reduce the harm by putting the car in reverse and running him over in the other direction.

The United Kingdom under Winston Churchill and most other countries chose to restore the prewar gold content to the monetary unit, which forced an ongoing deflation to reverse the remaining wartime price inflation (or at least that part in excess of the temporary global rise in gold prices). As Mundell put it, "The deflation of the 1930s was the mirror image of the war-time rise in the price level that had not been reversed in the 1920–1921 recession." Mazumder and Wood (2013) detail the economic logic of this reversal, and show how the post–First World War deflation parallels the pattern seen in resumptions of the gold standard at the old parity following the suspensions and inflations of the Civil War in the United States and (early in the 1800s) the Napoleonic War in the UK.

The global deflation of the interwar period, to summarize, could not have been due to the leading economies of Europe being on the gold standard, because they were not. The deflation was primarily due to European nations having *left* the gold standard, having *inflated massively* while off the gold standard, and then trying to *resume* the gold standard *at prewar parities* (refusing to devalue) starting from price levels that were unsustainably high at prewar parities. Put another way, the

---

[7] The 1913 CPI stood at 6.90, the 1920 CPI at 20.04. Multiplying 6.90 by the ratio of (35/20.65), that is, raising it by 69 percent, gives a new estimated equilibrium level of 16.3. The CPI reached that new level in 1942, not coincidentally the end of the Great Depression.

purchasing power of currencies emerging from the War was well below that of the quantities of gold to which they were equivalent at prewar parities. Deflation arose not from the automatic mechanisms of the gold standard but primarily from governments' decisions to resume the gold standard at prewar parities after large inflations. Universal resumption of the gold standard could have been achieved without deflations had governments devalued their national currencies.

3.4 "DEFLATIONARY PERIODS UNDER THE GOLD STANDARD CAUSED DEPRESSIONS"

Concern that a gold standard is deflationary and thereby depressing was voiced very soon after the end of the First World War. The Swedish economist Gustav Cassel (1920, p. 39) complained that mankind by adopting a gold standard had in recent decades "allowed a scarcity of gold to retard his economic progress and keep down the productivity of his work." More recently my George Mason University colleague Tyler Cowen (2011) wrote that "The most fundamental argument against a gold standard, is that when the relative price of gold is go[ing] up, that creates deflationary pressures on the general price level, thereby harming output and employment."

Eichengreen (2011) makes a related claim: If the stock of monetary gold grows less rapidly than the real output of goods and services, prices must fall, which (he says) raises real interest rates. Investment becomes more expensive, rendering job creation more difficult. Eichengreen writes: "The robust investment and job creation prized by the gold standard's champions and the deflation they foresee are not easily reconciled, in other words." In a nutshell, vigorous economic growth is at war with itself under a gold standard because the money stock will not keep up. Eichengreen's theoretical argument here is incorrect. A deflationary trend due to rapid growth does not inhibit growth. But before we examine the theory, it is critical to note the – perhaps surprising – simple fact that in the historical record of the gold standard periods of deflation are not associated with depressions.

Andrew Atkeson and Patrick J. Kehoe (2004) reviewed the historical record for a panel of 17 nations over 100 years. They found that deflation (falling prices) was not linked to depression (falling real output) outside of one extraordinary episode, the Great Depression period of 1929–1934. For the overall dataset, "nearly 90% of the episodes with deflation [65 of 73] did not have depression." (A measured "episode" was a five-year period in a nation.) Meanwhile 21 of 29 depressions occurred without deflation. They summarized the pattern as follows: "A broad historical look finds many more periods of deflation with reasonable growth than with depression, and many more periods of depression with inflation than with deflation. Overall, the data show virtually no link between deflation and depression."

Other researchers have similarly found that most deflations under the gold standard were not troublesome in themselves, nor symptomatic of problems elsewhere. Economic historians Bordo, Landon-Lane, and Redish (2010, p. 544) find that "deflation in the late nineteenth century was primarily benign," the result of rapid growth in the output of goods rather than negative monetary shocks. There *were* negative monetary shocks associated with late-nineteenth-century financial panics in the United States, but those panics were not caused by being on a gold standard. Evidence: Canada did not have them despite also being on the gold standard (and also having a heavily agricultural economy). The US panics were fundamentally due to bank-weakening legal restrictions. Canada avoided panics by not having those restrictions.

When prices fell under the gold standard, it was usually because the world's real output of goods and services grew faster than the world stock of gold. Relatively rapid real output growth is of course not a problem. Even workers with flat dollar wages enjoyed higher levels of real income when dollar consumer prices were falling.

The decade of the 1890s is sometimes identified as a "great depression" based on several years of high unemployment numbers. But while five years exhibited mild deflation, only three years (1893, 1894, 1896) also saw a decline in real GDP from the previous year, and thus exhibited both deflation and declining real income.[8] The decade as a whole was certainly not one of depressed output. US real GDP in 1900 was 32.5 percent *higher* than in 1890, for a healthy compound growth rate of 2.86 percent per year over the decade.

Without a doubt, deflation during the 1880s and 1890s had well-known contemporary critics in the United States. Groups that supported policies to raise the price level, namely the Greenbackers, Silverites and Bimetallists, appealed to farmers by blaming deflation for slow growth in farm incomes and heavy real debts. The regional popularity of these viewpoints has sometimes been mistaken for evidence that the gold standard was widely unpopular. It should not be forgotten that the voting American

[8] Real GDP and GDP deflator data are from MeasuringWorth.com.

public as a whole rejected the champion of using Bimetallism to generate inflation, the Democratic Party presidential candidate William Jennings Bryan, three times: first in 1896, again in 1900, and then again in 1908.

Deflation did coincide with depression during 1920–1921 and 1929–1934. These sharp deflations (like the gradual deflation of 1865–1879) were not due to the uninterrupted working of the gold standard, but (as noted earlier) followed from the high inflations that central banks (*off* the gold standard) had created during the First World War, combined with decisions to return to prewar gold parities (refusal to devalue) afterward, as spelled out most clearly by Mazumder and Wood (2013).

Eichengreen's theoretical claim that when prices go down "real interest rates become higher" with the result that "[i]nvestment becomes more expensive, rendering job creation more difficult," falls apart on inspection. A "real" interest rate is one adjusted for inflation. The identity that defines the real interest rate is: (1 + real interest rate) = (1 + nominal interest rate) / (1 + inflation rate). The identity has two distinct applications: ex ante (forward-looking) and ex post (backward-looking). The inflation rate in the identity can either be an *anticipated* rate or a *retrospective* rate. Correspondingly, the real interest rate can either be anticipated or retrospective. A standard proposition of monetary theory (the "Fisher Effect") tells us that if the anticipated annual inflation rate is 1 percentage point lower in one country (or one decade) than another, the nominal interest rate must also be approximately 1 percentage lower to keep the anticipated real interest rates the same. Eichengreen's claim is therefore untrue of anticipated interest rates: an anticipated deflation does not make it more expensive to borrow for investment. The real rate remains the same, and the nominal rate is lower.

Suppose instead that Eichengreen had the retrospective real rate in mind. If deflation of one percentage point occurs when zero was anticipated over the period of a loan, the loan is repaid in dollars more valuable than anticipated, which raises the *ex post* real interest rate paid on the loan by one percentage point. But such an *unanticipated* deflation, occurring after an investment loan was taken out, does not raise the interest rate at the time of the loan, and thus does not discourage investment or job creation. Eichengreen's claim is therefore also untrue about retrospective interest rates as well.

To be fair, there is one atypical set of conditions where Eichengreen's argument could apply. If the nominal interest rate is already near or at the zero lower bound, then the nominal rate cannot fall enough in response to a large downward shift in the anticipated inflation rate to keep the *ex ante* real interest constant. The *ex ante* real interest rate then does rise. This was a problem during the extreme deflation of 1930–1932. Three-month Treasury rates fell close to zero at the end of 1932. During the period of the classical gold standard, however, there were no cases of an anticipated deflation so great as to bring the nominal interest rate close to zero or create a lower-bound problem. The extreme US deflation of 1930–1932, to repeat, was not caused by the working of the gold standard (an "external drain"), but by the collapse of the money supply associated with bank runs and hoarding (an "internal drain") left untreated by Federal Reserve policy.

"The gold standard" stands accused of fostering interwar deflation and depression in another way. A number of authors (Eichengreen 1992, Irwin 2012) have persuasively attributed international deflationary pressure to the Federal Reserve System's and the Bank of France's policies of absorbing and sitting on ("sterilizing") large amounts of gold in the early 1930s. That the central banks acted harmfully is not in question. But in acting that way, they were not following any dictates of the gold standard. As Ben Bernanke (2010) has put it (emphasis added), "*in defiance* of the so-called rules of the game of the international gold standard, neither country allowed the higher gold reserves to feed through to their domestic money supplies and price levels." The Fed thereby blocked the equilibrating mechanism that would have satisfied the public's demand for currency and the banking system's demand for reserve money, and so would have moderated the downward pressure on prices. It was not the rules of the gold standard but the two central banks' discretionary actions that accelerated the global deflation that was already on the cards (from the attempted resumptions at prewar parities after the First World War inflations).

The contrast between the relative calm of the classical gold standard period and the chaos of the interwar period indicates that an international gold standard works best when it works most automatically, with least discretionary action by central banks to block its adjustment mechanisms. It would have been possible to restore a classically automatic gold standard if all resuming countries had devalued after the wartime inflations. Then exchange controls and other arbitrary measures that sought to reduce the use of gold, in order to prop up unsustainable price levels, could have been avoided.

In *Golden Fetters* (1992, p. 393) Eichengreen also charged that "the gold standard was responsible for the failure of monetary and fiscal authorities to take offsetting action once the Depression was underway."

In 1930–1933, the United States' banking system was hit with banking panics (clusters of bank runs). The public and the banks reacted to the threat of runs by hoarding paper and gold currency, which shrank the broad US money stock, accelerating deflation. Eichengreen (p. 393) wrote that the gold standard "was the binding constraint preventing policymakers from averting the failures of banks and containing the spread of financial panic." He acknowledged that the Fed had "extensive gold reserves," but nonetheless maintained that it "had very limited room to maneuver." Monetary historians who have taken a closer look, however, have shown that the Fed had enough room to maneuver, so that responsibility for not acting to stop the monetary contraction rests on the Fed's discretion, not on constraints imposed by its need to defend its gold reserves.

Three researchers (Bordo, Choudhri, and Schwartz 2002) have found that the Fed had more than enough spare gold reserves to offset the contraction of the money supply due to bank runs and thereby to offset the downward pressure on real output. They write that the Fed, "holding massive gold reserves," was "not constrained from using expansionary policy to offset banking panics, deflation, and declining economic activity." Had the Federal Reserve chosen a more expansionary policy "at two critical junctures (October 1930 to February 1931; September 1931 through January 1932)" it "would have been successful in averting the banking panics that occurred, without endangering convertibility" despite expected losses of some of its gold reserves. Their counterfactual simulations indicate that had the Fed chosen to offset the contraction of the broader money supply, "U.S. gold reserves would have declined significantly but not sufficiently to reduce the gold ratio below the statutory minimum requirement." The Fed, not the gold constraints on it, was responsible for overly tight money.

Other studies of the Fed's balance sheet and activities during the 1930s have likewise found that it had plenty of gold (Hsieh and Romer 2006, Timberlake 2008). The "tight" monetary policies it pursued were not forced on it by lack of gold reserves.

If not the constraints of the gold standard, namely the concern with having enough gold in its vaults to cover potential external drains, what stopped the Fed from expanding? To judge by its own pronouncements at the time, the Federal Reserve Board was following a misconceived monetary policy view known as the Real Bills Doctrine, hereafter RBD (Humphrey and Timberlake 2019). Discussed in more detail later in this chapter, the RBD directed the central bank to match the volume of its credit creation to the volume of business firms' legitimate demand to borrow at current interest rates. The legitimate demand to borrow was to be gauged by the volume of "real bills," short-term debt obligations that finance goods in process, offered by producers to commercial banks for discount (essentially, offered as collateral for loans). In a period of depressed production and hence low business borrowing, the RBD called for a low supply of credit. Hence the Fed saw no need to promote monetary expansion.

3.5 "DEFINING 'THE DOLLAR' AS SO MANY GRAMS OF GOLD IS PRICE-FIXING, INCONSISTENT WITH A FREE MARKET ECONOMY"

Barry Eichengreen (2011) argues that countries using gold as money "fix its price in domestic-currency terms (in the U.S. case, in dollars)." He suggests that this fixity is inconsistent with free-market principles:

> But the idea that government should legislate the price of a particular commodity, be it gold, milk or gasoline, sits uneasily with ... [a] commitment to letting market forces work .... Surely a believer in the free market would argue that if there is an increase in the demand for gold, whatever the reason, then the price should be allowed to rise, giving the gold-mining industry an incentive to produce more, eventually bringing that price back down. Thus, the notion that the U.S. government should peg the price, as in gold standards past, is curious at the least.

What is curious, however, is Eichengreen's description of a gold standard as a system to "peg the price" of monetary gold in terms of domestic currency, as though monetary gold and the most basic domestic money were distinct goods. A gold coin standard means that a certain mass of gold in coined form *defines* the domestic monetary unit. The monetary unit (dollar) is nothing other than a gold unit, not a distinct good with a potentially fluctuating market price against gold. That $1, defined as x grams of gold, continues to be worth the specified amount of gold – or, in other words, that x units of gold continue to be worth x units of gold – does not involve the pegging of any relative price. Under a gold standard, domestic currency notes and checking-account balances are denominated in and redeemable for gold, not priced in gold. They do not have a price in gold any more than Federal Reserve Notes or checking-account balances in our current system, denominated in fiat dollars, have a price in fiat dollars. Presumably, Eichengreen does not find it curious or objectionable that his bank maintains a fixed dollar-for-dollar redemption rate, base money for checking balances, when he withdraws cash at an automatic teller machine or makes an online payment from his account.

As to what a believer in the free market would argue, surely Eichengreen understands that if there is an increase in the demand for gold under a gold standard, whatever the reason, then the *relative* price of gold (the purchasing power of gold over other goods and services) *will* rise, that this rise *will* give the gold-mining industry an incentive to produce more, and that the increase in gold output *will* eventually bring the relative price back down.

3.6 "THE VOLATILITY OF THE PRICE OF GOLD IN RECENT YEARS SHOWS THAT GOLD WOULD BE AN UNSTABLE MONETARY STANDARD"

Eichengreen (2011) asserts that "gold's inherent price volatility" makes it unsuitable to "provide a basis for international commercial and financial transactions on a twenty-first-century scale." But the relative price of gold is not inherently volatile when gold is the world's basic money. Gold was demonetized in 1971 when US President Richard Nixon shut the gold window at which foreign central banks had been able to redeem dollars for gold at $35 per troy ounce. The volatility of the dollar price of gold since 1971 does not show that gold is an unstable monetary standard. The dollar price of demonetized gold rises and falls largely because of swings in the speculative demand for gold as an inflation hedge. These swings mostly reflect, in other words, the instability of fiat currencies.

Writer Ezra Klein (2012) similarly declares, "The problems with the gold standard are legion, but the most obvious is that our currency fluctuates with the global price of gold as opposed to the needs of our economy." It is not entirely clear what "our currency fluctuates with the global price of gold" means in this declaration. If it means that, for a country that is part of an international gold standard, the purchasing power of domestic currency moves with the world purchasing power of gold, then it is true, but it fails to identify a problem. The world purchasing power of gold has better behaved under the classical international gold standard than the purchasing power of fiat money has been since 1971. If it means to invoke the volatility of the dollar price of gold since gold was demonetized in 1971, it identifies a problem, but it is a problem experienced under a fiat standard and not under a gold standard.

The respected University of California–San Diego economist James D. Hamilton has made an argument that similarly fails to recognize that the price volatility of demonetized gold under a fiat standard is not an argument against a gold standard. Hamilton (2012a) charts how much the average dollar wage would have varied if it had been contractually fixed in ounces of gold but paid in the dollar equivalent as the price of gold varied between January 2000 and July 2012. He observes that "if the real value of gold had changed as much as it has since then, the dollar wage that an average worker received would need to have fallen from $13.75/hour in 2000 to $3.45/hour in 2012." That sounds alarming, but in fact it is of very little significance. Such a calculation would be relevant if (say) the Bahamas were considering a proposal to unilaterally adopt the gold standard today. A small open economy's unilateral adoption of a gold standard would not substantially reduce the volatility of the world price of gold, so that economy would experience a very volatile exchange rate. Not a good idea, which is why nobody advocates it. Hamilton's calculation is irrelevant, however, to proposals to reinstate an international standard encompassing all the world's major economies.

Hamilton's observations drawn from a world of fiat regimes are not informative about the behavior of the purchasing power of money under an international gold standard. In economics jargon, "the Lucas critique" applies. Hamilton anticipates such an objection and has a reply ready:

[G]old advocates respond with the claim that if the U.S. had been on a gold standard since 2000, then the huge change in the real value of gold that we observed over the last decade never would have happened in the first place. The first strange thing about this claim is its supposition that events and policies within the U.S. are the most important determinants of the real value of gold. According to the World Gold Council, North America accounts for only 8% of global demand.

It would be odd to imagine the United States being on a gold standard while the rest of the world is not. In any event, claims about such a system are not relevant to the evaluation of proposals for an international gold standard. It would not be strange to suppose that the real value of gold would have been relatively stable, as it was during the classical gold standard, if *all* the world's major economies had been on a gold standard and therefore speculation against fiat monies was minor or non-existent. Absent fiat inflation hedging, there is no obvious cause for concern about the volatility of demand for gold or the volatility of gold's relative price.[9]

In a follow-up blog entry posted a few days after the one just quoted, Hamilton (2012b) recognizes the historical record: "It is true that the

---

[9] Professor Hamilton's 8 percent figure, by the way, is North America's share of global purchases of new gold *jewelry*, a non-monetary and flow measure, rather than its share of the stock transactions demand to hold monetary gold, which under an international gold standard would presumably be closer to North America's 30 percent share of world output.

biggest concern I have about going back on a gold standard today – that it would tie the monetary unit of account to an object whose real value can be quite volatile – was not the core problem associated with the system of the 19th century."

Tyler Cowen (2011) also expresses concern about volatility in the real price of gold:

Why put your economy at the mercy of these essentially random forces? I believe the 19th century was a relatively good time to have had a gold standard, but the last twenty years, with their rising commodity prices, would have been an especially bad time. When it comes to the next twenty years, who knows?

In a later blog entry, Cowen (2012) adds, "I think a gold standard today would be much worse than the nineteenth century gold standard, in part because commodity prices are currently more volatile and may be for some time." Cowen does not directly address the possibility that the current volatility of several commodity price series, most importantly that of gold, is principally caused by the inflation- and tail-risk hedging prompted by our current fiat monetary systems. Inflation-hedging demand is volatile today because inflation expectations are volatile under an unanchored monetary system.

The answer to Cowen's first question – why put your economy at the mercy of "essentially random" supply and demand shocks for gold? – is that, to judge by the historical evidence, doing so engenders less volatility than the alternative of putting your economy at the mercy of a central bank's monetary policy committee (Selgin, Lastrapes, and White 2012). Money supply and demand shocks under fiat money systems have been much larger (more on this in Chapter 4).

Under the pre-1914 gold standard, changes in the growth rate of the base money stock were relatively small – perhaps surprisingly small to those who have not looked at the numbers. As noted in Chapter 2, even the California Gold Rush caused inflation of only 1.3 percent per year (as measured by the United Kingdom's RPI) stretched over eighteen years (1849–1867). Gold discoveries the size of California's are hardly likely today.

Eichengreen (2011) worries that volatility in the demand for gold would persist even under an international gold standard. He reckons that there could be violent fluctuations in the purchasing power of gold were it to again become the principal means of payment and store of value, because the demand for it might change dramatically owing to shifts in the state of confidence or general economic conditions. But the historical evidence shows that price levels fluctuated less during the UK gold standard of 1821–1914 than during the fiat money era 1971–2022.

There is a good reason why the demand for monetary gold changes more dramatically today than it did under the gold standard. Robert Barro (1983, pp. 104–106) notes that changes in the expected inflation rate are empirically a major driver of changes in desired money balances per dollar of income. The gold standard constrained inflation in a more credible way, thereby better pinning down inflationary expectations and better stabilizing the demand to hold money relative to income (stated inversely, it better stabilized the "velocity" of money) than the fiat money system that followed it. Barro explains:

Since the move in 1971 toward flexible exchange rates and the complete divorce of United States monetary management from the objective of a pegged gold price, it is clear that the nominal anchor for the monetary system – weak as it was earlier [under Bretton Woods] – is now entirely absent. Future monetary growth and long-run inflation appear now to depend entirely on the year-to-year "discretion" of the monetary authority, that is, the Federal Reserve. Not surprisingly, inflationary expectations and their reflection in nominal interest rates and hence in short-run inflation rates have all become more volatile.

The volatility of inflation and of inflation-rate expectations diminished during the "Great Moderation" after the double-digit inflation of the 1970s and 1980s subsided, but they have returned. In the fourteen years between August 1991 and August 2005, the annual US CPI inflation rate (year-over-year, observed monthly) stayed between 1 and 4 percent, a band of just 3 percentage points. But between July 2008 and July 2009, the year-over-year inflation rate went from a high of 5.5 percent to a low of minus 2.0 percent, a swing of 7.5 percentage points in a single year. The Fed in 2012 proclaimed a self-chosen target of 2 percent annual inflation, but later revised it to 2 percent on average over an unspecified time period. In June 2022, the price level was up 9 percent over June one year earlier. The durability of the Fed's commitment to the target remains to be seen. The same is true for other inflation-targeting central banks around the world. As long as central banks retain discretion, inflation expectations will remain variable.

To summarize, the stability of the purchasing power of *monetary gold* under a gold standard cannot be judged by observing the behavior of the price of *demonetized gold* under a fiat standard. We should instead look at the performance of historical gold standards. It might be noted that the argument applies with equal logic to judging a Bitcoin standard. The stability of the purchasing power of monetary Bitcoin under a Bitcoin standard cannot be judged by observing the behavior of the price of premonetary Bitcoin under a fiat standard. But because we cannot look to the performance of any historical Bitcoin standard, we will be limited in Chapters 5 and 6 to theoretical evaluation in light of Bitcoin's supply mechanism and its differences from gold's supply mechanism.

3.7 "A GOLD STANDARD WOULD FORCE THE FED TO LOWER AND RAISE INTEREST RATES SHARPLY TO PEG THE PRICE OF GOLD, WHICH WOULD DESTABILIZE THE ECONOMY"

A gold standard does not require that a central bank "peg the price of gold" by manipulating interest rates to tighten or loosen monetary policy.[10] Many countries (like the United States before 1913) have been on a gold standard without having a central bank at all. No gold standard in history has maintained its parity via interest-rate policy. Although the Bank of England in the nineteenth century did deliberately raise and lower its discount rate in response to gold flows, it did so not because the working of the gold standard demanded it, but on the contrary, because it wanted to *impede* or temporarily *overrule* the automatic gold flows through which the system maintained international price equilibrium.

Some economists in recent years have nonetheless imagined that a gold standard involves targeting the nominal price of gold through interest rate policy. Perhaps they are only familiar with how leading central banks operate today on fiat standards, setting and adjusting a short-term interest-rate target as a means to steer the economy toward a nominal goal like a 2 percent inflation rate, and think that the gold standard must use the same technique to pursue a different nominal goal. They imagine that when a central bank pursues a constant nominal price of gold (rather than 2 percent CPI inflation) it does so by varying its interest-rate target.

Paul Krugman (2019) reflects this misconception. He writes that when the dollar price of gold is rising, "gold standard advocates should be calling for the Fed to raise rates, not lower them." He adds that "if gold-standard ideology had any truth to it," then the rising price of gold in 2007–2011 "would have been a harbinger of runaway inflation, and the Fed should have been raising interest rates to keep the dollar's gold value constant. In fact, inflation never materialized, and an interest rate hike in the face of surging unemployment would have been a disaster."

Krugman's is a sensible criticism of people who want the Fed's monetary policy *under the current irredeemable fiat-money system* to target the dollar price of gold. Such a "gold price rule" would be foolish

---

[10] This section draws on White (2019a).

because, whenever (demonetized) gold's relative price rises on world markets, stabilizing its dollar price would require tightening the supply of dollars by enough to force the dollar prices of all other goods downward in proportion. (The reverse for a fall in the relative price of gold.) No system so destabilizing would survive as long as the gold standard has historically survived. But people advocating a "gold price rule" of this sort should not be called "gold standard advocates" because they are not advocating a switch from fiat money by defining the monetary unit as a fixed mass of gold.

There is no need to vary interest rates to "keep the dollar's gold value constant" under a gold standard. A gold coin's dollar value is kept constant by *containing* the defined amount of gold corresponding to its dollar value. Dollar banknotes and deposits keep a constant gold value by being *redeemable* in standard coins or bullion. There is no distinct floating dollar price of gold when the dollar is defined as a fixed mass of gold. Under a gold standard the central bank – if one exists – is obliged to redeem its own liabilities in gold and thus is obliged to focus on maintaining adequate gold reserves. The price-specie-flow mechanism, not interest-rate policy, continuously adjusts the local money stock to match local money demand at the given parity.

The economist Menzie Chinn (2019) thus begins from false premises when he takes it for granted that a gold standard requires a central bank and is implemented by having the central bank adjust interest rates as necessary to maintain a constant dollar price of gold. Chinn constructs an empirical estimate of how greatly the interest rate would have to vary to stabilize the dollar price of gold. But he does not look at US experience during the classical gold standard period in the United States. He instead gathers data on the dollar price of gold from 1968 to the present, and regresses the dollar price of (demonetized) gold on a short-term Treasury bond yield. He then draws conclusions about what he calls a gold standard. He writes:

Stabilizing the price of gold in US dollars requires adjusting the interest rate (akin to how the exchange rate is managed). ... [A] return to the gold standard would imply that the Fed funds rate would have to be about 15 percentage points higher than it was in January 2000 in order to keep the dollar's value stable at January 2000 levels – a rate 18 percentage points higher than actually recorded in March 2019.

At least two noteworthy historical facts contradict Chinn's conception of how a gold standard works and the interest rate range it entails. First, as already noted, the United States maintained a fixed dollar–gold parity during the classical gold standard era without any central bank. Although there is thus no *policy* rate to track, the observed range of rates on prime commercial paper in the United States remained between 3 percent and 6.5 percent during 1888–1914 (Smiley 1975). Second, the Bank of England, which did vary its discount rate to dampen gold flows, never had to raise its rate above 7 percent during the same period (Hanes 2020). There is no rate remotely approaching 18 percent to be seen.

It does not make sense to think that an observed statistical relationship between the dollar price of (demonetized) gold and the Fed Funds interest rate *under our current fiat system* gives us reliable information about the relationship between the dollar price of gold and interest rates under a gold standard regime.[11] The dollar price of gold bullion in the New York financial market did not vary from $20.67 per troy ounce under the classical gold standard, except within a narrow band (about 7 cents) between the upper price point that triggered gold imports and the lower price point that triggered exports. The *price* of gold was therefore insensitive to interest-rate differences between New York and London. Instead, an interest-rate difference would prompt gold to flow toward the higher-interest market, which changed the relative *quantity* of gold (or claims to London gold) in the New York market while keeping the price of gold within the gold points.

3.8 "A GOLD STANDARD CANNOT BE A GOOD IDEA BECAUSE SO MANY ECONOMISTS OPPOSE IT"

The statement as quoted is not a substantive argument, of course, merely an appeal to authority. But it raises the question: Why isn't the gold standard more popular with current-day economists? The simple answer is that very few economists have firmly grounded views on the gold standard. Never having seriously studied the theory or history of the gold standard (topics that rarely appear on graduate macroeconomics or monetary economics course syllabi), many monetary economists – and even more so economists in fields other than monetary theory and history – are prone to accept and repeat uncritically the popular mischaracterizations of the gold standard that are scrutinized above. Followers of John Maynard Keynes echo his dismissal of the gold standard as a "barbarous relic" in a modern age of policymaking by enlightened experts. On

---

[11] Economists will recognize this as an application of "the Lucas Critique."

this issue, they are aligned with those followers of Milton Friedman who share Friedman's early-career optimistic view that we can achieve a fiat standard governed by a rule that will provide greater price stability than a gold standard while avoiding its resource costs.

Monetary economists have a very understandable reason not to study the gold standard or other alternatives to the status quo: It would not be good for their careers. As Milton Friedman once suggested in an interview (Fettig 1993), monetary economists on the whole are reluctant to criticize the policy choices of the central bank because the central bank is by far their largest employer. (There are of course exceptions. Among the most notable in the United States are the handful of Monetarist critics of the Fed associated with the Shadow Open Market Committee.) For the same reason, it seems reasonable to suppose, most monetary economists would be reluctant to criticize the status-quo fiat monetary standard, which enables central banks to make those policy choices in the first place. In other words, career incentives may explain why so many monetary economists show a pro-status-quo bias (White 2005).

Most monetary economists accordingly focus their research efforts on how to improve policy under the current regime, and do not pursue research on alternative regimes. An automatic or market-regulated gold standard would drastically reduce the central bank's rationale for employing hundreds of economists in monetary policy research. If you value the option to be employed by or consult for a central bank (or a multinational agency like the International Monetary Fund or Bank for International Settlements), why investigate whether the current fiat regime is the best monetary regime? This may be a cynical take on economists' motives, but it is no more cynical than other economic explanations that focus on incentives and constraints. Speculating about the reasons why certain people are attracted to certain arguments is of course no rebuttal to those arguments. It is no substitute for taking on the arguments themselves, as the rest of this chapter does.

That many economists are prone to accept and repeat the most common mischaracterizations of the gold standard can be seen in the answers provided by a panel of prominent economists asked about the gold standard by the IGM Forum (2012). Here is the survey question, actually a statement to which panelists were asked to agree or disagree, with the option to explain why:

If the US replaced its discretionary monetary policy regime with a gold standard, defining a "dollar" as a specific number of ounces of gold, the price-stability and employment outcomes would be better for the average American.

All 38 respondents disagreed with the proposition. And yet for price-stability outcomes, at least in the senses of a lower average inflation rate and higher price level predictability at medium to long horizons, outcomes have historically been better under gold standards (Rolnick and Weber 1997; Selgin, Lastrapes, and White 2012). For employment outcomes, there are neither theoretical nor empirical reasons to suppose that a gold standard would bring a first-order improvement (or deterioration) in labor-market coordination. Nor are "better employment outcomes" a common claim on the gold standard's behalf, so that part of the proposition was an odd thing to include.

Offered the chance to elaborate, several panelists repeated misconceptions that have been criticized earlier in this chapter. Some version of "the volatility of the price of gold in recent years shows that gold would be an unstable monetary standard" was offered by three panelists (Darrel Duffie, Robert Hall, Kenneth Judd). Caroline Hoxby commented: "Since gold has supply and demand dynamics of its own, for reasons unrelated to its use as a store of value, Americans would be exposed to risk." This is true in an absolute sense but not in a comparative sense: It neglects the "better" part of the proposition. Historically the risk of purchasing-power instability from gold supply and demand volatility has been *smaller* than the risk from fiat supply and demand volatility. Anil Kashyap overlooked the classical gold standard's successful track record when he commented: "A gold standard regime would be a disaster for any large advanced economy. Love of the G.S. implies macroeconomic illiteracy." Richard Thaler replied with a snarky question: "Why tie to gold? why not 1982 Bordeaux?" While humorous, his reply mistakenly suggests that the proposition's "defining a 'dollar' as a specific number of ounces of gold" refers only to an arbitrary choice of a *numeraire* or unit of account, rather than to the adoption of a historically tested system in which units of a durable and divisible commodity also serve as the common medium of redemption.

Two exceptional panelists (Daron Acemoglu and Edward Lazear) made balanced comments recognizing both costs and benefits of a gold standard, despite voting "disagree."

Another example of a poorly informed historical critique is provided in a blog post by textbook authors Stephen Cecchetti and Kermit Schoenholtz (2016). They imagine that the international gold standard determined money growth and inflation in the United States *until 1933,* and so they count against the gold standard the US inflation rate in excess of 20% during 1917, followed by deflation in excess of 10% in 1921. As we have seen, these rates were actually produced by the abandonment of the international gold standard by European nations during the First World War. Even while Cecchetti and Schoenholtz mistakenly condemn "the gold standard" for producing a highly volatile inflation rate, they do note that average inflation was much lower and real growth slightly higher under the gold standard than under fiat standards.

Many mainstream economists today may be averse to the very idea of a gold standard because, although I grant that this is uncharitable, they have been trained as social engineers. They consider the aim of scientific economics to be the prediction and control of economic phenomena, not just their explanation. An automatically self-governing gold standard does not make use of their expertise at optimizing economic systems, so they find it primitive. Even barbarous, to echo Keynes.

3.9 "A PROPERLY MANAGED FIAT STANDARD CAN PROVIDE ALL THE PRICE STABILITY OF A GOLD STANDARD WITH SMALLER RESOURCE COSTS"

As already discussed in Chapter 2, there are two main problems with the usual accounting of the resource costs of gold versus fiat standards. First, the resource costs of a gold standard are commonly overstated by assuming reserve ratios much higher than sophisticated gold-standard systems have actually used. Second, the balance tips against fiat money once we recognize how much monetary gold has been accumulated for hedging under actual (rather than hoped for) fiat standards.

Of course, examining actual fiat standards does not directly address claims about a hypothetical "properly managed" fiat standard. Chapter 4 examines the theory of an ideal fiat money and to what extent it provides a relevant path to better money.

We now turn to prominent misunderstandings of the gold standard by its would-be defenders. The French classical economist Frederic Bastiat (1996, ch. 21) once observed, "The worst thing that can happen to a good cause is not to be skillfully attacked, but to be ineptly defended." In that spirit, the following criticisms of the weaknesses in some common pro-gold arguments are not attempts to dismiss gold-standard defenders but rather to improve the quality of their arguments.

3.10 "GOLD HAS OBJECTIVE VALUE"

Well before he became Chairman of the Board of Governors of the Federal Reserve System, Alan Greenspan was associated with the novelist-philosopher Ayn Rand, who called her philosophical system Objectivism. Two characters in her novel *Atlas Shrugged*, the entrepreneur Francisco D'Anconia and the smuggler Ragnar Danneskold, make spirited defenses of gold as money. D'Anconia declares that the forced substitution of irredeemable paper money for gold "kills all objective standards" and adds: "Gold was an objective value, an equivalent of wealth produced." Danneskold exclaims: "Gold is the objective value, the means of preserving one's wealth and one's future." In the context of Rand's philosophy, an "objective value" is something that really does promote a person's survival or flourishing. It is usefulness to an individual rather than a market value or relative price. A Rand-influenced author (Bates 2010, p. 109) distinguishes the two sorts of value when she writes: "Gold is real; it has objective value to people, and its market value is determined by free exchange." For D'Anconia and Danneskold, then, what has "objective value" is a medium of exchange that reliably indicates and stores wealth. Not gold as a metal, but as a money of reliable purchasing power. The use of gold as money promotes genuine well-being (thus has an "objective value" to its users) insofar it has a more reliable purchasing power than some alternatives.

Greenspan also appears to use the phrase in this way. In a non-fiction essay entitled "Gold and Economic Freedom" that first appeared in Rand's newsletter and later in a Rand-with-others anthology, Greenspan (1967) writes that an economy would be limited to barter unless people had "some commodity of objective value which was generally acceptable as money." The meaning would be clearer if he had written "of reliable market value."

Modern economists understandably avoid the phrase "objective value." Whatever its meaning in philosophy, it lacks a clear meaning in economics, and thus creates needless ambiguity when used in the midst of an economic argument. For an economist versed in the history of economic thought, the phrase may suggest the pre-modern "labor theory of value," in which a good's equilibrium market price follows from the objective fact of its necessary labor input, contrary to the modern preference-centered or "subjective" theory of price.

Gold's widespread acceptance as a medium of exchange, and hence its emergence as a commonly accepted medium of exchange or money, began with people subjectively valuing it as a beautiful material for jewelry and other ornaments. Greenspan fortunately recognizes this, and refers to the "artistic and functional uses" of gold. He also recognizes the role of network effects in the evolutionary process from which gold emerged as money: "Preferences on what to hold as a store of value, will shift to the most widely acceptable commodity, which, in turn, will make it still more acceptable." And he recognizes that some commodity other than gold might have emerged as money. The objective physical properties of gold that made it suitable as a hand-to-hand medium of exchange (durability, divisibility, and so on) promoted but did not pre-ordain its emergence as money, as seen by the emergence of shells, salt, silver, and other commodities depending on local circumstances.

3.11 "A GOLD STANDARD PROVIDES A STABLE MEASURE OF VALUE, JUST AS A YARDSTICK PROVIDES A STABLE MEASURE OF LENGTH, BECAUSE IT FIXES THE DEFINITION OF THE MONETARY UNIT"

Over medium to long horizons, gold standards have provided money with a *relatively* stable purchasing power, as indicated by lower inflation rates and lower price-level forecast errors, than fiat standards have provided (Rolnick and Weber 1997; Selgin. Lastrapes, and White 2012; more on this contrast in Chapter 4). That is a major advantage of a gold standard. But it would be an exaggeration to say or suggest that under a gold standard the purchasing power of money is *absolutely* stable, or as constant as the length of a yardstick. A gold standard fixes the *gold content of the dollar* or the pound, but this is not the same as fixing its purchasing power. Fixity of the dollar or pound in terms of gold content means that the purchasing power of dollar or pound *varies with the purchasing power of gold*, which is not fixed.

The distinction between a constant gold definition and a constant purchasing power for the dollar can be made clearer by seeing that the price level measured in dollars (the number of dollars need to purchase a reference basket containing a specified set of goods and services) can, under a gold standard, be understood as the product of two ratios: the defined dollar–gold parity (measured as dollars per troy ounce of pure gold, the inverse of the defined gold content of the dollar measured as gold ounces per dollar) and the market-determined relative price of gold (measured as the number of ounces of gold that it takes to buy the reference basket), that is,

$$P = (\$X / \text{oz. Au}) \cdot (Y \text{ oz. Au} / \text{goods-basket}) = \$XY / \text{goods-basket} \quad (3.1)$$

For example, if the defined parity makes \$20.67 equivalent to 1 ounce of gold, so that X = \$20.67, and 1 ounce of gold buys 4.84 baskets at base-year relative prices, so that Y = 4.84, then the dollar price level XY = (4.84 oz. Au / basket)(\$20.67 / oz. Au) = \$100 per basket. If prices in gold fall 10 percent, so that now Y = 4.35, then the dollar price index falls to 90. The number X, although sometimes called "the official price of gold," is not really a price. It does not vary with supply and demand, but is fixed by definition. The gold price index Y *is* a relative price. It is the inverse of the purchasing power of gold (ppg, measured in baskets / oz. Au), the variable measured in the vertical direction on the figures in Chapter 2, and thus varies with shifts in the stock supply and demand curves for monetary gold.[12]

To recap the lessons of the model of Chapter 2, the ppg varies whenever the stock supply and demand for monetary gold do not shift in the same direction at the same rate. Alterations to the ppg from shocks to stock demand (e.g., a large country joins or leaves the gold standard) are eventually reversed by long-run supply responses, but that takes time. Shocks to flow supply or demand have permanent effects on the ppg. Historical variations in the ppg from these sources have been small in comparison to changes in the purchasing power of fiat monies, as will be shown in Chapter 4. But it is easy to show that changes have not been *zero*.

Leland Yeager (1984, pp. 651–652) has offered an amusing example of the common confusion between a fixed definition and a fixed purchasing power. When critics of putting Austria on the gold standard in 1892 complained that gold had recently been unsteady in purchasing power, legislative Deputy Anton Menger (brother to the economist Carl Menger, but not his equal in economic thinking) replied that if the critics would look at the gold market in London, they would see that gold has *consistently* traded against Bank of England notes at prices very close to £3 17s. 10-½ p. per ounce! This was the parity implied by the defined gold content of the pound sterling and the coin redemption value of the Bank of England notes. It said nothing about the purchasing power of gold or of the pound.

Writers who draw an analogy between a gold standard and a system of weights and measures unfortunately sometimes suggest that the purchasing power of gold is constant. For example, authors Steve Forbes

---

[12] The equation and surrounding discussion are drawn from White (1999, ch. 2).

and Elizabeth Ames (2014), in a book advocating a "twenty-first-century gold standard," write:

Just as we need to be sure of the number of inches in a foot or the minutes in an hour, people in the economy must be certain that their money is an accurate measure of worth. ... Remember that gold, a measuring rod, is stable in value. ...

We don't let markets each day determine how many ounces there are in a pound or how many inches there are in a foot.

Forbes and Ames might have had the following sound argument in mind: "Prices are expressed in units of money. Consumers and businesspeople do not want the information conveyed by money prices to become noisier (less reliable) due to erratic shrinkage in the purchasing power of the monetary unit. A money with a more stable and predictable purchasing power is therefore better, and along this dimension gold standards have historically outperformed fiat standards." But calling money a "measure of worth" is not the best way of expressing the argument. There is no "worth" or "value" inherent in goods to be "measured." The money prices realized in the market for potatoes do not reveal any inherent property of potatoes. They reveal only that at the realized price sellers valued getting the money over keeping the potatoes, and buyers preferred getting the potatoes over keeping the money. And the same is true for any set of goods whose money prices are used to construct a price index basket.

The declaration that "gold, a measuring rod, is stable in value," is somewhat cryptic. Presumably gold serves as "a measuring rod" only when prices are expressed in units of gold, namely in a gold-standard economy, not when gold is demonetized as it is today. But if gold were "a measuring rod" by virtue of its serving as the medium of account under a gold standard, it would be equally true that the fiat dollar is "a measuring rod" under a fiat dollar standard, so that serving as "a measuring rod" identifies nothing special about gold.

Again, the phrase "stable in value" here may refer either to (a) the *definition* of the monetary unit as a mass of gold (troy ounces of pure gold per dollar), or (b) the *purchasing power* of the monetary unit. But not both. That is, it may either refer to X or instead to Y in Equation 3.1. If it refers to X, again the statement says nothing about the superiority of a gold standard over any other standard. It is true under *any* monetary standard that prices are normally expressed in money units, and the monetary unit is "stable" in terms of itself. If instead "stable in value" here means "stable in purchasing power," then the authors seem to be attributing stability to gold money (but not to other monies) without reference to historical evidence. By contrast to the final quoted sentence, we *do* let markets each day determine how many bundles of goods an ounce of gold will buy. The superior purchasing-power stability of gold money over fiat money can only be established by historical data, not by definition or by analogy to measuring devices.

In the midst of a thought-provoking monograph, George Gilder (2015, p. 64) uses a celestial analogy to suggest that gold can be regarded as having a perfectly (rather than comparatively) constant purchasing power, though at least he initially phrases it as an "if-then" proposition:

If gold's value is constant, then all other prices can become variables around that constant. Just as the North Star provides a fixed reference for celestial navigation and astronomy, gold provides a fixed reference for the value of the galaxy of goods and services.

The simple fact of the matter is that gold's purchasing power over other goods cannot be fixed so long as supply and demand conditions for gold, *or for other goods*, do not remain fixed.

We discussed earlier in this chapter an anti-gold-standard argument that blames the deflation of the early 1920s and early 1930s on "the gold standard." We argued in rebuttal that what created the deflation was actually the wartime suspension of the gold standard, enabling wartime paper money inflation, followed by the postwar attempt to return to the prewar parity (rather than devalue), which required a return to the prewar price level starting from well above it. A bad defense of the gold standard results from skipping this complicated set of facts, and instead *taking it for granted* that gold has a perfectly stable purchasing power, based on the confused notion that a fixed gold *definition* for the dollar is sufficient to make the dollar's *purchasing power* stable. Then the interwar deflations can be simply defined away! This at least is the line of defense that columnist John Tamny (2019a) suggests in the following passage:

Hiltzik makes the odd argument that the gold-defined dollar caused a "deflation" in the 1930s and that because it allegedly did, it's not a worthy way to define money. Except that's not what happened. The dollar's value held at 1/20th of an ounce of gold until FDR devalued in '33. Inflation is a decline in the value of the monetary measure, while deflation is a rise. The purpose of a gold-exchange standard is to avoid either scenario by virtue of monetary authorities abiding a currency price rule in terms of a commodity most known for stability.

Tamny's reply seems to deny the fact that there *was* a deflation in the United States. It thereby fails to answer the false indictment of the gold standard as the cause of that deflation.

The price level fell in 1930–1933 from its 1929 level (or, alternatively, the purchasing power of the US dollar in terms of goods and services rose), as indicated by the CPI or any other broad price index. It will not do to suggest that there *could not* have been a deflation in the ordinary sense of the term (a falling price level) because the par value of the dollar *in terms of gold* did not change. The purchasing power of gold rose. Even if we suppose that the purpose of instituting an international gold or gold-exchange standard is to avoid both inflation and deflation, it remains the case that deflation was *not* avoided between 1930 and 1933 despite the Federal Reserve System adhering to a gold standard at a constant parity. The global purchasing power of gold rose because European central banks, having driven the purchasing power of gold down by dumping their gold standards and inflating during the First World War, began trying to accumulate gold to return to their prewar parties from postwar price levels too high to be consistent with those parities. And because of the hoarding of gold by the American public following bank runs.

Another poor argument for the gold standard exaggerates the instability of the purchasing power of the fiat dollar by citing the volatile prices of individual commodities rather than a broad index of prices like the CPI. For example, Tamny (2019b) writes:

The problem is that since the early 1970s, money has floated without definition. While a dollar was exchangeable for 1/35th of an ounce of gold in August of 1971, it now buys roughly 1/1300th of an ounce. A dollar that used to purchase almost ½ of a barrel of oil now purchases 1/60th. Readers get the picture.

It took $631 in 2019 to buy the CPI basket that $100 bought in 1971. The purchasing power of the dollar declined by about 86 percent against consumer goods in general, which is bad enough. It undermines rather than strengthens the argument to reach for a larger figure (a 93 percent decline against gold alone or a 97 percent decline against oil alone) by cherry-picking those commodities whose dollar prices rose more than average.

A rise in the dollar price of demonetized gold alone is not an accurate measure of general dollar price inflation. Tamny (2010) has nonetheless remarkably claimed that the fiat price of gold by itself is "the objective indicator of inflation" in a fiat regime, and that this is so "no matter what" the CPI tells us:

When the price of gold moves, what is changing are the values of the currencies in which it's priced. Gold is the objective indicator of inflation: When its price in any currency rises substantially, that means the unit of account is weakening and that we're inflating. ... As the rising price of gold has revealed throughout the decade we've been inflating, no matter what the more quiescent government measures of consumer prices have been telling us. ... Money quantities, economic growth and consumer prices are poor measures of inflation, but the dollar's price in terms of gold is.[13]

Is the claim that gold is "the objective indicator of inflation" an empirical claim? Or is it supposed to be true by definition? Tamny here seems to be merely re-defining "inflation" to correspond to a sustained rise in the price of gold (or a "weakening" of the currency unit *against gold alone*). A rise in the nominal price of gold thus indicates inflation "no matter what" the CPI indicates. If we were to adopt this novel use of terms, we would need some other term to refer to a sustained rise in the prices of goods in general. Needless to say, redefining "inflation" in an idiosyncratic way provides us with no evidence of whether a gold standard or a fiat standard gives greater stability to money's purchasing power in relation to a broad array of goods and services. If instead Tamny is making an empirical claim that gold is "the objective indicator of inflation," whatever that might mean, he has failed to provide the empirical evidence.

As a somewhat technical aside, some economists have long recognized a theoretical case for constructing a broader price index than the CPI, including the prices of producer goods and financial assets along with the prices of final goods and services, to better measure changes in the purchasing power of the monetary unit (Alchian and Klein 1973; Goodhart 2001). But reducing the scope of the index to a single asset price, the price of gold alone, is not consistent with the case for a broader index. The dollar price of gold is less rather than more informative than a larger set of prices. The case for a gold standard over a fiat standard is not strengthened by spotlighting the performance of unrepresentative numbers and ignoring representative numbers.

3.12 "THE QUANTITY OF MONEY IS SELF-REGULATING UNDER A GOLD STANDARD – BUT ONLY IF WE OUTLAW FRACTIONAL-RESERVE BANKING IN FAVOR OF ONE HUNDRED PERCENT RESERVES"

Some economists in recent decades – most notably followers of the late Murray N. Rothbard (1962, 1990) – have supported a gold standard that

---

[13] Tamny criticizes the accuracy of the CPI for measuring inflation on the grounds that (his example) the makers of Skippy peanut butter sometimes put fewer ounces in a jar while charging the same price. The Bureau of Labor Statistics, however, takes note of product weight and treats this kind of downsizing as an increase in the price of Skippy.

is constrained by a major legal restriction on banking contracts. Deposits or circulating notes that are redeemable on demand must be backed 100 percent by gold in the vault. They view fractional-reserve arrangements as fraudulent, and thus not to be allowed for liabilities that are payable on demand. Checking deposits may not be used to finance lending. Checking accounts must be backed by "full reserves" in the vault, a strict warehousing operation.

Some of Rothbard's followers would generalize the restriction to outlaw other modern banking practices. Barnett and Block (2009) would prohibit anything but perfect matching between the days-to-maturity of a bank's liabilities (time deposits only) and its assets (loans and securities). Jesus Huerta de Soto (1999) would outlaw any loan contract that grants the borrower an option to prepay (a feature very common today on home mortgages), or that grants the lender an option to call in the loan.

Although Rothbardians have bundled 100-percent-reserve restrictions on demand deposits together with advocacy of a decentralized gold standard, other economists have proposed similar restrictions on demand deposits under a central bank fiat standard. Some members of the early Chicago School like Henry Simons (1934), and more recently Laurence Kotlikoff (2010), have called for an end to fractional-reserve banking for the sake of greater financial stability. They want to eliminate bank runs and debt crises by eliminating banks and other intermediaries that finance their asset portfolios by issuing debt claims. They would require that all intermediaries be equity-financed in the manner of mutual funds.

The abolition of fractional-reserve banking under a gold standard would not be beneficial or innocuous. It would abridge freedom of contract, impede financial innovation, eliminate beneficial responsiveness in the quantity of money to changes in the market demand to hold money, and eliminate gains from economizing on the use of physical gold in the payment system. When the restriction is built into a gold standard proposal, it limits the benefits and appeal of the gold standard. Fortunately, it need not be built in.

Some full-reserve advocates invoke supposed principles of natural law or Roman law.[14] I will skip jurisprudential arguments here in favor of

---

[14] Classics scholars Andrew Collins and John Walsh (2014, pp. 183, 191, 192) find that Huerta de Soto seriously misrepresents Roman law in respect to banking: "J. Huerta de Soto has recently declared that fractional reserve banking was outlawed in Classical Roman law, but, as will be seen below, this is patently untrue. ... Huerta de Soto distinguishes between the *mutuum* and *depositum* contracts, but defines the *mutuum* in a manner that is inconsistent with Roman law. ... In short, Huerta de Soto's definition of both the *mutuum* and the irregular deposit will not stand, nor will the view that fractional reserve banking was against the principles of Roman Law."

focusing on two objections, which claim that fractional-reserve banking disrupts the stable functioning of a gold standard.[15] The first argument claims that fractional-reserve banks are inherently fragile and cannot survive without government support. The second argument claims that a fractional-reserve banking system produces swings of monetary over-expansion and contraction in the economy, enlarging business cycles.

Some historical background on fractional-reserve banking under silver and gold standards, supplementing Chapter 1's account, may be helpful in answering the first objection. Taking coins "on deposit" emerged in medieval Lombardy as a sideline for coin-changers, specialists who would buy your foreign coins with local coins. In London, goldsmiths came to play the same vault-keeping role. There were two types of depositors. A customer who merely wanted his silver or gold coins safely stored, with the very same coins to be returned on demand, would bring the coins to the vault-keeper in a sealed bag, and had to pay a storage fee. The bag was not to be opened, and the coins were to remain undisturbed in the vault (Mueller 1997, pp. 12–13). This arrangement, akin to renting a safety deposit box, is sometimes described as "100 percent reserve banking." Strictly speaking, it is not a *banking* arrangement at all, because there is no lending of the money collected, but only warehousing, though the vault-keeping firm may *also* do banking with funds obtained from time depositors.

A second type of medieval customer, who primarily wanted economical payment services, made a different arrangement with the vault-keeper. The new arrangement differed in three important particulars. First, the vault-keeper gave the customer not a warehousing contract entitling her to get the very same coins back, but a demandable debt contract, a claim to *equivalent* coins on demand. Accordingly, she would bring *loose* coins to the vault, which the vault-keeper would evaluate for pure metallic content (weight times percentage purity) before adding the coins' metallic value to the customer's account credit, and mingling her coins with those brought by other such depositors. Second, the debt claim had the feature of *transferability* to other customers, allowing payment by deposit transfer. The depositor could now direct the banker to transfer a designated sum, say 2.1 troy ounces of silver, from her account balance to a payee's account balance. A money warehouse could in principle take these first two steps, provided that customers accepted debt claims in

---

[15] For critiques of the jurisprudential arguments, see Selgin and White (1996) and White (2003).

place of bailments. But, third, the vault-keeper became a banker rather than a warehouser when the agreement allowed him to invest some of the deposited coins by purchasing securities or making loans. The customer took on a somewhat increased risk of default by becoming a lender rather than bailee to the bank, presumably deeming the risk of loss smaller than the flow of benefits (reduced or zero annual account fees and/or interest income on account balances).

Following the market acceptance of fractional-reserve deposits, banks began to issue a second kind of liability. These were general claims on the bank (not a claim that might bounce against a particular customer's account) that could be signed over to another party, something like cashier's check today. For their customers' convenience, banks soon provided the claims in bearer form (no signing-over necessary) and in round denominations. These were now banknotes, circulating paper currency claims on banks that were payable on demand in silver or gold to the bearer (whoever presented them). As currency, they could be transferred anonymously, and without bank involvement (unlike deposits transfers, which need to be recorded on the books). London goldsmiths were issuing banknotes in the mid-1600s.

Banks by necessity held fractional reserves against their banknote liabilities. There was no practical way to charge storage fees to holders of circulating banknotes because they were anonymous to the bank of issue (White 2003). The costs of issuing banknotes were instead defrayed by the interest income from loans financed by notes in circulation.

The demandable liabilities of a solvent bank with fractional reserves are 100 percent backed by the bank's *assets*, but they are less than 100 percent backed by its monetary gold in the vault. The monetary gold that it holds is an *immediate* reserve for meeting redemption demands. Its most liquid (readily saleable) earning assets form a secondary reserve. Should redemption demands begin to deplete the coin on hand, the most liquid interest-earning assets would be sold to replenish reserves and allow the uninterrupted payment of depositors. In the extreme case of a bank run, a bank without other resources might be overwhelmed by redemption demands and be unable to pay.

An example offered by the economist Ludwig von Mises (1980 [1912]) helps to explain the circumstances under which fractional reserves are feasible. Suppose that a bakery issues 100 tokens, each stamped "good for one loaf of bread," which are useless for any other purpose. Leaving aside lost tokens, the bakery will find that it cannot get by on fractional reserves. It will need 100 loaves of bread, because all the tokens will be redeemed. By contrast, suppose that a bank issues 100 banknotes, each redeemable for a gold coin. Once they are widely accepted in payments, the banknotes can make almost all the payments for their holders that coins can make. Unlike the bread tokens, which themselves cannot be eaten with butter and jam, the banknotes themselves serve as a medium of payment. They do not need to be redeemed to be useful to most holders.

Once banknotes and checkable deposits are popular, a few redemptions will still be made. Banks into which banknotes and checks have been deposited will present them for redemption at the clearinghouse. Largely offsetting inflows of monetary gold will go into the bank from depositors who sell goods abroad and from other banks whose customers have written checks or given banknotes to customers of the bank in question. The bank will find that *net* outflows of gold amount to only a fraction of all its banknote and checkable deposit liabilities during any week, so it does not need "full reserves" to meet the net redemption demands that it actually faces. As Mises (1980, pp. 299–300) put it, a banker "is therefore in a position to undertake greater obligations than he would ever be able to fulfill; it is enough if he takes sufficient precaution to ensure his ability to satisfy promptly that proportion of claims that is actually enforced against him."

To avoid breaching the contractual obligation to repay, the banker needs to keep *enough* monetary gold in reserve (and enough liquid assets as a secondary reserve). How can the banker figure out how large a gold reserve is large enough? It is a matter of practical calculation: The banker needs to err on the side of caution at the outset, and learn over time from experience the probability of any given amount of gold flowing out on a given day. If he wants to be 99.9999 percent safe each period (so that the expected time to default is 500,000 periods), he needs to hold reserves (or have ways of quickly replenishing the reserves) sufficient to cover 99.9999 percent of cases. For a numerical example, consider a very small bank with only 1000 demand deposit accounts, each initially containing $10. Each day every account either has $10 withdrawn (–$10), which has a 50 percent probability, or has $10 added (+$10). Net withdrawals will form a bell-shaped distribution (high probabilities in the middle close to zero net outflows, low and declining probabilities at the tails representing large inflows and large outflows). The probability that 600 or more accounts are emptied on the first day, so that the net outflow ((600 – 400) × $10)) is $2000 or more, is the same as the probability that a fair coin turns up heads 600 or more flips out of 1000, which turns out to be less than 0.00001 percent. Thus, $200 or 2 percent reserves against the $10,000 in deposits will cover net outflows on more than 99.9999 percent of such days. The expected time to default is more than one thousand years. (Of course, the example assumes that depositors act independently, so it does not deal with bank runs, which we discuss in the following text.)

To quote Mises (1980, p. 362) once more: the banker in deciding on the amount of reserves to hold "has to rely upon an uncertain empirical procedure which may easily lead to mistakes. Nevertheless, prudent and experienced bank directors – and most bank directors are prudent and experienced – usually manage pretty well with it." To provide the incentive to hold enough reserves, it is important that the banker who miscalculates, holds too little in reserves, and fails to pay when obligated to pay, be subject to the legal penalties for breach of contract.

A money warehouse or 100 percent reserve institution could also offer payments by account transfer, but its services would be significantly more expensive because of the cost of storage and the absence of interest income. Redeemable banknotes circulating anonymously in round denominations simply cannot exist without fractional reserves. Banknotes are feasible for a fractional-reserve bank because the bank does not need to assess storage fees to cover its costs. It can let the notes circulate anonymously and at face value, unencumbered by fees, and cover its costs by interest income. An issuer of circulating 100-percent-reserve notes would need to assess storage fees on someone, but would be unable to assess them on unknown note-holders. There are no known historical examples of circulating 100 percent reserve notes unencumbered by storage fees. Historically money warehouses were not outlawed, but were out-competed by fractional-reserve banks offering more attractive and more economical payment services to customers who wanted bank accounts and banknotes for making payments (rather for storing coins).[16]

The introduction and public acceptance of fractionally backed demand deposits and banknotes under a gold standard means that the economy needs less gold in its vaults to supply the real quantity of money balances (commonly accepted media of exchange) that the public wants to hold. Money is supplied at a lower resource cost, that is, with less labor and capital devoted to mining or importing precious metals and fashioning them into coins or bars. Contrasting the balance sheets of fractional reserve banks to those of money warehouses, we see that loans to productive enterprises take the place of warehoused metal. Some gold can be exported, and productive machinery imported. This development in

---

[16] I make this argument at greater length in White (2003).

Scotland was praised by Adam Smith as an important contributor to his country's economic growth. As Mises put it, "fiduciary media," meaning demand deposits and banknotes in excess of reserves, "enrich both the person that issues them and the community that employs them."

Jesus Huerta de Soto (1995, p. 30) calls the above account of the feasibility of fractional-reserve banking "the trite argument that the 'law of large numbers' allows the banks to act safely with a fractional reserve," and rejects it on the grounds that "the degree of probability of an untypical withdrawal of deposits is not, in view of its own nature, an insurable risk." It is true that the atypical clusters of withdrawals known as bank runs have not historically been random events. But this means that runs have identifiable causes. If uninsured banks with fractional reserves take the necessary steps to minimize their susceptibility to these causes, as seen historically in free banking systems, few will fail on account of runs. History shows that modern fractional-reserve banking spread from medieval Lombardy throughout Europe and the rest of the world, and thrived, for centuries before deposit insurance. The idea that fractional-reserve banks are inherently fragile and cannot survive without government protection is an armchair theory contradicted by history.

Rather than being been random, a run on the bank has almost always been triggered by bad news severe enough to give customers good reason to suspect that the bank has become insolvent.[17] It follows that a bank able to credibly assure the public of its solvency can avoid being run upon. Fractional-reserve banks are not inherently run-prone where they are allowed to adopt (and do adopt) run-resistant strategies, primarily diversification of assets and adequate capitalization (advertised to the public) to absorb potential asset losses. Runs on individual insolvent banks did not spill over to other banks or give rise to panics in countries like Scotland, Canada, and Sweden where (unlike the United States in the nineteenth century) banks were not weakened by legal restrictions on note-issue or branching and were held accountable for any failure to meet their contractual obligations to pay. The vast majority of well-known banks with fractional reserves did not experience runs, but continually met all their redemption demands for decades (Dowd 1992; Selgin 1994a).[18]

---

[17] The historical timing and clustering of runs is not well explained by the canonical bank run model of Diamond and Dybvig (1983). In their account, many customers withdraw from an otherwise solvent bank merely due to the (collectively self-justifying) fear that too many other customers might withdraw.

[18] For a more detailed discussion of the notion that banks are inherently run-prone and of historical run-proofing strategies, see White (1999, ch. 6).

We now turn briefly to the second objection made by proponents of a gold standard that excludes fractional-reserve banking, the argument that a fractional-reserve system fosters over-expansion of money and credit, creating an unsustainable boom that ends in a bust. While a government-sponsored central bank can certainly engage in excess monetary expansion despite a gold standard, and can indeed generate a boom–bust cycle, it is not the case that competing fractional-reserve commercial banks on a gold standard can over-issue (or under-issue) for long or to a great extent. Any bank that over-issues while surrounded by rival banks will quickly lose gold reserves to those rivals when they collect and redeem more of its liabilities. Should (implausibly) all banks expand together, the system as a whole would be disciplined by reserve losses to the rest of the world. The clearing system and the price-specie-flow mechanism thereby limit the expansion of the banking system's monetary liabilities to the volume consistent with the public's demand to hold them, and correspondingly limit the aggregate stock of bank-issued money. A competitive system avoids the excessive credit expansion that can create an unsustainable business cycle boom. Adverse clearings and the price-specie-flow mechanism preserve monetary equilibrium.

It is an attractive feature of free banking with fractional reserves that the quantity of bank-issued money expands when there is an increase the demand to hold bank-issued money, but does not expand otherwise (Selgin and White 1994, p. 1725). Free banking thus works against short-run monetary disequilibrium (excess supply or unsatisfied excess demand) and its business-cycle consequences. An increase in the volume of bank-issued money matched by an increased demand to hold it is not disturbing but on the contrary avoids a potential disturbance. A banking system that accommodates an increased demand to hold its gold-denominated demand liabilities by expanding their quantity does not drive market interest rates away from their natural values, spur excessive investment, or set in motion a boom–bust cycle. On the contrary.

Before leaving the topic of mandatory 100 percent reserves, it should be noted that even a country that has retained its gold reserves since the demonetization of gold, like the United States, could not back its money supply 100 percent in gold without great expense. The US volume of money in narrow terms (currency plus demandable bank deposit) is measured by the aggregate M1. In April 2020 (before a redefinition that expanded the aggregate), M1 stood at about $4.3 trillion. The stock of monetary gold held by the US government, meanwhile, had a market value of less than half of $1 trillion (261.5 million troy ounces

@ $1,735 per ounce is about $454 billion).[19] To provide 100 percent backing of M1, based on these figures, Americans would have to buy another $3.8 trillion worth of gold – a very expensive proposition. And that is only the one-time cost. In an economy with 2 percent per annum real GDP growth, assuming a flat trend in the ratio of gold to GDP, a constant purchasing power of gold implies the domestic extraction or importation each year of 2 percent of the gold stock. For a gold stock equal to 100 percent of $4.3 trillion in M1, that 2 percent would require an annual expense of $86 billion. With a 5 percent fractional reserve against M1, the needed stock of gold would already be more than provided, and the annual expense would be only $4.3 billion – slightly less than the Federal Reserve's annual budget.

3.13 "THE QUANTITY OF MONEY IS SELF-REGULATING UNDER A GOLD STANDARD – BUT ONLY IF BANKS OF ISSUE LEND EXCLUSIVELY ON REAL BILLS OF EXCHANGE"

The "Real Bills Doctrine," a viewpoint common among economists one to two centuries ago, contained ideas that still echo in some places today. The RBD misunderstood how market forces regulate the quantity of money under a gold standard.[20] It overlooked the corrective role of adverse clearings among banks in a region, and specie flows among regions, suggesting instead that a region's money stock would be self-regulating if and only if the banking system focused exclusively on acquiring a certain type of asset, namely purchasing commercial IOUs known as "real bills." So long as it did not advocate legal restrictions on banking to force compliance with its recommendations, and directed its advice only to commercial bankers in a competitive system on a gold standard, the RBD was harmless enough. As David Glasner (1992) has noted, it provided a prudential rule of thumb to bankers: Acquire safe, short-term, and liquid earning assets to match demandable liabilities

---

[19] The Fed's gold certificate entry as reported on its balance sheet (H.4.1, October 6, 2011) is $11,041 million, the product of the bookkeeping price of $42.22 times 261.511 million fine troy ounces of gold. See also Federal Reserve Bank of New York (2008: 17), which notes: "A majority of these reserves are held in depositories of the Treasury Department at Fort Knox, Kentucky, and West Point, New York. Most of the remainder is at the Denver and Philadelphia Mints and the San Francisco Assay Office." I ignore the United States share of gold held by the International Monetary Fund.

[20] Although the RBD is less popular than it once was, George Selgin (1989) has warned us that "it would be a mistake to think of the real-bills doctrine as a 'dead horse'" because "dead horses of economic theory have a habit of suddenly springing back to life again."

and thereby enable redemption of any excess issues. The role of primary gold reserves in correcting an over-issue, however, should not be eclipsed. Any banker in a competitive system who has issued a greater volume of its monetary liabilities than his clientele wants to hold will find the over-expansion soon corrected by reserve losses in the form of adverse clearings to surrounding banks. Liquid assets are for replenishing primary reserves when necessary (they provide a secondary reserve). They supplement and do not replace gold reserves. And the set of liquid assets is not limited to real bills.

The RBD became a dangerous idea, however – and this was the source of its historical notoriety – when it was used as a guide to central bank policy.[21] Limiting a central bank to real-bills discounting did not effectively prevent it from over-issuing or under-issuing, and adverse clearings would not promptly correct it because it was not surrounded by rivals collecting and redeeming the excess. RBD adherents on the Federal Reserve Board in the 1920s were responsible for the Fed excessively expanding money and credit in the 1922–1929 period, rather than letting interest rates rise to reach a new equilibrium level as the business demand for credit rose. They were later responsible for the Fed's non-response to excessive monetary contraction in the early 1930s because the business demand for credit was low (Humphrey and Timberlake 2019).

To explain the Real Bills Doctrine more clearly, we need to identify what is a "real bill." To use a common example, a miller sells $1000 worth of flour to a baker and presents a bill due in 90 days. The baker endorses the bill, making it a transferable bond-like IOU pledging to pay $1000 in 90 days. The baker plans to pay off the bill out of the revenue she will earn by producing and selling bread from the flour. The miller need not wait 90 days to get paid but can immediately sell the endorsed bill to a bank (one that considers the baker creditworthy) at its present discounted value, say $980. The bill is "real" in being associated with tangible goods in process, unlike a personal consumption loan or a government bond. Thus, real bills in the eighteenth and nineteenth centuries were short-term commercial IOUs that financed goods through stages of production. High-quality real bills were low in default risk and liquid. They had a thick secondary market with small bid-ask spreads.

---

[21] Thomas Sargent and Neil Wallace (1982) and Sargent (2011) have recommended what they call "the real bills doctrine" over the quantity theory of money as a monetary policy guide. David Laidler (1984) has shown, however, that what Sargent and Wallace have recommended is not the traditional Real Bills Doctrine.

The view that adherence to real-bills lending is necessary and sufficient for self-regulation of the money stock under a gold standard can be found in the work of the late Antal Fekete (2002), a long-time RBD advocate. Fekete calls a system where banks make loans or buy bonds other than real bills an "adulterated" gold standard.[22] He asserts that an "adulterated" gold standard, like a fiat standard, fails to stabilize the purchasing power of money:

> The gold standard is called unadulterated if the stock of circulating medium has no fiduciary component. This means that the banks issue no bank notes and create no bank deposits except when buying gold or discounting a bill of exchange. ... The price level under the adulterated gold standard and, for the stronger reason, under the regime of irredeemable currency, is no longer stable. If a country wants a stable price level for consumer goods, it will have to adopt the unadulterated gold standard.[23]

The claim that an "adulterated" gold standard fails to stabilize the purchasing power of money amounts to claiming that the adverse-clearing and price-specie-flow mechanisms somehow become ineffective if banks hold assets of the wrong types. Yet these mechanisms do not in fact depend on the specific types of assets that banks hold. The adverse clearing mechanism depends rather on the public shedding excess monetary liabilities issued by particular banks, and the various banks redeeming at the clearinghouse the claims they acquire upon one another. The price-specie-flow mechanism depends on the public in the aggregate spending off excess money balances partly in net imports paid for with gold.

The ordinary operation of both mechanisms assumes that banks maintain solvency and liquidity. While prudence requires a bank to hold levels of primary reserves (monetary gold) and secondary reserves (readily saleable assets) appropriate to the risk of redemption of its demandable liabilities, experience and the general requirements for prudent banking show that real bills are not the *only* assets appropriate to the role of secondary reserves. Secondary reserves need not be 100 percent of demandable liabilities minus primary reserves. In other words, a bank portfolio of real bills does not have special advantages over a portfolio of other assets with equivalent default risk, liquidity, and duration.

---

[22] The Spanish economist Juan Ramón Rallo has defended propositions that he identifies with the real-bills doctrine, citing Fekete. But what Rallo defends are guidelines for prudent banking rather than the real-bills doctrine as a guide to monetary policy or as a proposal for legal restrictions.

[23] https://professorfekete.com/articles/AEFMonEcon101Lecture13.pdf.

Viewed as a formula for maintaining equilibrium between the supply and demand for money, the Real Bill Doctrine has several shortcomings. (a) It wrongly takes the quantity demanded by a particular type of *business borrowing* as a reliable guide to the quantity of bank-issued *money* that the public wants to hold. Not only are these quantities different but, as economist Henry Thornton (1802) noted long ago, a central bank not subject to immediate redemption of its liabilities can increase the nominal quantity of credit demanded simply by expansionary money policy. In the short run, the expansion lowers the real interest rate, which raises the real quantity of credit demanded. In the medium term, the increased supply of money raises price level and thereby all nominal quantities. (b) It wrongly takes the *quality* of bank assets acquired as a reliable governor of the *quantity* of monetary liabilities issued. (c) It makes redeemability of bank liabilities (in gold or otherwise) an inessential "fifth wheel" in the process that determines the quantity of money. It is in fact the banks' obligation to redeem their monetary liabilities in gold, and not what the economist Melchior Palyi (1936, p. 5) called "the backflow of their automatically self-liquidating, short-term credits" that fundamentally limits the volume of bank-issued money. If gold reserve losses were not a constraint, expiring short-term credits could always be rolled over.

To elaborate on the first flaw, an increase in the quantity of bills offered at a given lending rate, associated with more goods in process, does not signal that the banks can prudently purchase the entire increased volume of bills. A rise in the discount rate is called for to ration the scarce supply of deposited savings that the banks have to lend. With greater demand for savings, competing banks will bid up the deposit rate, which will increase the quantity of deposits supplied. The Real Bills Doctrine, however, calls for accommodating all offers of real bills for discount, presumably at an unchanged interest rate, and is silent on the need for equilibrating changes in interest rates.

A sounder account of the self-regulation of the quantity of bank-issued money in a competitive banking system on a gold standard begins with the proposition that profit-seeking banks must carefully attend to their reserve positions. Running out of reserves and defaulting incurs a costly legal or reputational penalty. A bank that issues an excessive volume of demandable liabilities will soon experience adverse clearings (will lose reserves to other banks). To lower the risk of payment default it will be compelled to stop its expansion, thereby stopping the outflow, and then reverse it to rebuild its reserves. Conversely, a bank that issues less than its clientele wants to hold will gain reserves and find it profitable to expand. These responses to adverse or positive clearings will return the quantity of money issued by an individual bank to the quantity demanded. Economy-wide, for a region that is part of an inter-regional gold standard, reserves flow into and out of the system to maintain monetary equilibrium (the price-specie-flow mechanism operates).

The sounder account of the self-regulatory properties of a gold standard with bank-issued money does not require that banks exclusively hold a single type of earning assets against demandable liabilities. The system self-regulates even where bills of exchange are uncommon. Accordingly, the gold standard can continue to govern the quantity of money appropriately when financial progress brings other types of assets that banks find more advantageous to hold. The self-regulating properties of a gold standard are not limited to a world of nineteenth-century financial assets.

4

How a Fiat Standard Works

Under a metallic standard, as discussed in Chapter 2, the monetary unit is conventionally or legally defined as a specified mass of a particular metal or alloy. For example, the Gold Standard Act of 1900 confirmed the previously established definition of the US dollar as "consisting of twenty-five and eight-tenths grains of gold nine-tenths fine," in other words 23.22 grains of pure gold, and declared that "all forms of money issued or coined by the United States shall be maintained at a parity of value with this standard." (56th Congress, Session 1, Chapter 41, 1900). The dollar of defined gold content was the *unit of account*, and gold coins were the *medium of redemption* that dollar-denominated banknotes and bank accounts promised to pay. Dollar-denominated and standard-conforming gold coins were sometimes privately issued (while private issue was legal before 1864), and paper currency was predominantly privately issued.

In a fiat standard, by contrast, the monetary unit established by fiat (government decree) is merely one unit of itself. It is not defined in terms of, or redeemable for, any commodity that has non-monetary uses.[1] Governments issue units of basic fiat money in the form of coins and central bank currency notes (e.g., Federal Reserve Notes or Bank of England notes) and as digital ledger entries on the balance sheets of central banks. A *privately* issued irredeemable medium of exchange like Bitcoin will not

---

[1] On 4 March 2022, while the Russian ruble was sharply dropping in value on foreign exchange markets following the Russian army's invasion of Ukraine, a tweet appeared from "President of Russia" declaring "1 RUBLE = 1 RUBLE." It was from a fake account, but it was accurate as to what defines the fiat ruble.

here be called "fiat money" because it is not established by government decree nor issued by government.

Coins under a fiat standard are tokens made of non-precious metal, valued for their interchangeability with paper notes or deposit dollars.[2] Fiat currency notes carry the same name and may visually resemble formerly gold-redeemable notes, even bearing the same portraits, especially when a government has created a fiat currency by making its formerly gold-redeemable notes suddenly irredeemable. Checking account balances that the public holds at commercial banks are claims to fiat money, not themselves basic fiat money. Fiat money has thus been aptly described as "money consisting of mere tokens which can neither be employed for any industrial purpose nor convey a claim against anybody" (Mises 2007, vol. 2).

Some economists have confusingly departed from this terminology, even while recognizing it as the standard terminology. Milton Friedman (1951, p. 210, n. 7) wrote: "I shall use the term 'fiat' to refer both to inconvertible government-issued currency (to which alone the dictionary restricts the term) and to other types of currency that have one essential feature in common with the former, namely, that they are evidences of debt rather than of the existence of specified physical amounts of the currency commodity." Inconvertible currency is not evidence of debt, however. As the former central banker John Exter (1972) liked to say, since the Bretton Woods regime ended the fiat dollar is not an IOU but rather an IOU-nothing. Neither is it "fiduciary" (trust-based), another term that Friedman (1960, p. 68) used for it, nor "debt-based." Quite unlike the commercial bank as issuer of banknotes or checking account balances, the government as issuer of fiat money has no contractual obligation to repay the money-holder. Lumping government-issued irredeemable fiat money together with bank-issued redeemable debt leads to confusion rather than clarification. While the quantity of bank-issued money is limited by market forces, the quantity of fiat money is not.

A model of the supply and demand for money under a fiat standard necessarily differs from our model of a gold standard. Fiat money does not have a *market-governed supply*, or a standard upward-sloping supply curve indicating increasing marginal cost of production, since the supply is exclusive to government (apart from counterfeiting) and the marginal

---

[2] Although made from non-precious metals, inflation has sunk the purchasing power of small denomination coins in the United States below the value of the metal they contain. For example, a US penny contains more than one cent's worth of zinc. Other nations have abolished low-denomination coins once they became unprofitable to make.

cost of production for nominal units is negligible. On the demand side, because fiat money units are neither composed of nor redeemable claims to any useful commodity, there is not any non-monetary demand. Monetary theorists accordingly say that a fiat money is "intrinsically useless" for non-monetary purposes.

4.1 HOW FIAT STANDARDS AROSE

Because it does not consist of a commodity or a claim to a commodity, fiat money could not have emerged in the same way that a commonly accepted commodity money emerged from indirect exchange. That is, pieces of fiat money could not have first proven suitable to a few traders for paying others who wanted to consume or wear them (as was the case with salt or silver or shells), their use as media of exchange then spreading as others observed the success of the first group and imitated them. Instead, fiat money was historically established by government intervention into the monetary system.

The typical historical path to the establishment of a fiat money came in three steps, beginning and ending with government policies.

1. The central government gave a legal monopoly of note-issue to a single institution, which consequently became a central bank (Smith 1936). In the UK, the Bank of England was chartered in 1694. Legislated restrictions on other banks (via the Acts of 1708, 1833, and 1844) gave the Bank of England a monopoly on note-issue in greater London, then in the entirety of England and Wales. The Federal Reserve, created by 1913 legislation, gained a note-issuing monopoly in the 1930s via additional legal restrictions that ended note-issuing by commercial banks.

2. The liabilities of the central bank became so widely accepted that they displaced specie as the reserves for other banks. In the case of the Bank of England this development was unplanned, but was reinforced by law. In the later case of the Federal Reserve, it was part of the legislated plan.

3. Government suspended the redemption of central bank liabilities permanently.[3] Central bank notes and deposits thereby became fiat money. Although the unit of account has been divorced from its specie definition, it continues to use its traditional married name

---

[3] In the cryptocurrency world, this kind of project abandonment is known as a "rug pull."

("Dollar"). Introductions of new fiat monies in recent decades have followed a similar pattern. Initially they are redeemable for a pre-existing money. Once they achieve wide circulation, redeemability can be ended, and they continue to circulate (Selgin 1994). In newly independent Lithuania, for example, the new central bank first introduced the Talonas in the form of notes and deposit balances redeemable for rubles, then ended redemption and floated it against the ruble.

In no known historical case has an irredeemable money standard resulted from a free-market-driven evolution of bank reserves from a positive fraction of liabilities down to zero, contrary to a scenario envisioned by the economist Kevin Dowd (1996). The reasons are economic and legal. Economically, money-users understandably prefer bank-issued money with a fixed value in units of the standard money, where redeemability provides the fix, over bank-issued money with a floating nominal value. Imagine what would happen if a bank in a competitive system were to announce that it will be removing the option to redeem its notes and deposits after a specified future date, leaving its liabilities to float against standard money. Its note- and account-holders would want to cash out and move their funds to other non-floating banks before that date arrived. When money-users prefer par acceptance, and we have seen historically that most do, a switch to fiat money must be involuntary. Legally, only a bank that the government protects from ordinary contract enforcement has the immunity to unilaterally end its contractual obligation to "pay the bearer on demand" in basic money.[4]

Economic theorists Joseph Ostroy and Ross Starr (1990) have proposed: "Since the opportunity cost of holding real goods in inventory will generally be non-negligible, there is an efficiency gain through the use of fiduciary (bank) or fiat money in place of commodity money." In standard Paretian welfare economics, an "efficiency gain" means the capturing of additional mutual gains from voluntary trade (or, to be technical, gains on at least one side and no losses on the other). Bank-issued money issued competitively, without legal privileges, presumably provides an

---

[4] English and Welsh country banks, and Scottish banks, also suspended gold redemption between 1797 and 1819, surprisingly without legal challenge. These banks continued to redeem in Bank of England notes or deposits, which were now the basic money in Great Britain's financial center. In the early United States, state governments often sanctioned suspensions of gold payment in financial crises.

efficiency gain: If the bank or its customer considered bank-issued money inferior to available alternatives, they would choose not to issue or use it. But given that *fiat* money – money by decree – is involuntarily imposed, we cannot presume a Paretian efficiency gain. At least some customers historically objected when redeemable fiduciary money issued by the central bank became fiat money by the central bank unilaterally breaking the redemption contract on its notes.

Here is an example. In 1797, when the privileged Bank of England temporarily suspended gold redemption (not to be restored until 1819), it did so with the legislated permission of Parliament. When Bank of England notes depreciated against gold, it became clear that compulsion would be required to make creditors and landlords accept paper pounds at par for debt or rent payments contracted in pounds before the suspension. Lord King, a critic of the Bank of England's expansionary behavior that drove the depreciation during the suspension period, notified his tenants in 1811 that they must now pay in gold coin or "by the payment in Bank notes of a sum sufficient to purchase the weight of standard gold requisite to discharge the rent" (quoted by Fetter 1950, p. 244). Parliament responded with legislation that effectively declared Bank of England notes a legal tender for old debts and rents, no matter the contractual terms.

The case of Bitcoin, a private irredeemable asset, will concern us in Chapter 5. Bitcoin has been irredeemable from the start, and its use is entirely voluntary (at least outside of the country of El Salvador, whose government has mandated its acceptance by retailers, although it does not seem to be actively enforcing the mandate).

Economics textbooks, much like Ostroy and Starr, have sometimes rationalized the switch from a gold standard to a fiat standard, or treated it *as if* voluntary on the public's part, on the grounds that fiat money saves the public the real resources consumed by mining or storing gold for monetary use. We noted in Chapter 2 that economists have often severely exaggerated the resource cost of a gold standard. But even if many economists believed that a well-run fiat standard would have lower resource costs than a gold standard, a concern for social efficiency is inconsistent with governments' behavior during and after the switch. Governments concerned with monetary efficiency would have wanted to avoid the inefficiencies caused by inflation, and so would not have gone on to produce the higher monetary expansion rates and correspondingly higher price inflation rates we have seen under fiat standards by contrast to commodity standards.

Further, a concern for reducing the resource cost of the monetary system does not explain the *timing* of the switch. Governments that left the gold standard during the First World War had something else in mind: Suspending gold redemption would allow them to print additional money, which would provide revenue to pay for soldiers and war materiel. The US federal government's restrictions against private gold ownership beginning in 1933, and its final closing of the gold window in 1971, were motivated not by the desire to improve the efficiency of the monetary system but by macroeconomic and political concerns, the desire to loosen and finally escape the constraints that gold redeemability put on expansionary monetary policy. Economists Michael C. Keeley and Frederick T. Furlong (1986, p. 59) of the Federal Reserve Bank of San Francisco have rightly noted that governments have reasons to favor fiat money over a gold standard even if the switch brings no resource cost saving: "a fiat system does differ importantly from a commodity based system in that it makes the social control of money, prices and credit possible, and it provides a source of tax revenue."

Compared to textbook accounts, the motive that actually produced the switch to fiat money has been better explained by humorist Dave Barry (2006, p. 10) in *Dave Barry's Money Secrets*: "Over the years, all the governments in the world, having discovered that gold is, like, rare, decided that it would be more convenient to back their money with something that is easier to come by, namely: nothing."

Accounts that identify governments' political and fiscal motives for switching to fiat money have sometimes been ridiculed for supposedly depicting fiat money as a kind of "establishment conspiracy." But President Richard Nixon and his advisors (indisputably "the establishment") had then-secret discussions (a "conspiracy" if you like) between May and August 1971 about their options for dealing with dwindling US gold reserves, and the consequences for Nixon's re-election of choosing to tighten monetary policy to stop the gold outflow, leading to his decision to end US dollar redemption for gold and thereby to establish a fiat currency. We know this because the discussions were taped, and transcripts are available (Abrams and Butkiewicz 2012). No country we know of switched to a fiat standard following an open public discussion of its benefits and costs.

4.2 WHY IS A FIAT MONEY VALUED?

Why do units of fiat money have a positive market value despite being intrinsically useless outside of a monetary role? At one level, the answer is simply supply and demand. Items (deposit balances and paper notes denominated in "dollars") that are intrinsically useless for non-monetary purposes can be suitable for use as a medium of exchange (uniform, cheap to store, easy to transfer, and so on). If we assume that these items are held and used as money, we can plot the intersection of a money demand curve with the money-item's supply curve to determine the purchasing power that clears the market for money balances. We can conduct thought experiments in which we shift one curve or the other, and find the new equilibrium intersection, to analyze the impact of events on its purchasing power. Supply–demand analysis of this sort is illustrated in the following text.

At a deeper level, however, it begs the question to *begin* the analysis with the assumption that an intrinsically useless good serves as money. It assumes what needs to be explained. It does not answer the question of how the convention arose of treating a particular intrinsically useless item as money.[5] Approaches to answering *that* question usually pursue one of the two lines of argument. The first line invokes sovereign powers: People value fiat dollars because the US government compels creditors to accept it in payment of debts (the government gives it legal tender status or debt-discharging power) or compels people to use it to pay taxes (gives it exclusive public receivability or tax-discharging power). The second and perhaps less obvious line is a path-dependency argument: The historical developments described earlier habituate people to accept redeemable paper money, with the result that, when redemption ends, they continue accepting it so long as it works, and it works (given moderate supply growth) so long as others follow the same strategy.

Some unusual evidence that sovereign powers are not strictly necessary for the continued circulation of fiat money at positive values comes from the case of the Somali shilling, a fiat money issued by the government of the nation of Somalia in northeast Africa. The Somali government collapsed during a civil war in 1991 and effectively disappeared. De facto control fell to "a variety of overlapping and fluid local authorities that included private militias, clan elders, and fundamentalist mosques" (Marshall and Jaggers 2008, p. 2). Somalia's central bank was

---

[5] As Kiyotaki, Lagos, and Wright (2016, p. 2) have written of economists' efforts to explain why an intrinsically useless item is valued: "Some work resorts to taking short cuts (i.e., giving up on the fundamental problem) by assuming money enters utility or production functions, like goods or inputs. Other work imposes the restriction that agents cannot trade *A* for *B*, but must first sell *A* then buy *B* with cash. While this may be realistic, it is a failure for monetary economics to have this as an assumption rather than a result."

"destroyed and looted" (Mubarak 1997, p. 2031). The central state no longer existed to enforce legal tender status or to collect tax payments. And yet the shilling continued to circulate. Given the shilling's history of common acceptance, continuing to accept shillings was a self-fulfilling strategy: Everyone found it useful to continue accepting them as long as others did so and were expected to continue to do so. It was in no individual Somali's interest to refuse shillings and insist on paying or being paid in some other money that his or her trading partners were not using (Luther and White 2016). Sheer momentum thus appears to be enough to keep a fiat currency circulating once it has been successfully launched. Sovereign power might be necessary to launch a fiat money, but it is not necessary to keep it circulating at a positive value.

Self-reinforcing expectations of acceptance can be fragile, however. A negative shared expectation is also self-reinforcing. If the common expectation arises that most others will not accept an item as money, then its acceptance will indeed stop. Accordingly, there are two potential equilibria: The item that would be currency can have a positive value (acceptance) or a zero value (non-acceptance). Such fragility is presumably what commentators have in mind when they speak of money as a "shared illusion" or an "arbitrary social construct." Popular author Yuval Noah Harari (2015, pp. 195–6) has written that "Money isn't a material reality – it is a psychological construct." People treat something as money "when they trust the figments of their collective imagination." Such a view was parodied by *The Onion* (2016) with the headline "U.S. Economy Grinds to Halt as Nation Realizes Money Just a Symbolic, Mutually Shared Illusion." That the gold coin or the fiat US dollar bill or any other specific material or non-material item has become the focus of a common expectation or "psychological construct" regarding its use as money, however, is the product of lived experience. It is not merely a figment of collective imagination. Its real properties and its history matter.

There is a germ of truth to the "shared illusion" view when applied to a fiat money or a cryptocurrency: The value of an "intrinsically useless" item would go to zero without a shared expectation of its future use as a medium of exchange. When the public abandons a fiat money in which prices are denominated, like the Confederate States dollar after 1864 or the Ecuadorian sucre in early 2000, the result is a high or hyper-inflation in which the price level rises even faster (the purchasing power and foreign exchange value of the money unit falls even faster) than its quantity grows. With rapid central-bank monetary expansion feeding rising inflation expectations, Ecuador's sucre lost a quarter of its exchange value in

US dollars during the first week of 2000 (Beckerman 2001, p. 1). The purchasing power of the irredeemable Confederate dollar likewise collapsed as the Confederacy lost the US Civil War (Cutsinger and Ingber 2019).

Similar effects can be seen when optimism about the future of a cryptocurrency evaporates. From a peak market cap of $175 million in December 2014, PayCoin (XPY) fell to under $1 million six months later as rosy expectations of its future faded. In February 2022, its market cap was under $100,000. Emercoin (EMC) dropped to $2 million from a peak above $300 million in 2018, and in February 2022 was worth about $2.5 million. The IOTA cryptocurrency was valued above $10 billion for five weeks in December 2017–January 2018, at which time it was the seventh-highest cryptocurrency in market cap, but by December 2018 it was valued below $700 million and ranked 28th. Its market cap recovered somewhat to reach $2.5 billion in February 2022. Many examples of other coins that have lost 99 percent of their peak value might be cited.[6]

The shared-illusion view is less applicable to a commodity money. A commodity like gold, valued for its usefulness in jewelry and electronics, with additional units costly to produce, retains a positive value even when demonetized. Only part of the demand for it rests on its use or potential use as money. The World Gold Council estimates that about 40 percent of the above-ground gold stock is in the quasi-monetary forms of coins and bullion held by private investors or central banks. The rest is in jewelry and other forms like inventories for industrial use.

In a classic article, the economist John Hicks (1935) asked why fiat currency notes are demanded despite their financial return (zero) being lower than that of risk-free bonds issued by the same governments. He offered a general answer: Money is more readily or conveniently transactable than bonds. Money overcomes "frictions" that impede paying with bonds or other financial assets. Researchers in monetary theory in recent decades have built a variety of interesting models based on specific assumptions about the relevant frictions (for a survey of the literature, see Lagos, Rocheteau, and Wright 2016). A counterfactual implication of some models (e.g., Kiyotaki and Wright 1991), however, is that an intrinsically useless money can prevail in equilibrium without reference to the economy first adopting a commodity money and then

---

[6] Market cap information from coinmarketcap.com. See coinopsy.com for a list of "dead" cryptocurrency projects. Some deaths are attributed there to the coins having simply been scams, but many are attributed to "abandoned or no volume."

commodity-redeemable money. This cautions us against regarding such models as explanations of the historical path to fiat money.

4.3 SUPPLY AND DEMAND FOR FIAT MONEY

A central bank (like the Federal Reserve System, the ECB, or the Bank of England) controls the supply of a fiat money (dollars, euros, pounds sterling). Detailed accounts of the operating procedures of central banks can be found in many textbooks and central bank publications. In a nutshell, the central bank controls the quantity of basic fiat money (also known as the "monetary base," on which bank deposits are "built") by expanding or contracting its own balance sheet. The US monetary base is the sum of currency in circulation plus commercial bank reserve deposits at the Fed. Suppose that the Federal Reserve buys $5 million in bonds from the securities dealer Honest Joan by wiring $5 million into her account at Megabank. When the payment settles, Megabank has an additional $5 million in its reserve deposit at the Fed, matching the addition to Joan's deposit balance at Megabank. The monetary base has grown by $5 million because no other bank has lost reserves. The Fed simply created $5 million in new claims against itself. Under a fiat standard, by contrast to a gold standard, the central bank can create as many claims against itself as it chooses, being unconstrained by any obligation to redeem its liabilities for an asset it cannot create. There is no built-in limit to amount of fiat money.

The stock of money held by the public, as measured by the M2 aggregate (roughly, the non-bank public's holdings of currency plus all bank deposits plus checkable mutual fund balances), is a multiple of the monetary base. For example, in March 2022, M2 was $21.8 trillion while the monetary base was $6.1 trillion. When the Fed increases the monetary base by 1%, other things equal (the ratio of M2 to the base remaining the same), it causes M2 to expand by 1%. The mechanism for the expansion of M2 is that the commercial banks typically choose to hold less than 100% reserves against additional M2 deposits, enabling the banking system to make additional loans and securities purchases when it receives additional reserves, actions that expand the public's holdings of deposits. So long as the Fed can predict the ratio of M2 to the monetary base (a ratio known as the "M2 money multiplier"), the Fed can control the size of M2 by controlling the size of the monetary base.

Since 2008, the Fed does more than try to predict the money multiplier: It strongly influences it by choosing the interest rate it pays on bank reserve deposits held on its books. Commercial banks' desired

holdings of reserves relative to other assets depend on the rate of interest on reserves (IOR) the Fed pays them relative to the rates that they
can earn by lending or by holding bonds. A higher IOR rate, relative to
these opportunity-cost rates, makes it more attractive at the margin for a
bank to hold reserves rather than make loans, which shrinks the money
multiplier and consequently M2 for a given monetary base. The Federal
Reserve thus has two main tools for controlling the growth of the quantity of money held by the public: (1) The Fed can arbitrarily expand or
contract the monetary base through bond purchases and sales, hence (for
given money multiplier) can make M2 whatever size it wants; (2) the Fed
can influence the money multiplier by setting the interest rate on reserves
above or below other rates, hence (for a given monetary base) can vary
the size of M2.

The central bank controls the supply side of the market for nominal
money balances held by the public. Although the commercial banks can
take actions that (unintentionally) change the money multiplier, the central bank can offset any such change.

As we did in the case of a gold standard, we can represent the determination of the quantity and purchasing power of a fiat money using
supply and demand curves. As before, the horizontal axis of Figure 4.1
measures the nominal quantity of money, while the vertical axis measures the purchasing power of money (hereafter ppm, meaning bundles
of goods per money unit, the inverse of the price level). The supply curve
for fiat money is vertical, indicating that (by contrast to gold) no greater
quantity of money automatically comes forth at a higher purchasing
power per unit of money. Rather, the central bank chooses the quantity. Expansionary monetary policy shifts the vertical supply curve to the
right. The vertical supply curve stands in contrast to the upward-sloping
stock supply curves for monetary gold that we saw in Chapter 2.

What about the demand curve? As in Chapter 2, we draw the money
demand curve as a rectangular hyperbola. In a fiat system too, it makes
sense for the level of nominal money balances that each individual
wants to hold, and thus that the public as a whole wants to hold, to
vary inversely and proportionally with the ppm. If prices are 10 percent
higher, a money-holder will want to hold 10 percent more dollars to have
the same amount of purchasing power. Alternatively put, if each dollar
buys 10 percent less in goods and services, a money-holder will want
to hold 10 percent more dollars. On the nominal money demand curve
drawn, desired *real* money balances ($M^D \times$ ppm) are the same at every
point on the curve.

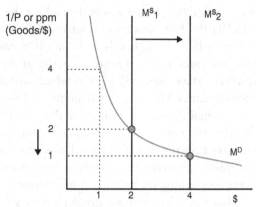

FIGURE 4.1 Doubling the nominal fiat money supply halves the equilibrium purchasing power of money.

From the property that desired real money balances are independent of the price level follows the proposition that when the central bank increases the nominal stock of money by Z percent, equilibrium between money supply and demand will not be restored until the general level of prices has risen by Z percent (or equivalently, the purchasing power of money has fallen to 100/(100+Z)). We illustrate this in Figure 4.1, which shows that a doubling of the nominal money stock results in a halving of the equilibrium ppm (or equivalently a doubling of the price level).

The implication of this analysis is that the central bank, because it is able to control the level of the money supply, is responsible for the price level. Because it can control the *rate of growth* of money supply, such a central bank can control the rate of growth of the price level, also known as the rate of inflation. Under a fiat standard, the central bank is responsible for the inflation rate. If the inflation rate is too high this year, it is because the central bank has been expanding the money supply too rapidly (given this year's behavior of velocity and real income). As Scott Sumner (2021, p. 43) puts it:

[U]nder a fiat money system, the long-run rate of inflation is whatever the government wants it to be, ... because the government has an essentially unlimited ability to vary the growth rate of paper money. It gets to pick the average inflation rate over extended periods of time, even if month-to-month changes are hard to control.

Before the Fed began in 2008 to pay interest on commercial banks' deposits held at the Fed, there was a clear distinction between the monetary base and the interest-bearing debt of the federal government.[7] With

[7] The remainder of this section draws on White (2018).

banks not incentivized to hold excess reserves, higher base growth translated into higher growth in M2. Faster M2 growth in turn meant more units of money chasing each unit of goods and services, causing faster price level growth. Domestic money-holders bore the burden of a higher inflation tax.

Since gaining authority to pay IOR in 2008, by contrast, the Fed has raised the interest rate it pays on excess reserves as necessary to persuade commercial banks to hold them rather than to create additional deposits by "lending out" the excess reserves, and thus was able to keep M2 growth from rising along with the higher base money growth during 2008–2015 (White 2016). The dramatic base growth 2008–2015 consequently did not raise the inflation rate. Instead, insofar as the Fed acquired Treasury rather than private securities, and paid banks the full Treasury yield rate on their depository reserves, growth in the monetary base has been merely a fiscally pointless swap of one interest-bearing government liability in the hand of the public (interest-bearing commercial bank deposits on the Fed's books) for another (interest-bearing Treasuries held outside the Fed).

Interest on the reserves that the Fed issues to buy Treasuries means that Fed purchases of Treasuries no longer in effect retire them. That is, Fed acquisition of Treasuries no longer reduces the consolidated Fed-Treasury burden of debt service to the public. The Treasuries held by the Fed are now properly counted as federal debt held by the public. Rising Fed holdings of Treasury debt, financed by interest-bearing reserves, are part of the rising ratio of federal debt to GDP.

In 2020–2021, the Fed chose not to raise IOR as it dramatically expanded the monetary base, and thus let M2 grow dramatically, to offset a temporary sharp rise in the demand to hold money accompanying the uncertainties of the COVID-19 pandemic. Failing to moderate the expansion of M2 promptly enough as money demand returned to normal, the Fed fueled a rise in the CPI inflation rate to 9 percent, June 2022 over one year earlier, the highest inflation rate in forty years.

4.4 THE QUANTITY-OF-MONEY THEORY OF THE PRICE LEVEL

The "quantity theory of money" (QTM) proposition that the price level is proportional to the quantity of money, other things equal, applies to a fiat standard. (A clearer label would be "the quantity-of-money theory of the price level.") Expositions of the QTM explain how the price level P is linked to the quantity of money M by using an accounting identity known as "the equation of exchange": $MV = Py$. (It is an identity because we define V such that V = Py/M.) The equation says that the economy's nominal income, decomposed one way into the product of M time V, equals the economy's nominal income decomposed another way into the product of P times y.

In the equation of exchange, M can represent a narrow monetary aggregate (Mo) or a broader measure of money held by the public (M1 or M2). V is the "income velocity of money," meaning how many times per year the average dollar of M is spent in transactions that generate final income or GDP, so that MV equals nominal GDP. ("Final" indicates sales of newly produced goods and services to final users, excluding such intermediate transactions as an oil extractor selling crude oil to a refinery.) M is measured in dollars, and V in times per year, so the product MV is in dollars per year. The price level P is an index of dollars per basket of newly produced final goods, such as the consumer price index or the GDP deflator, while y measures real final income or real GDP, measured in index baskets per year. The product Py is thus also in dollars per year.

From MV = Py it follows mathematically that holding V and y constant, P must be proportional to M. This truism alone cannot establish, however, that in a particular real-world monetary system M varies exogenously, real-world V and y are unchanging parameters, and only real-world P changes as a result. The QTM, therefore, has to go beyond the accounting identity of the Equation of Exchange. It requires three key conditions to justify running the thought experiment in which a fiat-issuing central bank varies M, any resulting changes in V or y are only transitory, and only P changes in the long run. Namely, it assumes that (1) a monetary authority can exogenously vary the nominal quantity of money M held by the system; (2) the public's desired ratio of money balances to income (desired M/Py, or, stood on its head, "desired V") is determined by real factors, independent of the nominal quantity of money (except for transitory effects following changes in M), and in the long run, the actual ratio converges to the desired ratio; and (3) real income y is determined by real factors (such as labor and capital supplies, technology, institutions) that are independent of the nominal quantity of money M in the long run (any supply effects following changes in M are transitory).

All three conditions are reasonable for a fiat money regime, and the last two are reasonable for any monetary regime. The first condition, however, excludes the changes in M that come about endogenously under a commodity money standard, namely regional gold inflows driven by the price-specie-flow mechanism and new gold production induced by a growing global demand for money. Thus the quantity theory is not generally applicable to the operation of a commodity money regime. The first condition does apply, however, when a sovereign exogenously debases (reduces the metallic content of) the local monetary unit. Raising the dollar value of a given mass of coined silver will raise the dollar prices of goods proportionally.[8]

The equation of exchange provides a framework for understanding the inflation rate in a fiat money economy, meaning the growth rate of the price level.[9] Converting the equation of exchange expressed in levels to a "dynamic" equation of exchange expressed in growth rates, we get $gM + gV \approx gP + gy$, where gM is the growth rate of the money stock and so on.[10] Holding velocity growth gV and real income growth gy constant, the new equation says that the inflation rate must rise by one percentage point with each percentage point increase in the growth rate of the money stock. A central bank accordingly can control the inflation rate by varying the fiat money growth rate. Overly expansionary central banks are to blame for cases of persistently high inflation.

We can use the dynamic equation of exchange to dig beneath the surface of Milton Friedman's (1970, p. 24) famous statement that "Inflation is always and everywhere a monetary phenomenon in the sense that it is and can be produced only by a more rapid increase in the quantity of money than in output." The statement says that $gP > 0$ can only occur when $gM > gy$. The equation $gM + gV \approx gP + gy$ does not *exactly* tell us that. It rather says that $gP > 0$ reflects the combined influences of positive money growth gM plus positive velocity growth gV, together in excess of positive real income growth gy. Friedman's statement mentions the growth rates of the price level, money stock, and real output, but makes no mention of the growth rate of velocity.

---

[8] For advancing this idea, Bernardo Davanzati (1696 [1588]) and John Locke (1692) can be considered pioneers of the QTM. I discuss the history of the theory in more detail in White (2012, ch. 12).

[9] In the nineteenth century, economists used "inflation" to refer to expansion of the money stock, gM, rather than the growth rate of the price level, gP. There is no good reason to cling to the old usage. Any theoretical and empirical proposition about gM and its relationship to gP can be expressed in the current terminology.

[10] To covert, we take natural logs of both sides and differentiate with respect to time. The equation is exact for continuously compounded growth rates, approximate for growth rates over discrete intervals.

It remains a *logical possibility* that a particular period's positive inflation rate could be produced without "a more rapid increase in the quantity of money than in output" provided there is high enough velocity growth gV. Hence Friedman's "can be produced only" is not strictly correct.

Here it should be noted that Friedman used "inflation" to mean a *sustained* period of positive price level growth, not just one year's upward blip. The predominance of money growth in accounting for inflation is then an empirical matter: It rests on money growth being larger and more persistent in practice than velocity growth or shrinkage in real income. In US postwar history, recession periods with negative real income growth have been short and relatively few (there have been only ten such years since 1948, and two consecutive years of negative real GDP growth only in 1974–1975). The trend in velocity has been downward in every decade except for the 1950s and 1990s. In only one postwar case has velocity growth been positive for four or more consecutive years and high enough to create positive inflation despite money growth being *less* rapid than output growth, namely 1992–1995.[11]

These sorts of exceptions noted, Friedman's statement is by and large an accurate summary of the historical record of fiat monies. A central bank that issues a fiat money can make the nominal money stock grow persistently at an arbitrarily high rate, while velocity growth and real income growth are determined by technological change and other real forces. They may be cyclically disturbed by monetary policy, but overall, their changes make relatively modest contributions to explaining changes in the inflation rate.[12] Countries with persistently high inflation are almost always countries with persistently high fiat money growth (rather than persistently high-velocity growth or real output shrinkage, because those are rare). In any single country, high inflation decades are almost always decades with high money growth.

---

[11] In 1991–1995, cumulative M2 velocity growth was about 16 percent, allowing positive inflation (about 9 percent) despite M2 money growth (6 percent) below real income growth (13 percent). Annual velocity data from FRED, https://fred.stlouisfed.org/series/M2V#0. Annual real income and price level data from Louis Johnston and Samuel H. Williamson, "What Was the U.S. GDP Then?," www.measuringworth.com/datasets/usgdp/result.php.

[12] It follows that the lower the inflation rate, and the smaller its variation, the greater the relative contributions of changes in velocity growth and real income growth to explaining its level and variation.

4.5 HOW FIAT STANDARDS HAVE PERFORMED ON INFLATION

15 August 2021 marked the fiftieth anniversary of President Richard Nixon closing the "gold window," formally ending the US commitment to redeem dollars held by foreign central banks for gold at $35 per ounce. Nixon's action ushered in a floating fiat money regime. The closing of the gold window followed a period of rising inflation rates after 1965. During successive five-year periods beginning August 1961, the US Urban Consumer Price Index rose at average annual rates of 1.62 percent, 4.35 percent, 7.1 percent, and 10.0 percent. The Federal Reserve had loosened monetary policy to reduce unemployment rather than maintaining moderate money growth to keep inflation close to zero and thereby consistent with continuing redemption of dollars at $35 per ounce. The Fed could not both produce a rapidly rising price level, reducing the purchasing power of the dollar relative to that of gold, *and* sustain a constant redemption rate of the dollar for gold. Redemptions by foreign central banks, over-supplied with US dollars of diminishing purchasing power, progressively drained gold from the US Treasury. The loss of gold reserves forced Nixon to choose between tightening monetary policy and shutting the gold window. He chose the latter.

The formal end of redemption at $35 per ounce in August 1971 – the adoption of a fully fiat monetary standard – enabled still greater monetary expansion, driving inflation rates still higher. Year-over-year inflation rate peaks were reached at 12.2 percent (November 1974) and 14.6 percent (March 1980). In subsequent decades the Fed moderated money growth, and the inflation rate fell. Over the fifty years after August 1971, the Consumer Price Index for All Urban Consumers (CPI-U) rose a cumulative 569 percent, for an average annual inflation rate of 3.9 percent.[13] The average annual US CPI inflation rate during the period of the classical gold standard (1879–1913), by contrast, was 0.13 percent.[14]

Fiat money regimes have resulted in even higher inflation rates in most other countries. For the UK, average inflation since 1971 has been 5.2 percent per year, with peak year-over-year rates of 26.9 percent (August

---

[13] Monthly data from FRED, fred.stlouisfed.org/series/CPIAUCSL. The reported averages are geometric averages. The geometric average is the rate that, if prevailed every year during a period, compounded annually, would yield the period's cumulative growth. It is the g that solves the equation $P_{t+n}/P_t = (1 + g)^n$, where P_t is the starting date's price level and P_{t+n} is the price level n years later.

[14] Historical CPI data from the Federal Reserve Bank of Minneapolis, www.minneapolisfed .org/about-us/monetary-policy/inflation-calculator/consumer-price-index-1800-.

1975) and 21.9 percent (May 1980). For Mexico, inflation has averaged 19.9 percent per year, with year-over-year peaks of 117 percent (April 1983), 180 percent (February 1988), and 52 percent (December 1995).[15]

In mid-2021, according to the IMF, the three countries with the highest annual inflation rates were Venezuela at 5,500 percent, Sudan at 197 percent, and Zimbabwe at 99.3 percent. Six more countries had inflation rates above 20 percent per year, and another ten had inflation rates above 10 percent. Of 169 countries with reported inflation rates, only 9 had inflation rates below the classical gold standard benchmark of 0.13 percent.[16]

A cross-country study by Arthur J. Rolnick and Warren E. Weber (1997) provides systematic historical evidence. The authors computed inflation rates for fifteen countries, contrasting the rates experienced while those countries were under commodity standards (silver, gold, or bimetallic) with the rates experienced while they were under fiat standards. During the commodity-standard periods in their sample, the average annual inflation rate was 1.75 percent, while during fiat-standard episodes the average was 9.17 percent (*excluding* the one hyperinflation in the sample). Every country in the sample had higher inflation under fiat money than it had under commodity money.

4.6 INFLATION IS BURDENSOME EVEN WHEN THE INFLATION RATE IS CORRECTLY ANTICIPATED

A monetary regime that produces a higher average inflation rate, as fiat standards historically have relative to commodity standards, imposes at least four burdens on money-holders. First, it erodes the purchasing power of money balances and thereby transfers wealth from money's holders to its issuers. Second, in response to the tax, households and firms adopt costly strategies for keeping real currency balances at a lower level. Third, higher inflation enlarges economic deadweight losses where higher effective tax rates result from the tax system not being fully indexed to the price level. (In the United States, capital gains taxes are not indexed, although income tax brackets are.) Fourth, a higher average inflation rate is associated with a more variable inflation rate, increasing noise in the price system and thereby reducing the efficiency with which the price

---

[15] UK and Mexico CPI data from FRED, series fred.stlouisfed.org/series/GBRCPIALLMINMEI and fred.stlouisfed.org/series/MEXCPIALLMINMEI.
[16] www.imf.org/external/datamapper/PCPIPCH@WEO/ARE/GBR/IND/LBN/EGY/CAN.

system allocates resources. The following paragraphs say a little more about each of these effects.

1. *The transfer from public to government.* As noted above, ongoing price inflation is normally due to ongoing expansion in the quantity of money. Under a fiat standard, government can produce new money units at practically zero cost. Introducing new units dilutes the value of existing units. The process transfers wealth from money-holders to the government. Government undertakes more spending with newly introduced money, or retires debt, at the expense of money-holders who see the purchasing power of their existing balances diminished. (The technical name for the government's profit from money creation is "seigniorage.") The government buys up a larger share of the economy's output, leaving less for households and firms in the private sector.[17]

2. *The deadweight burden on money-holders.* By increasing a distorting tax on money-holding, a higher inflation rate makes it worthwhile for the public to expend the time and effort necessary to accomplish any given amount of spending with smaller average money balances. Households lose benefits ("consumer surplus") and business firms lose net income by operating with smaller real money balances. At a higher inflation rate, a household or firm is more heavily penalized for holding those types of money (currency and some deposits) that do not pay interest (or more generally, do not pay an after-tax interest rate that rises one-for-one with the inflation rate).

3. *Unindexed taxes.* In the presence of taxes that are not fully indexed to remove the effects of inflation, higher inflation can significantly increase effective tax rates and amplify the distortive effects of those taxes. In the present-day US tax system, nominal capital gains are taxed. This means that if an asset's dollar price rises only just enough to keep up with inflation, so that there is no gain in real terms, taxes are nonetheless due on the purely nominal gain. The asset owner receives a negative after-tax return in real terms. The higher the inflation rate, the greater the real tax burden, and the greater the discouragement to investment and capital formation. A lower inflation rate in such a tax system conversely lowers the cost of capital and thereby encourages capital formation, leading to higher real output per capita. The United States and many other countries also tax merely nominal interest income, which means that a higher inflation rate lowers the after-tax real return to owning bonds

---

[17] For more on seigniorage, see Section 4.10 below and White (1999, ch. 7).

and interest-bearing savings accounts, and makes the after-tax real return negative when the nominal return just matches inflation.

Because savers and investors care about after-tax real returns, if two countries have the same tax rates on nominal capital gains, or the same tax rates on nominal interest income, the country with the higher inflation rate will have lower after-tax returns. It will become poorer as savers and investors respond by moving their financial and real capital to the country with lower inflation and correspondingly higher after-tax returns. An empirical study by Tamim Bayoumi and Joseph Gagnon (1996) found that this effect – capital flight prompted by higher inflation – is large. Countries with chronically higher inflation rates have noticeably less capital per head – fewer machines per worker – and therefore lower real incomes.

4. *Ragged price adjustments.* Lower inflation rates are associated with less "raggedness" in price adjustments (some prices rising early in the process and others catching up later) and thereby less "noise" in relative prices. By increasing the reliability of observed relative prices, a low inflation environment permits more accurate savings and investment decisions (Leijonhufvud 1981, pp. 227–269; Heymann and Leijonhufvud 1995, pp. 84–108; Horwitz 2003, pp. 71–95).

4.7 UNANTICIPATED INFLATION IS EVEN WORSE THAN ANTICIPATED INFLATION

Inflation harms the public in the four ways listed earlier even when the public correctly anticipates the inflation rate. Additional harms are added when the inflation rate is surprisingly high. A well-known harm arises from the effects of unanticipated inflation on the real burden of debt: When inflation over the course of the loan contract is higher than anticipated, reducing the value of dollars repaid below what was reckoned, it harms the creditor (and benefits the debtor). When inflation is lower than anticipated, increasing the real value of the debt, it harms the debtor (and benefits the creditor, if the debtor is still able to pay). A more variable inflation rate, imposing a greater risk that the inflation rate will be significantly higher or lower than its anticipated average, deters both borrowers and lenders.

Risk surrounding the inflation rate means that the lenders and borrowers face an inflation risk in addition to a default risk. The greater the risk about the future value of the dollars to be repaid, when some lenders and borrowers are risk-averse, the smaller the number of willing lenders and borrowers. Financial markets shrink, harming both potential borrowers and potential lenders. Looking across countries, it is evident that countries with higher and more variable inflation have shallower financial markets (Rousseau and Wachtel 2001; Boyd, Levine, and Smith 2001; Berentsen, Breu, and Shi 2012).

The price level under fiat standards has not only risen at a faster average rate than under the classical gold standard, it has been less predictable at medium to long horizons. Conversely, the classical gold standard era had lower price level uncertainty. Whereas fiat standard price levels drift with no tendency to return to a predictable underlying trend, deviations of the gold standard price level were followed by a return to the flat trend established by the flat long-run supply curve for gold. Higher price level uncertainty under fiat money means that savers and financial intermediaries are less able to predict what a dollar will be worth in ten to fifty years.[18] They are accordingly less eager to buy ten- to fifty-year bonds, as shown by the fact that corporate bonds issued since 1971 have a much shorter average maturity than bonds issued during the classical gold standard era. Butler, Gao, and Uzmanoglu (2021, p. 1) report: "From 1975 to 2015, the average maturity of new corporate bond issues in the U.S. declined from 20 years to 10 years." Fifty-year bonds, commonly issued by railroads during the classical gold standard era, have practically disappeared. Under a less predictable regime, a borrowing firm must pay a larger purchasing-power-risk premium when it issues medium- to long-term bonds, so entrepreneurs find it more costly to finance medium- to long-term investment projects. It is hard to put a number on the size of the effect, but it stands to reason that by raising a barrier to long-term investments the reduced predictability of the price level over medium to long terms has harmed economic growth.

4.8 FISCAL DISCIPLINE UNDER FIAT MONEY

Under a gold standard, government bonds are nearly free of inflation risk but not of default risk. Under a fiat standard, the reverse is true.

Under a gold standard, government borrowing creates an obligation to repay in gold, a medium that the borrowing government cannot

---

[18] For empirical evidence, see Selgin, Lastrapes, and White (2012), who measured price-level predictability in the United Stated under gold and fiat in two ways: (1) the size of the errors from a simple moving-average forecast; (2) the six-year rolling standard deviation of the quarterly price level. The price level during gold standard era, at horizons of ten years and greater, was better on both scores.

simply print into existence. There is consequently always a danger of default. The amount the government can borrow at reasonable rates (with a low default risk premium) is limited to the amount that the government can credibly commit to repay by raising more tax revenue than it spends on things other than debt service. (This is also known as running primary budget surpluses. We assume that there is no prospect of the government's bondholders being bailed out by some multinational entity.) A reduction in the credibility of the government's repayment plan forces upward the yields it must offer when rolling over its debt and when issuing new debt. Accordingly, as the economist Joseph Schumpeter (1954, pp. 405–406) commented: "An 'automatic' gold currency ... is extremely sensitive to government expenditure ... . This is the reason why gold is so unpopular now and also why it was so popular in a bourgeois era. It imposes restrictions on governments or bureaucracies."

The credibility constraint is much the same for a government that has to borrow in a fiat currency that it does not issue (and that likewise has no likelihood of being bailed out). Such a country might be one that issues its own fiat money, for example, Argentina, but because the devaluation risk is so great, the global bond market makes borrowing in US dollars cheaper in real terms. Or it might be a country that does not issue its own currency, for example, Greece using the euro issued by the ECB, or Panama using the US dollar.

The effectiveness of the default risk premium at limiting over-borrowing is weakened if creditors to a government think that they are likely to be bailed out by some supranational agency. Greece in recent decades provides an object lesson. Before Greece joined the Eurozone in 2001, the bond market imposed a 500 basis-point (5 percentage-point) default risk premium on Greek sovereign two-year bonds, measured by the spread over the yield on two-year German bonds. After joining, the premium fell to only about 40 basis points (4/10 of one percentage point) and stayed there until 2008 (Gibson, Hall, and Tavlas 2014). There had been no fiscal reform in Greece. Buyers of sovereign Greek bonds evidently placed a high probability on being bailed out, should the Greek government be unable to pay, by some combination of the ECB, the European Union, and the IMF. When the cost and unpopularity of a full bailout became clear to other ECB and EU member nations in 2011, however, the limited bailout actually provided was too little to prevent a Greek default. Commercial banks that held Greek sovereign debt lost €100 billion.

A government that borrows in its own currency, like the federal government of the United States, can issue sovereign debt that is free of nominal default risk. Meaning, it can always issue as many new dollars as it needs to pay what it has promised as principal and interest on its bonds. Such a government's debt is not free of *inflation risk*, however. A monetary expansion that enables the government to repay the number of dollars owed, but that causes the dollar to decline in purchasing power by 10 percent, is equivalent in real terms to repaying creditors only 90 percent of the debt owed. With higher inflation comes devaluation against foreign currencies (holding their inflation rates constant), so devaluation risk accompanies inflation risk. It is thus a mistake to call US Treasury debt denominated in fiat dollars "risk-free."

4.9 BUSINESS CYCLES HAVE NOT BEEN MILDER UNDER FIAT MONEY REGIMES

It has often been claimed that a fiat standard valuably enables a central bank to conduct a counter-cyclical monetary policy that dampens business cycles (reduces the volatility of real output or the average level of unemployment). Under the influence of Keynesian macroeconomic thinking, the Bretton Woods conference did not reinstate the classical gold standard, but promised to give central banks more leeway to practice counter-cyclical policies. The Keynesian approach calls for a data-driven central bank to vary its monetary policy as needed to stimulate an economy that is operating below its sustainable full-employment output path, or to dampen an economy that is operating above it. In theory, by appropriately tailoring policy to changing conditions in a timely manner, the central bank will dampen business cycles.

Greater macroeconomic stability is not evident in the historical record of fiat standards, however. For the United States, volatility in real output and unemployment have been nearly the same in the post–Second World War period as they were during the classical gold standard period (Selgin, Lastraptes, and White 2012). Postwar output volatility through 2009 (measured as percent standard deviation of real GDP from its trend using Christina Romer's GDP estimates) is insignificantly different from pre-1913 output volatility (2.6 percent vs. 2.7 percent). This despite the postwar US economy having a more diversified mix of agriculture, industry, and services, and thus smaller real supply shocks, which by itself should have produced improvement without any change in the monetary regime.

Stated in terms of the dynamic equation of exchange, stabilization policy could actually dampen cyclical swings in the economy if it could alter gM in a timely manner to offset changes in gV just as they occur, thus stabilizing growth in aggregate demand MV, and thereby keeping real output y near its full-employment or natural rate y_n. (Note that such a monetary policy cannot keep y from changing when y_n changes, for example, when there are real productivity shocks like the shrinkage of output by the COVID-19 pandemic and policy responses to it. No monetary policy can.) Such a stabilization of aggregate demand would be desirable *if* it could be achieved. But achievement requires timely and well-measured application, shifting M to offset changes in V, thus avoiding changes in aggregate demand that would otherwise occur. Alternatively put, when people want to hold larger money balances relative to income, and M remains constant, they have to cut spending to build up money balances. The aggregate demand for goods falls, and a recession with unsold inventories and unhired labor ensues in a world of sticky prices and wages. If the Fed provides enough extra money (as in 2020), aggregate demand for goods does not have to fall. But the Fed, to keep stabilzing, has to withdraw the extra M when people start spending off the money balances they have built up and V rises. Failure to tighten monetary policy promptly (as in 2021) brings about a higher rate of inflation (as in 2021–2022).

Central banks in practice, whether due to political pressure from elected officials or due to bureaucratic inertia, tend to err on the side of tightening policy too late rather than too soon.[19] At the very onset of the fiat money era, the French economist Jacque Rueff (1972, p. 42) warned: "I do not believe, as a matter of fact, that the monetary authorities, however courageous and well-informed they may be, can deliberately bring about those contractions in the money supply that the mere mechanism of the gold standard would have generated automatically."

4.10 SEIGNIORAGE: THE PROFIT FROM ISSUING FIAT MONEY

As noted earlier, a national fiat money offers a national government a quick and easy way to fund its spending: merely issue new units of money. Because an obligation to redeem on demand in gold coin constrained money-creation, it is not a coincidence that the European combatant

---

[19] Binder (2021) quantifies political pressure on central banks and its inflationary consequences.

nations suspended redeemability into gold with the onset of the First World War. Outbursts of irredeemable money and high inflation followed. Nor is it a coincidence that the gold standard was suspended only later by initially non-combatant nations such as Switzerland and the United States (Selgin and White 1999).

Unlike the cumbersome medieval process of generating seigniorage revenue by calling in the existing silver coins and reminting them into a larger number of coins with less silver in each coin, enlarging the stock of fiat money is easy. A central bank can expand the nominal stock to whatever extent it desires, with practically zero production cost, if it is prepared to accept the resulting rise in the price level.

Under modern arrangements, the fiscal authority (the Treasury or Finance Ministry) is distinct from the central bank. Spending in excess of tax revenues is seldom *directly* financed by paying government employees or suppliers or transfer recipients with newly created money.[20] The process is indirect: The Treasury finances deficit spending by borrowing, selling new IOUs in the bond market. To the extent that the central bank subsequently buys bonds from the market with newly created money, the two transactions add up to the same result: Deficit spending is financed by seigniorage, the profit from money creation.

Hyperinflations in history have all happened under fiat regimes. Peter Bernholz (2014) lists thirty hyperinflations, using the definition of a hyperinflation as an episode in which the inflation rate reaches 50 percent per month. Only one episode (the hyperinflation of the French Revolution's paper assignat) preceded the twentieth century. (Monthly inflation rates of the paper continental during the American Revolution peaked at 47 percent.) To Bernholz's list may be added Venezuela in 2018, which had a December inflation rate of 142 percent.

A hyperinflation requires a hyper-rapid expansion of the money supply. Such rapid monetary expansion has usually been driven by the deliberate use of money-creation to finance deficit spending (Bernholz 2003; Sargent 1982). Hyperinflating nations, and more broadly nations with triple-digit annual inflation rates, are nations in desperate fiscal conditions, effectively unable to borrow, such that enormous money-creation is the only way left to fund their enormous budget deficits. Triple-digit and higher inflation rates are almost never fully anticipated in financial

---

[20] An exception, when we count purchases of private-sector liabilities as expenditures, was the 2020 Fed-Treasury lending and asset-purchase programs (Payroll Protection Program Liquidity Facility, Primary Market Corporate Credit Facility, Secondary Market Corporate Credit Facility).

contracts. Citizens who enter a triple-digit inflation holding government bonds paying nominal returns only in single digits or low double-digits see the real value of their bonds wiped out. In the Weimar hyperinflation, Hall and Sargent (2019, p. 39) note, the 1923 price level in papiermarks rose "to approximately 12 orders of magnitude of the 1913 price level (that is, 10^{12} in scientific notation)," by which means the German government effectively wiped out its domestic debt denominated in papiermarks. (Much of its foreign debt was denominated in gold.)

The good news is that fiat monetary expansions rapid enough to generate triple-digit inflation rates have been relatively rare. At least in higher-income countries, national governments rely almost entirely on other taxes and borrowing to finance their spending. Money-creation typically supplies only a small amount of their revenue, for example, only 1 to 2 percent of US federal expenditure. When budget deficits grow, however, and correspondingly the ratio of public debt to GDP rises, there is an increasing danger that budget deficits will be covered by printing money, leading to higher inflation.

4.11 THE DANGER OF FISCAL DOMINANCE OVER MONETARY POLICY

The danger of "fiscal dominance" over monetary policy, whereby chronically high budget deficits compel an inflationary monetary policy, has been famously analyzed by Thomas Sargent and Neil Wallace (1981) under the label of "unpleasant monetarist arithmetic." To summarize their analysis, we begin with a government budget constraint:

$$G - T = \Delta D + \Delta M, \tag{1}$$

where G is government expenditure, T is ordinary tax revenue, ΔD is the change in government debt held by the public, and ΔM is the change in government-issued money. The stock of government debt in the hands of the public, D, is the accumulation of all previous years' budget deficits (net of any years' surpluses). The constraint says that a budget deficit requires financing from some combination of bond finance (borrowing) and seigniorage finance (money creation). Equation (1) implicitly rules out financing government spending by receiving gifts from multinational agencies or by selling off government assets.

We can modify the budget constraint by expressing G, T, ΔD, and ΔM as fractions of national income, and defining ΔD as borrowing proceeds *net* of debt service (thus moving debt service out of G). Then:

$$G - T = (\delta - r)D + \mu M, \qquad (2)$$

where δ is the growth rate of government debt ratio, r is real after-tax interest rate on government debt, and μ is growth rate of fiat money. Equation (2) says that a primary deficit (net of debt service) must be financed by some combination of the net proceeds from bond issue plus money creation. The net proceeds from bond issue become zero when a government so saturates the market for its debt that the interest rate on its debt rises to match the growth rate of the government debt ratio. Issuing new debt yields no net revenue because it raises the interest rate in equal measure. With $(\delta - r)$ falling to zero, only money-creation remains as a way to finance the stream of budget deficits. The government is reduced to defaulting outright or defaulting in real terms by producing an inflationary rate of monetary expansion.

Is there any relevance to this scenario in which fiscal deficits compel money creation? It follows simply from the market demand curve for debt sloping downward (like all other demand curves) such that issuing more government debt (relative to the ability to repay in real terms) will lower the market price of that debt relative to its promised payouts, and thereby will raise the market yield (r) on that debt. Put another way, as the debt ratio grows, the marginal buyers will be increasingly reluctant investors who will not buy without a higher yield, because they attach a higher probability to default or to equivalent depreciation of the currency. The idea that bond finance "maxes out" at some high ratio of debt to GDP (where GDP indicates the ability to repay) follows from remaining potential lenders beyond some point being increasingly reluctant, and the rate that the marginal buyers require having to be paid to all bondholders as bonds are rolled over.

Of course, it does not follow from the theoretical existence of a point beyond which no more bond revenue can be had that a particular government is currently near to that point. But the real-world relevance of the scenario in which a government saturates the market for its debt became plain at the peak of European sovereign debt crisis. In November 2011, the *Washington Post* ran the headline, "Jump in European borrowing costs adds to debt crisis" (Schneider and Faiola 2011). The story noted that "Spain's sale of short-term, one-year bonds fell short of its target, and the interest rate jumped to 5 percent, compared with 3.6 percent in a similar sale last month." Spain's ratio of sovereign debt to GDP had nearly doubled in the previous four years during the global financial crisis, to 70 percent from 36 percent.

The ratio of US total federal debt to GDP also rose during the recession of 2007–2009. In the first quarter of 2011, it stood at 93 percent, well above Spain's contemporary 70 percent debt ratio.[21] During the subsequent period of economic recovery, the US debt ratio did not shrink (as used to be common during recovery periods) but continued to rise due to chronic budget deficits. In 2020 Q1, it reached 108 percent. Then came unprecedented peacetime budget deficits associated with the COVID-19 pandemic. In 2021 Q3, the US debt-to-GDP ratio stood at 123 percent, up by 15 percentage points in less than two years. The dramatic rise in US federal debt has not, however, brought much of a rise in its sovereign bond yields yet. In fact, the real yields on ten-year US Treasury bonds have been lower over the last twenty over than they were over the previous twenty years, suggesting that demand has grown (presumably because Treasuries are considered safer than other assets in turbulent times) even more than supply, so that the international market for US Treasuries has not yet begun to become saturated.

But an approach to saturation must eventually come if the federal government continues on its current fiscal path. Budget deficits that continually exceed real GDP growth (both as shares of GDP) means that debt outgrows GDP. In the last twenty years, the US federal budget deficit has never been in surplus, and has only twice come in below 1.94 percent of GDP, which has been the compound average annual growth rate of GDP during the same period. Nominal debt growing faster than nominal gross domestic product means an ever-rising ratio of debt to GDP, as seen in the numbers of the previous paragraph. To avoid the inflationary "solution" to mounting US federal debt, dollar-holders must somehow lower the path of the ratio of debt to GDP, or somehow credibly constrain the Federal Reserve such that it cannot create money to cover fiscal deficits even should the Treasury begin to saturate the market for its debt.

4.12 THE CASE FOR A FIAT STANDARD

Given the checkered history of fiat monies, why do so many economists defend fiat standards? Mostly they defend an ideal version of how a fiat standard could perform, not how the typical fiat standard has performed in practice. In principle, appropriate management of the quantity of fiat money can achieve whatever nominal target the economist thinks best for the macroeconomy. Leading proposals call for a stable price level, a

[21] fred.stlouisfed.org/series/GFDEGDQ188S.

stable growth path of the price level, a stable level of nominal income, or a stable growth path of nominal income. The most widely discussed proposal in the pure theory of fiat monetary policy is Milton Friedman's "optimum quantity of money" proposition (Friedman 1969) that efficiency calls for a negative inflation rate to bring the nominal interest rate on Treasury bills down to the zero nominal rate paid on Federal Reserve Notes.[22] Under a gold standard or a Bitcoin standard, by contrast, the supply of money is governed by market forces or by a program, and its behavior does not guarantee the achievement of any of these policy targets.[23]

4.13 CAN FIAT CENTRAL BANKS BE CREDIBLY CONSTRAINED?

But will a central bank in practice successfully pursue the nominal target assigned to it? The problem is not technical; it has the ability. A large technical literature in macroeconomics spells out models and empirical coefficients that can be used to manage monetary policy to hit various nominal targets.

The problem is getting the central bank to stick to its assigned task rather than neglecting it while pursuing other goals. Many central banks have been assigned – or like the Federal Reserve System have assigned themselves – the goal of keeping the annual rate of inflation close to a target rate, typically 2 percent. In January to March 2022, the Federal Reserve's preferred measure of the inflation rate, the year-over-year percentage change in the Personal Consumption Expenditures deflator, was above 6 percent and rising, while the Fed's inflation target was 2 percent. (The more commonly reported CPI-U rose above 8 percent during the same period.) In mid-March 2022, the Fed's monetary policy committee (the Federal Open Market Committee, FOMC) released a Summary of Economic Projections[24] indicating that the FOMC's own PCE (Personal

---

[22] For more detailed discussion of the "optimum quantity of money" proposal, see White (1999, pp. 105–16).

[23] In the wider set of cryptocurrencies, some "algorithmic stablecoins," unlike banknotes because unbacked by dollar reserves, have pursued a stable exchange rate against the US dollar by using a preset feedback mechanism to manage quantity. In May 2022, one major coin of this type, UST, lost its peg and crashed. One might conceive of an algorithmic stablecoin that pursues stability in purchasing power over the CPI basket, in other words seeks to achieve zero price inflation rather than matching the inflation rate of the dollar. Or even a coin designed to pursue a stable path for nominal GDP. But no such coin has come to market, and designing a robust version of such a coin remains an unsolved problem.

[24] www.federalreserve.gov/monetarypolicy/files/fomcprojtabl20220316.pdf.

Consumption Expenditure) inflation-rate forecast for 2022 had risen to
4.3 percent. The Fed did not expect to tighten monetary policy during
2022 by enough to produce a 2 percent inflation rate by the end of the
year. Or even by the middle of the following year, given that its projections for 2023 and 2024 were, respectively, 2.7 and 2.3 percent. Clearly,
the Fed's inflation target did not closely constrain monetary policy in
practice in the sense that even an inflation rate 4+ percentage points
above target did not prompt timely corrective action.

In the Eurozone, the March 2022 inflation rate hit 7.4 percent, well
above the ECB's formal target of 2 percent. In the United Kingdom, the
inflation rate was 7.0 percent, despite the Bank of England's target of 2
percent. All three currencies – US dollar, euro, and UK pound – saw their
inflation rates rise rather than fall between March and the end of 2022.

The Fed adopted its inflation target at its own initiative. The target is
not embodied in any binding legislated mandate. There is no penalty for
the Fed missing its target. Accordingly, the Fed can suspend or modify its
target at its own initiative, as it did by announcing in August 2020 that
it was switching from "not above 2 percent" to "2 percent on average."
The Fed calls its modified approach "flexible average inflation targeting," where "flexible" indicates that "the Federal Reserve will seek an
inflation rate that averages 2% over a time frame that is not formally
defined" (McCracken and Amburgey 2021). The speed of returning to
the preferred average rate following an overshoot is unspecified, leaving
market participants to guess. Fed Chair Jerome Powell at first declared
the overshooting of the inflation rate in fall 2021 to be "transitory," but
later withdrew the description. His use of "transitory" was transitory.

The Bank of England's Monetary Policy Committee is slightly more specific, explaining that "[t]he Committee's approach is to set monetary policy
so that inflation returns sustainably to its target at a conventional horizon
of around two years."[25] Its target was assigned to the bank by legislation.

Even a legislated inflation target (rather than one self-adopted by the
central bank) seems a weak bar against fiscal or financial pressures on
the central bank. The Congress or Parliament that imposed the inflation
target on its central bank can suspend or neglect the target whenever
the legislature finds that issuing new money is a faster and easier way to
finance spending beyond its current tax revenue than enacting and collecting new taxes. Consider the limiting case of a national government

---

[25] www.bankofengland.co.uk/-/media/boe/files/letter/2021/september/governor-cpi-letter-
september-2021.pdf?la=en&hash=72EA4C295408124B9F55B4F04A9A9A646167B0DF.

with a legislated inflation target that has saturated the global financial market for its debt. That government has a stark problem: If it adheres to the rate of money creation consistent with keeping the price inflation rate to 2 percent, it will have to default on its sovereign debt, because it cannot borrow more and there is not enough ordinary tax revenue to service the debt. It seems likely that a government in such circumstances would consider it the lesser evil to abandon its inflation-rate target.[26]

The ECB initially had something that was supposed to be even stronger than a legislated inflation target: It had a written constitution that made price stability its sole target. The ECB board declared that price stability meant that inflation rate was not to exceed 2 percent. This experiment might be considered the last great hope for constitutionally constrained fiat money. It has not kept Eurozone inflation from exceeding 10 percent in 2022.[27]

When it was first advanced in the 1980s, the "fiscal policy dominance" scenario of Sargent and Wallace (in which rising debt saturates the market and thereby compels inflationary money creation) seemed empirically irrelevant to contemporary monetary policy, at least for nations like the United States that can borrow as much as they want at low real interest rates (Darby 1984). In a review of a book by Sargent, Milton Friedman (1987) wrote:

In any event, it is worth emphasizing how far we are in fact from the kind of crisis that Sargent and Wallace envisage. In 1945, the ratio of U.S. government interest-bearing debt to national income was 1.18; by 1979, it was down to 0.26. Since then it [debt] has been rising more rapidly than national income, and by 1985, it was 0.41. No doubt, if that recent upward trend were to continue, the debt would raise serious problems. However, there is every sign that it will not continue, both because of a continued decline in the real interest rate and because government deficits will be brought under control.

Needless to say, government budget deficits were not brought under control. The ratio of total debt to GDP rose from 41 percent in 1985 to 65 percent in 1995. Today it is triple 41 percent, at 123 percent. If the United States is not yet into the "serious problems" zone where real interest rates on sovereign debt are rising, it must at least be closer to that zone.

Situations of fiscal dominance driving rapid money creation are more common in lower-income countries, where money-printing often finances a much larger share of government expenditure. A table compiled by Reid

---

[26] Jeff Hummel (2010), however, has argued for expecting such a government to choose default, at least in the case where most of the bond-holders are foreigners.

[27] The Euro area HICP index hit 10.6 in October 2022 (over October 2021). On the politics behind the initial ECB Constitution and inflation target, and their decline in force over the years, see Vaubel and White (2013).

Click (1998) shows that thirty-four nations relied on money creation to finance more than 10 percent of their expenditure during 1971–1990. Ten of those nations financed more than 20 percent of expenditure with seigniorage. Argentina and Yugoslavia were the most seigniorage reliant, and both had hyperinflations at the end of the period. In nations with seigniorage-dependent governments, the convenience of revenue from money-creation makes high inflation a serious danger to money-holders. Money-creation levies a tax on holders of currency and any other form of money that pays a return that does not fully compensate for inflation. The tax burden is felt as a shrinkage in the purchasing power of a household's money balances.

4.14 IS A PRIVATE FIAT-LIKE MONEY FEASIBLE?

Monetary theorists at one time imagined systems where private irredeemable monies would promise a competitive interest return (Klein 1974) or stable purchasing power (Hayek 1976). But no such projects have been successfully launched. In addition to legal restrictions, such monies might lack credibility because the private issuer would be tempted – absent a contractual buy-back commitment – by the profit from unexpected monetary expansion (for a detailed discussion, see White 1999, ch. 11). Instead, we have seen the launching of Bitcoin, followed by other cryptocurrencies, which directly constrains expansion in the number of units and – at least before widespread monetary use – leaves their purchasing power unstable.

5

How a Bitcoin Standard Works

Before Bitcoin, monetary theorists imagined systems where private non-commodity monies would provide a competitive interest return (Klein 1974) or a stable purchasing power (Hayek 1976). But the launching of Bitcoin in 2009, followed by many other cryptocurrencies, has brought us private irredeemable would-be monies that instead are programmed to follow a pre-determined quantity path. In practice these currencies have provided high investment returns by appreciation, rather than by interest or dividends, and have exhibited great volatility in purchasing power.

For convenience we will focus in this chapter on Bitcoin, the first and still most successful cryptocurrency, to represent cryptocurrencies in general, just as we focused in the previous chapters on gold to represent commodity monies in general. Bitcoin has the most developed ecosystem of ancillary services. It is more credibly committed than later cryptocurrencies like Ethereum are to maintaining its originally programmed quantity path. It has this greater credibility in part because, unlike Ethereum, it has no active founder who can gather a consensus on significantly amending the source code.

Our focus will be on the economic and monetary aspects of Bitcoin, and not on its cryptographic technology or internal governance.[1] We are interested here in Bitcoin as a potential monetary standard, not as a personal investment.

---

[1] For a primer on Bitcoin's technology and governance, see Schär and Berentsen (2020, pp. 36–46 and 50–56).

5.1 WHAT BITCOIN IS

Bitcoin is an intangible digital asset. An owner of Bitcoin units ("unspent transaction outputs" or UTXOs) can transfer some or all of them to others using Bitcoin's native ledger system or "blockchain." The blockchain associates each UTXO with a specific address that either mined it or received it from another address. An unspent balance is transferable only by the holder of its cryptographic private key. (The use of private-key cryptography to secure the system is what puts the "crypto" in cryptocurrency.) The blockchain system prevents the illegitimate "double spending" of units (analogous to the counterfeiting of currency notes) without a centralized ledger-keeper. The ledger is not kept by any single central administrator but is distributed across a network of nodes that jointly validate transactions by consensus.

Bitcoin currently functions as a medium of exchange (is acquired in order to be spent) in some transactions. I myself once accepted Bitcoin for a speaking fee, and later spent it, so in that set of transactions it served as a medium of exchange for me. But Bitcoin does not yet serve as a *commonly* accepted medium of exchange, so it does not yet meet the standard economic criterion for being considered a *money*.[2] Less spendable cryptos might be better labeled "cryptoassets" rather than "cryptocurrencies," had the latter term not become so common.

Bitcoin's best-established niche use derives from the fact that Bitcoin transfers do not go through government-controlled central banks, and in that way avoid censorship. For example, if you want to donate funds to the dissident Belarusian human rights organization BYSOL, you cannot wire them fiat money. Wire payments go through the Belarusian government's central bank, which has frozen the bank accounts of known dissidents. The funds won't get to their intended destination. Human rights advocate Alex Gladstein (2020) reports that BYSOL has, however, received more than half a million dollars' worth of Bitcoin, and distributed it to striking workers. The workers can sell it on the black market for local currency, which they can use to buy groceries. Activists in Nigeria, Hong Kong, and Russia have similarly used Bitcoin for international fundraising. Dissidents within China use Bitcoin to make remote transactions outside of the surveillance of the government-owned banks. Residents of Cuba, blocked from credit-card networks by US sanctions, use Bitcoin to make online purchases (Sobrado 2021). Gladstein (2022, p. 8) estimates that

---

[2] On the distinction between "medium of exchange" and "money," see White (1999).

in the developing world "tens of millions of people are using Bitcoin to escape from broken financial systems." Over 80 million Bitcoin-capable wallets have been downloaded, according to Statista (2022).

To appreciate its novelty, it helps to contrast Bitcoin to other assets used as media of exchange. Unlike a gold coin, Bitcoin is intangible. It cannot be melted down for use as an electrical conductor (a production good) or as jewelry (a consumption good). Unlike a banknote or bank account balance, Bitcoin is not a debt contract or IOU. It is rather an "IOU-nothing," an asset itself like a fiat currency note, but not issued by a government.

Nor is Bitcoin issued by a business firm (although many later cryptocurrencies are). Bitcoin was launched by "Satoshi Nakamoto" (a pseudonym) in 2009 as a kind of hobby project, to demonstrate that a secure system for transferring a scarce private non-commodity money could work in practice. Early participants in the project came from a community of "cypherpunks" who were enthusiastic about the concept. The real identity of the author (or authors) of the Bitcoin White Paper and program remains unknown, Nakamoto never having appeared in public and his online activity having ended. With Bitcoin's success in getting off the ground, an ecosystem of ancillary for-profit enterprises has grown up around it, creating a new payment infrastructure. Daily trading of Bitcoin against fiat currencies, in large volumes, is now facilitated by numerous for-profit exchanges such as Binance, Coinbase, and Kraken. Merchant acceptance of Bitcoin in payments, still uncommon is facilitated by exchanges and by payment processors such as BitPay.

New coins are issued by the Bitcoin source code, distributed as rewards to those who devote their computers to transaction validation. The program releases quantities of new Bitcoins according to a fixed schedule, at an ever-slowing annual rate, with the quantity of Bitcoin set to max out at 21 million coins around the year 2140. At the end of 2021, about 19 million (or 90 percent) had been released. The source code that governs the issue schedule is changeable only by consensus of the validators. Thus, by contrast to a gold standard or any fiat standard in practice, the Bitcoin system has a strict quantity precommitment. Because they earn Bitcoin rewards for their work, the validators have been called "miners" by analogy to gold miners. But unlike gold miners, a larger number of Bitcoin miners or greater computing power per miner does not mean faster growth of the number of units in circulation. It rather means increased competition to win the predetermined number of new units that will be released.

5.2 THE BACKGROUND TO BITCOIN

A cryptographer named David Chaum launched a product called DigiCash in 1989. The DigiCash technology enabled a financial institution that licensed it to issue a peer-to-peer electronic currency denominated in dollars or another fiat currency, cryptographically secured against double-spending by having the institution's ledger validate all transactions. At the same time, like an electronic version of circulating paper banknotes, DigiCash would preserve the user's privacy by keeping his or her activity unknown to the bank. Transfers of "Chaumian banknotes" were "blinded" from the issuer. Chaum was unsuccessful in signing up enough financial institutions to keep the project going, because the early-adopting banks were unable to recruit many consumers. Concern for privacy in online shopping, and the volume of online shopping, were much smaller at the time (Pitta 1999).

A subsequent technology for peer-to-peer digital fiat payments was Mondex, a prepaid card system developed at National Westminster Bank (UK) in the early 1990s. Money balances loaded on to a Mondex card's chip could be transferred peer-to-peer to another holder's card without bank involvement, another electronic version of the banknote. Although licensed to Mastercard and Chase Manhattan Bank in the United States, and test-marketed, the project was never launched in the United States, having few apparent attractions to consumers over using a debit card. In Germany, a similar system called GeldKarte was launched in the late 1990s. It gained some adoption in small offline transactions (mostly vending machines) and continues in use today. Note that neither DigiCash nor Mondex nor GeldKarte introduced a new currency unit. All were intended for adoption by existing commercial banks on existing fiat standards, and provided new ways of transferring fiat-denominated claims on banks.

A different set of technological developments made Bitcoin possible. "Hashcash" was first proposed by Adam Back in 1997 (and spelled out in Back 2002) for blocking junk emails. Using the Hashcash program stops an email from reaching your inbox until the sender demonstrates having incurred a small (maybe one-second) computing cost. The cost is trivial for the sender of a single email but prohibitive in the aggregate for a mass spammer. The "hash" in the name refers to the kind of math problem (a "cryptographic hash function") that the sender must solve, one that can only be solved by "brute force" that consumes CPU time. A similar "proof of work" is required of Bitcoin miners to win block-validation awards. Before Nakamoto began coding Bitcoin, three distinct proof-of-work-based cryptocurrency systems had been proposed and discussed in online forums: Wei Dai's "b-money," Nick Szabo's "Bit gold," and Hal Finney's RPOW (Reusable Proof of Work).

A different ideology motivated these developers. Dai, Szabo, Finney, and to some extent Nakamoto were members of "Cypherpunk" and libertarian online communities. Dai (1998) even self-identified as a crypto-anarchist.[3] Their projects aimed to enable financial privacy at a deeper level than Chaum's, which operated within the status quo system in which bank accounts are subject to government surveillance. Regulators could readily have shut down DigiCash adoption by ruling that blinded bank payments run afoul of banks' know-your-customer and anti-money-laundering requirements. The new crypto-money projects aimed not only to create an alternative payment system free of government surveillance and censorship, by operating outside of status-quo banks, but also to provide an alternative to the inflation-prone fiat monies issued by central banks. On an email list, Nakamoto (2009b) explained the motivation for Bitcoin's alternative design:

> The root problem with conventional currency is all the trust that's required to make it work. The central bank must be trusted not to debase the currency, but the history of fiat currencies is full of breaches of that trust. Banks must be trusted to hold our money and transfer it electronically, but they lend it out in waves of credit bubbles with barely a fraction in reserve. We have to trust them with our privacy, trust them not to let identity thieves drain our accounts.

Evidence of joint importance of technology and ideology can be found in the following timeline of how Bitcoin came to be created and to acquire market value.

5.3 A TIMELINE OF BITCOIN DEVELOPMENTS

- 1976: F. A. Hayek (1976) publishes *The Denationalisation of Money*, arguing that private initiatives – if governments let them – will provide sounder money than fiat central banks do. He envisions competition among branded private non-commodity monies. Historical and theoretical research on (relatively) unregulated market money systems ("free banking") follows (White 1984b, Selgin 1988, Dowd 1992). An earlier tradition (Rothbard 1962) continues to focus on a private gold coin standard without fiduciary payment media.

---

[3] For a useful attempt to piece together Nakamoto's political views, see McElroy (2020, pp. 54–61).

- 1979–2001: Various researchers develop the cryptographic tools that would be used to build the Bitcoin program. Gwern (2011) lists the Merkle tree (1979), public key cryptography (1980), cryptographic timestamps (1991), the Hashcash proof-of-work system (1997), Peer-to-peer networks (1999), Byzantine fault tolerance (1999), and Secure Hash Algorithm 256 (2001). Narayan and Clark (2017) provide a helpful history of the enabling ideas from computer science and cryptography.
- 21 September 1992: The Cypherpunks mailing list gets underway. "Cypher" was a combination of "cyber" with "cipher" (Quereshi 2019). The list will continue until 1998. There Wei Dai, Hal Finney, Nick Szabo, and others including Tim May will discuss the intersection of cryptography and digital money. Initially most of the discussion refers to DigiCash, "blinded notes" for anonymous payments, and digital bearer certificates. It is taken for granted that all are denominated in existing fiat money units.
- 22 November 1992: Active Cypherpunk poster Tim May (1992), in a 499-word "Crypto Anarchist Manifesto," envisions an internet where user cryptography allows anonymous internet trade and contracts: "Computer technology is on the verge of providing the ability for individuals and groups to communicate and interact with each other in a totally anonymous manner. Two persons may exchange messages, conduct business, and negotiate electronic contracts without ever knowing the True Name, or legal identity, of the other."
- 1993: Hal Finney (1993) writes on cryptographic methods for "Protecting privacy with electronic cash" in *Extropy*, a libertarian futurist magazine. He describes Chaum's advances in e-cash systems for securely and privately transferring claims to existing reserve assets. The reserves "would likely be dollars or other government currency, but they could be gold or other commodities."
- 1995: Five issues later in *Extropy* I discuss Finney's and other accounts of private digital currency (White 1995). My piece is skeptical that "new methods of transferring payment" would "promote the use of some monetary unit better than the currently predominant government fiat unit (the Federal Reserve dollar, in the United States)," citing the network-effects advantage of an incumbent monetary standard absent high inflation. In the next issue Finney (1996) criticizes my piece, raising the possibility that "the net will offer an opportunity for new financial instruments." He likens the internet to "a new ecological niche" in which "it may be that the stodgy old currencies of the past won't be the strongest to colonize." With lower transaction costs

"it may not matter that much what currency you get paid in online, you can easily switch it to the local currency of whatever you want to buy." These remarks hint at the idea of a new internet-native currency, but Finney does not further elaborate.

- 1996: Douglas Jackson founds E-gold, a private system for online transfer of digital warehouse claims to gold. The gold itself was warehoused in London. In 2008, despite gold not then being money in law or in practice, and despite Jackson cooperating with the authorities, the US federal government prosecutes and convicts Jackson for operating an unlicensed money transmission business. The government shuts down E-gold (White 2014). A lesson is taken to heart by Cypherpunks: An alternative payment system that rests on an identifiable central institution has a single point of failure. It is vulnerable to government seizure. Jackson's fate may have influenced Nakamoto's decision to remain pseudonymous.

- 26 November 1998: Wei Dai announces on the Cypherpunks list the availability of his essay providing a "description of b-money, a new protocol for monetary exchange and contract enforcement for pseudonyms." Dai (1998) begins: "I am fascinated by Tim May's crypto-anarchy." He briefly sketches a distributed ledger system intended to provide "pseudonymous entities" with "a medium of exchange" created by proof of work. B-money is envisioned as creating its own currency standard, not as a system for transferring fiat money.

- 1998: On the libtech discussion list founded by Nick Szabo, as later recollected by Szabo (2019b), Finney and Szabo each propose their own privacy-preserving payment systems in which a digital currency based on proof-of-work provides the settlement layer for banks issuing retail-friendly "Chaumian digital cash" (Szabo 2017), somewhat akin to how free banking systems operated on a gold standard.[4] About the settlement medium, Szabo (2019a, 2019b) recollected: "The whole

---

[4] No archive of the libtech list seems to be available online. Szabo would later write that the idea of a speedy low-cost payment layer on top of a cryptocurrency layer was "inspired by [George Selgin's] and Lawrence White's historical research about free banking." Szabo (2019c) added: "Selgin, White, Finney, Dai, and myself were on the libtech list where we discussed these ideas in mid-1998. It seems to only be implicit in my public bit gold writings, but Hal later expressly proposed it for bitcoin." Finney (2010), citing Selgin (1988), proposed a free banking system on a Bitcoin standard to serve as "a secondary level of payment systems which is lighter weight and more efficient" than processing small Bitcoin-denominated payments on the blockchain. Szabo (2019b) would come to prefer something like the Lightning Network as a more secure second layer than Bitcoin-denominated bank liabilities: "We now have more trust-minimized versions of this 'layer 2' technology, e.g. Lightning, which is fully & more securely collateralized than mere IOUs." For a recent account of second-layer Bitcoin payments see Bhatia (2021).

idea of having an independent currency, rather than just more private or censorship resistant payments for existing currencies, didn't exist among either cypherpunks or academic cryptographers until libertarian futurists introduced it. ... Later bit gold & b-money were both first proposed on the libtech-l list, something of an intersection of libertarian futurists and cypherpunks."[5]

- 2004: Hal Finney (2004) describes and produces executable software for a payment system ("Reusable Proofs of Work") in which digital tokens created by proof-of-work can be spent or "reused" (once) by their recipients. The system runs on a single "transparent" central server, its ledger publicly observable such that any user can "verify its correctness and integrity in real time." Finney cites Nick Szabo's concept of "bit gold," which had not yet been published.

- 2005: In a working paper, Ian Grigg (2005) discusses the implications of financial cryptography for accounting and digital cash.

- 27 December 2005: Nick Szabo (2005) posts a description of "Bit gold," which he envisions as a "protocol whereby unforgeably costly bits could be created online with minimal dependence on trusted third parties," securely kept on a "distributed property title registry," and transferred with an "unforgeable chain of title." The proof-of-work costliness of Bit gold units keeps them scarce and valuable, allowing them to serve as money.[6] Szabo says that he "hit upon the idea" a "long time ago," presumably meaning 1998.[7] He cites Hal Finney's RPOW system, which he calls "a variant of bit gold."

- Early 2007: "Satoshi Nakamoto" begins writing the Bitcoin source code (Nakamoto 2009c).

---

[5] Szabo told interviewer Peter McCormack (2019) that Bit gold "was certainly a way out there, fringe idea at the time I was working on it and there was only a handful of people in the world I can talk to about it that even have any clue what I was talking about. We were on a mailing list, so the cypherpunks mailing list and then myself, Wei Dai, Hal Finney, Larry White, George Selgin and a few others were on a mailing list I created called libtech and that's where I came up with Bitgold and Wei Dai came up with B-money and we had great discussions on there." Archives show that Dai announced b-money on the Cypherpunks list, but lacking a libtech archive or confirmation by Dai himself it remains unclear that Dai proposed b-money on the libtech list.

[6] Szabo notes that Bit gold is vulnerable to a flood of money creation should a technological breakthrough cause a sudden drop in the computation cost of creating Bit gold units. The system does not have a pre-set release schedule, a novel feature introduced by Bitcoin. Szabo suggests that there could be a floating exchange rate between old units and new cheaper units, though this would create other hassles by destroying the fungibility of various Bit gold units.

[7] Szabo (1999) referred to "bit gold" in print in 1999 without elaborating.

- 31 October 2008: Nakamoto (2008a) posts the now-famous white paper, *Bitcoin: A Peer-to-Peer Electronic Cash System*, outlining a proposed cryptocurrency. In an announcement on the Cryptography Mailing List, Nakamoto (2008b) writes: "I've been working on a new electronic cash system that's fully peer-to-peer, with no trusted third party." The white paper cites Dai (1998) and Back (2002) but not Finney or Szabo. Nakamoto (2010) would later write that "Bitcoin is an implementation of Wei Dai's b-money proposal on Cypherpunks in 1998 and Nick Szabo's Bitgold proposal" [citing Dai 1998 and Szabo 2005].[8] Dai (2011), however, would comment that "my understanding is that the creator of Bitcoin, who goes by the name Satoshi Nakamoto, didn't even read my article before reinventing the idea himself. He learned about it afterward and credited me in his paper."[9]
- 8 November 2008: Hal Finney (2008a) responds to the Bitcoin white paper with questions. He applauds its supply mechanism: "Bitcoin seems to be a very promising idea. ... there is potential value in a form of [an] unforgeable token whose production rate is predictable and can't be influenced by corrupt parties. This would be more analogous to gold than to fiat currencies. Nick Szabo wrote many years ago about what he called 'bit gold' [cites Szabo 2005] and this could be an implementation of that concept." Finney does not mention his own RPOW proposal.
- 13 November 2008. Hal Finney (2008b) observes that the Bitcoin program solves two problems: It creates a distributed database and then uses it "for a system similar to Wei Dai's b-money (which is referenced in the paper) but transaction/coin based rather than account based. Solving the global, massively decentralized database problem is arguably the harder part ... The use of proof-of-work as a tool for this purpose is a novel idea well worth further review IMO." In an email to Wei Dai, Nakamoto quoted this comment and called it "a good high-level overview" (Gwern 2017).
- 17 November 2008: Nakamoto (2008c) comments on The Cryptography Mailing List that "The functional details are not covered in the paper, but the sourcecode is coming soon." The main files are available on request, "full release soon."

[8] For comparison and contrast of b-money and Bit gold with Bitcoin, see Van Wirdum (2018) and Quereshi (2019).

[9] Nakamoto-Dai emails, formerly private but now public (Gwern 2017), support Dai's understanding. It was after Adam Back told Nakamoto to cite the Dai proposal that Nakamoto wrote to Dai, seeking citation information that he would add to the Bitcoin white paper.

- 10 December 2008: Nakamoto welcomes users to bitcoin-list, a small mailing list to which only Nakamoto, Hal Finney, and seven others contribute over the coming year.
- 3 January 2009: Nakamoto begins running the first version of the Bitcoin software client, bitcoin.exe v.0.1.0. The program issues the first 50 Bitcoin units as a reward for mining the "genesis block."
- 8 January 2009: Nakamoto (2009a) announces on The Cryptography Mailing List "the first release of Bitcoin, a new electronic cash system that uses a peer-to-peer network to prevent double-spending. It's completely decentralized with no server or central authority." A download link is provided. Nakamoto remarks: "You can get coins by getting someone to send you some, or turn on Options->Generate Coins to run a node and generate blocks." List members begin to download the Bitcoin client, enabling them to generate, accumulate, and send Bitcoin.
- 10 January 2009. Hal Finney (2009a) tweets two words: "Running bitcoin." Finney (2013) later recalled: "I carried on an email conversation with Satoshi over the next few days, mostly me reporting bugs and him fixing them."

Given this timeline, some have speculated that Satoshi Nakamoto is a pseudonym for some combination of Dai, Szabo, and Finney (who died in 2014). As Gwern (2011) has asked about the field of potential candidates, "how many genius libertarian cryptographers are there?" Szabo (2011) commented: "The overlap between cryptographic experts and libertarians who might sympathize with such a 'gold bug' idea is already rather small, since most cryptographic experts earn their living in academia and share its political biases. Even among this uncommon intersection as stated very few people thought it was a good idea." If Finney was Nakamoto, he was very coyly masking it by conducting sock-puppet online conversations with himself even before Bitcoin was up and running. Evidence from Nakamoto-Dai emails (Gwern 2017) provides persuasive evidence that Nakamoto was neither Dai nor Szabo.

- 12 January 2009: Nakamoto sends fifty Bitcoin to two Bitcoin addresses owned by Finney. This was merely a test of the system rather than a payment or a value transfer. At the time, and for nine months thereafter, Bitcoin had no observable market value. As Luther (2019, p. 195) notes, "There were no market exchange rates with existing monies and no known transactions of bitcoin for goods or services."
- 12 October 2009: In the first known exchange of Bitcoin for fiat currency, Martti Malmi, then a Finnish computer science student who

has been helping Nakamoto with improvements to the software, sends 5,050 Bitcoin, obtained by mining, to a fellow list member who uses the pseudonym "NewLibertyStandard" (NLS). Malmi (2014) would later report that he made the sale to NLS "to help him get the world's first bitcoin trading service started." NLS pays Malmi $5.02 via PayPal, pricing one Bitcoin at just below 0.1 US cent (Popper 2015).

- 19 November 2009: Nakamoto welcomes users to a new online Bitcoin forum, bitcointalk.org, set up by Martti Malmi to supersede bitcoin-list. Nakamoto will post there 575 times, mostly responding to suggestions for upgrades and bug fixes. He last posts there on 13 December 2010.

- 28 December 2009: NewLibertyStandard (2009) posts the following bid and offer pair on a page of his website:

  We Sell 1,578.76 Bitcoins for $1.00 USD Plus PayPal Transaction Fee.
  We Buy 1,578.78 Bitcoins for $1.00 USD Minus PayPal Transaction Fee.
  $100.00 USD Available
  15,100.00 Bitcoins Available.

The listing of USD and Bitcoin inventories means that NLS is a market-making dealer, not an exchange broker. The page explains that the posted dollars-per-Bitcoin exchange rate equals the estimated dollar electricity cost per Bitcoin mined by NLS's own home computer. Electricity cost does not determine the equilibrium market price of Bitcoin, because the quantity of Bitcoin released is pre-scheduled and is independent of the size of mining costs incurred. But even an arbitrary price called out by a market maker – what the general-equilibrium theorist Léon Walras (1954, p. 169) called a *prix crié au hasard* – can be a useful starting point for discovery of the market-clearing price. If there's an excess of demand over supply at that price, raise the price and try again. Fostering price discovery seems to have been NLS's objective, since the posted spread (possibly a typo) was too miniscule to turn a profit.

The NLS exchange rate page reports selling/buying rates dating back to 5 October. The rate varies, apparently due to variations in NLS's mining success. It does not report the volume of trades in either direction, but elsewhere NLS indicates that the volume is not zero.[10] While

---

[10] NewLibertyStandard (2010a): "I have had people buy bitcoins from me and sell bitcoins to me. Supply and demand, albeit only a small amount, already exists."

28 December is the earliest capture of the page by the Internet Archive Wayback Machine, the bid and offer listings presumably started on 5 October. The blockchain address (presumably NLS's) that received Malmi's 5,050 Bitcoin had previously received 700 Bitcoin on 6 October, although from whom and in exchange for what we don't know.[11]

- 15 January 2010. Bitcoin Talk user dwdollar announces his plan to launch a new exchange, The Bitcoin Market, "a real market where people will be able to buy and sell Bitcoins with each other." On 6 February he announces that a demonstration model is up, where those who register "will get 10 phoney [sic] dollars and 10,000 phoney [sic] bitcoins to trade." In subsequent discussion, dwdollar explains that his aim is to create "a market for buyers and sellers and a way to track demand versus the US Dollar," that is, to enable discovery of, and provide observability to, a market price of Bitcoin in dollars. On 16 March he announces that the market is open for real trading; on 17 March he announces that a first trade has occurred, though not its price or quantity.[12]

- 25 April 2010: Bitcoincharts.com registers a trade on The Bitcoin Market of 1000 Bitcoin for $3 (thus $0.003 per BTC).[13] The BTC daily closing price surpasses $0.01 for the first time on 12 July, which is also the second date on which the trading volume exceeds $100.

- 18 May 2010: Laszlo Hanyecz posts an offer to the Bitcoin Talk list to pay BTC 10,000, then worth about $45 on The Bitcoin Market, in exchange for two pizzas. On May 22 he reports having made the trade, receiving two large Papa John's pizzas. This is the first known purchase of goods using Bitcoin (Luther 2019, p. 195).

- 17 July 2010: Jed McCaleb, having read media coverage of Bitcoin, opens the MtGox Bitcoin/USD exchange, using a domain name he once used for trading "Magic: The Gathering Online" game cards (Gwern 2014).[14] In its first trade BTC20 are sold for $0.9902, about 5 cents per

---

[11] These transfers are viewable at www.blockchain.com/btc/address/1CBXL5tBSqJZyyCT WVkrLiQsKm4KULBfPA.

[12] https://bitcointalk.org/index.php?topic=20.msg100#msg100, https://bitcointalk.org/index .php?topic=20.msg265#msg265, https://bitcointalk.org/index.php?topic=20.msg671#msg 671, https://bitcointalk.org/index.php?topic=20.msg726#msg726.

[13] This is the earliest Bitcoin trade reported on bitcoincharts.com, https://bitcoincharts .com/charts/bcmPPUSD#czsg2010-01-01zeg2010-08-17ztgSzm1g1ozm2g25zv.

[14] MtGox (aka Mt. Gox) is a quasi-acronym for "'Magic: The Gathering Online' Exchange."

Bitcoin. The price of BTC rises above 10 cents on 14 September 2010, crashes to 1 cent on 8 October, then recovers (Moody 2020).

• 6 November 2010: Bitcoin reaches a price of $0.50 on MtGox, giving the stock of Bitcoin a value above $1 million (Luther 2019, p. 196). The MtGox exchange came to handle some 70 percent of Bitcoin trading volume before it closed due to insolvency in February 2014, having had a large number of Bitcoin stolen.

5.4 HOW BITCOIN ACQUIRED A POSITIVE MARKET PRICE

Most simply, Bitcoin acquired observable market value from some early-adopter enthusiasts who were willing to pay to acquire it. Economists (myself included) have sometimes struggled to understand why anyone would pay to acquire Bitcoin when it was not yet being used as a medium of exchange. The best short answer: Enthusiasts were willing to pay because they placed some positive probability on Bitcoin becoming useful as a medium of exchange and/or trading at a higher price at some future date. To the extent that early market demand for Bitcoin was based on anticipation of its future market value, we might say that the market price of Bitcoin picked itself up by its own bootstraps.

A real-life "bootstrap equilibrium" is surprising and puzzling if we try to understand Bitcoin along some familiar lines of monetary theory. The idea is an old one that a scarce fiat money has a positive purchasing power *assuming* that it serves as the only commonly accepted medium of exchange for an economy (Patinkin 1965), and that it alternatively has a zero value when the market rejects it as a medium of exchange (as demonstrated by the wheelbarrows full of worthless currency notes left behind after the German hyperinflation of the 1920s). Any potential fiat money thus has at least two equilibrium values, positive and zero. But there is no established theory of a bootstrapping process by which a potential asset *switches* from a zero to a positive value *in anticipation* of its use as a medium of exchange, or in anticipation of a future positive value (however grounded).[15]

A well-known backward-looking theory of how a new money can attain value (called "the regression theorem") was long ago provided by Ludwig von Mises (1980 [1912]), building on Carl Menger's account of the emergence of money from barter. Mises' account says that (a) any money's purchasing power today is determined by today's supply and

---

[15] On multiple equilibria in fiat money and in cryptocurrency see Berentsen and Schär (2018).

demand, (b) today's quantity demanded depends on its expected purchasing power per unit, and (c) today's purchasing-power expectation derives from its observed purchasing power on yesterday's market (McCulloch 2014). That is, an individual (and the market in the aggregate) chooses to hold a number of units of an intended medium of exchange that depends inversely on each unit's expected current purchasing power, and the process of forming the purchasing-power expectation refers back to previously observed purchasing power. By extension, a seller offered payment in a *new* medium of exchange (such as a new fiat currency) will refuse it without some observed basis (such as its use yesterday in redeemable form) for believing that he can use it successfully to buy from others.

Observation of earlier trades is certainly one basis for accepting a new money at a positive value. But Mises (2007) seemed to consider it the only logically conceivable basis, and to deny that any medium of exchange could be launched in an exclusively forward-looking way:

> The regression theorem establishes the fact that no good can be employed for the function of a medium of exchange which at the very beginning of its use for this purpose did not have exchange value on account of other employments. ... In this sense it says that there is a historical component in money's purchasing power.

He added: "Neither a buyer nor a seller could judge the value of a monetary unit if he had no information about its exchange value—its purchasing power—in the immediate past." But purchasing-power expectations can also be forward-looking. When they are, prior "exchange value on account of other employments" is not necessary. Alternatively put, that Alice chooses today to hold x units of good J as a medium of exchange (to be spent tomorrow) implies that Alice has an expectation of J's purchasing power tomorrow. But the expectation needn't rest (even if historically it typically or even always has rested) on observing J's purchasing power yesterday.

Mises's historical-component hypothesis accounts for a fiat currency's initial purchasing power when it is launched by suspension of redeemability for gold, by referring to market traders' nominal demand for money based on expectations of purchasing power extrapolated from the previous day's gold-redeemable currency.[16] The same logic applies

---

[16] J. R. Hicks (1935) commented that the historical component in Mises's theory makes the value of any fiat paper money the "ghost of gold." Note that when Mises' story explains the purchasing power of the newly fiat dollar by appealing to continuity with the purchasing power of yesterday's redeemable dollar it *takes for granted* that transactors think the latter is relevant to the successor fiat currency. But why do they? An explanation is needed.

to the launch of a new fiat money that is initially a redeemable claim for an established fiat money. The post-Soviet Lithuanian currency unit the talonas, for example, was introduced as a claim redeemable 1:1 for the Russian ruble. Once the public came to expect common acceptance of the talonas at a more or less predictable purchasing power against goods, redemption was ended and talonas-denominated notes and checks continued to be accepted. The historical-component hypothesis helps to explain why all governments that have successfully launched new fiat monies have in similar fashion first given them a fixed redemption value in terms of a commodity or an established fiat money (Selgin 1994). But while all irredeemable *government currencies* that have successfully launched have first had a fixed redemption value, Bitcoin has never been redeemable at a contractually fixed rate for another money or commodity.[17]

To explain Bitcoin's positive value as a medium of exchange along backward-looking Misesian lines, then, we would need to show that it already had "exchange value on account of other employments." But what employments would those have been?[18] Today Bitcoin is used as an investment or "store of value," but it had no such use before it achieved a positive market value. Fortunately, there is an alternative to positing that Bitcoin must have had another employment: We can allow forward-looking expectations to have played an enabling role. Thus Nick Szabo (2011) has justifiably complained about the "common argument coming ironically from libertarians who misinterpreted Menger's account of the origin of money as being the only way it could arise (rather than an account of how it could arise) and, in the same way misapplying Mises' regression theorem."

William Luther (2019, p. 189) helpfully distinguishes two views about how Bitcoin initially established a positive market value. (1) The "use-value view" attributes Bitcoin's initial positive value (like monetary gold's) to a valued non-monetary use, along Misesian lines. (2) The "coordination view" attributes the initial positive value to a group of early adopters who chose (with or without explicit collaboration) to buy Bitcoin in the anticipation that others would join in. The second view requires forward-looking expectations but does not require prior

---

[17] Luther and Sridhar (2021) further elaborate on the problems that the successful launch of Bitcoin creates for Mises' regression theorem, at least in its backward-looking version.

[18] One hypothesized use-value candidate is that early acquirers were willing to pay for Bitcoin simply because they liked what it stood for. But presumably people who liked what it stood for, a secure and privacy-protecting non-governmental medium of exchange, did not assign a zero probability to its *actually serving* as a medium of exchange in practice.

non-monetary use. Surveying messages posted to bitcoin-list, the online Bitcoin forum founded by Nakamoto, Luther finds that "early participants in the bitcoin community understood the importance of coordination and took steps to coordinate users." They talked almost exclusively about Bitcoin as a potential money, not as an innovation useful for something else nor as an ideological badge. They worried about how to achieve wider acceptance. Nakamoto suggested that Bitcoin might first develop a niche payment use where it would be more efficient than existing payment mechanisms (Luther 2019, p. 200). In Nakamoto's scenario, once a core group accepts Bitcoin in payment, new users who want to trade with them can be attracted and a Mengerian positive feedback loop of trade acceptance (monetary network effects) can begin.

5.5 WHAT WAS NAKAMOTO TRYING TO ACHIEVE, AND HOW WELL HAS BITCOIN ACHIEVED IT?[19]

While Bitcoin's rise to a market valuation of hundreds of billions of dollars is certainly a remarkable accomplishment, the founder had other aims. Nakamoto (2009b) emphasized three institutional problems with the status quo payment system that Bitcoin would address. First, inflation from central banks that issue fiat money:

The root problem with conventional currency is all the trust that's required to make it work. The central bank must be trusted not to debase the currency, but the history of fiat currencies is full of breaches of that trust.

Second, a lack of privacy and security from commercial banks (*"We have to trust them with our privacy"*). Third, the high cost of bank-mediated payments that made online micropayments infeasible.

Nakamoto wanted to create a currency with less risk of inflation and devaluation. It is of course true that the history of fiat currencies is full of breaches of trust in purchasing-power stability, as Chapter 4 noted. Bitcoin's source code, which predetermines the quantity path of the stock of Bitcoin units, solves that problem by ruling out any unexpectedly rapid expansion. The code provides a valuable object lesson in how to write a constitutional monetary rule that is fully automatic and free from discretion.

Nakamoto suggested that Bitcoin would behave like gold under a gold standard: "In this sense, it's more typical of a precious metal. Instead of the supply changing to keep the value the same, the supply is

---

[19] This section draws heavily on White (2018).

predetermined and the value changes." Chapter 6 will discuss the extent to which this comparison is accurate.

Bitcoin's fixed quantity path creates a different problem that inhibits its widespread use as currency. With the number of Bitcoins unresponsive to demand shifts, all the burden of adjustment to those shifts falls on the relative price (purchasing power). As a result, the market price of Bitcoin is enormously volatile week-to-week and even day-to-day. This makes it very risky to hold or accept BTC as a payment medium for monthly bills that are denominated in anything other than BTC (whether US dollars, other fiat currencies, or commodity index baskets).

Bitcoin is also risky over six-month and longer horizons. Between its November 2021 peak ($67,566) and its November 2022 trough ($15,709) Bitcoin's market price in dollars declined by more than three-quarters. A pseudonymous wag tweeted: "With inflation at 7.5%, you lose half your money in 9 years. The only way to outperform that consistently, that I have found, is crypto. Just this year I've already lost half my money" (rcm___. 2022). It is quite possible that they weren't exaggerating.

Nakamoto anticipated that Bitcoin's fixed supply path makes possible an enormous appreciation in its price:

As the number of users grows, the value per coin increases. It has the potential for a positive feedback loop; as users increase, the value goes up, which could attract more users to take advantage of the increasing value.

He seems not to have anticipated the problem of high-frequency volatility of price. He did not design Bitcoin to have an automatically demand-responsive supply because, he wrote, he did not know how to do it without creating the need for a trusted authority:

[I]ndeed there is nobody to act as central bank or federal reserve to adjust the money supply as the population of users grows. That would have required a trusted party to determine the value, because I don't know a way for software to know the real world value of things. If there was some clever way, or if we wanted to trust someone to actively manage the money supply to peg it to something, the rules could have been programmed for that.

What Satoshi didn't know how to do – create a software oracle that responds to data without human input – is still not known. The problem remains unsolved of how to feed a program with real-world data in a tamperproof way. Users who are willing to trust a party to "actively manage the money supply to peg it to something" now have stablecoins available. It remains a future challenge to create a programmed cryptocurrency with a supply that responds to demand so as to stabilize its purchasing power over goods and services, in the fashion of the gold standard but even more rapidly, rather than to stabilize its exchange rate with a fiat currency (ordinary stablecoins) or with demonetized gold (gold stablecoins).

Attracting investors who want an appreciating asset (and are willing to overlook short-term volatility) conflicts with attracting everyday medium-of-exchange users, who normally seek short-term predictability of purchasing power. The analysis of supply and demand provided below shows that fixed supply and its potential for rising price, which attracts long-term investors ("hodlers"), unfortunately brings with it the short-term price volatility that discourages the use of Bitcoin as a transaction medium.

5.6 TRANSACTIONS DEMAND FOR BITCOIN

We can personify the motives for holding Bitcoin by dividing Bitcoin holders into spenders and investors. The distinction is roughly between those who treat Bitcoin holdings as a checking account and those who treat Bitcoin as a retirement account or portfolio asset. Any real-world person can have a mix of the two motives, of course.

Bitcoin-denominated spending on goods remains very small relative to financial transacting (exchanges for other cryptocurrencies, fiat currencies, or financial claims), from all available indicators. But the exact volume of retail spending is unknowable. During December 2021, confirmed BTC transactions of all kinds averaged about 250,000 per day. The largest BTC retail payment processor, BitPay, reported only 67,423 cryptocurrency transactions that month, or about 2175 per day. Of those BitPay transactions, 58 percent were in Bitcoin, leaving us at about 0.5 percent of all BTC transactions. For comparison, Visa averaged 564 million retail transactions per day during the 12 months ending June 30, 2021.[20]

The BitPay service enables a purchaser who wants to spend BTC to buy from a retailer who wants to receive USD. For a $100 sale, BitPay calculates and receives from the purchaser BTC worth $100 plus exchange fees, and provides $99 to the retailer. The exchange-plus-invoicing service is akin to what Visa does when it provides dollars to a US retailer after a European tourist charges a purchase that will (together with interchange and foreign-transaction fees) be billed to the tourist's credit-card account

---

[20] Confirmed Transactions Per Day, www.blockchain.com/charts/n-transactions; Blockchain Payment Statistics, bitpay.com/stats/; Visa Fact Sheet, usa.visa.com/dam/VCOM/global/about-visa/documents/aboutvisafactsheet.pdf.

in euros. The largest category (44.46 percent) of items purchased using BitPay is gift cards, which are designed to be spent on final goods.[21] In a chain of transactions where a merchant (1) acquires Bitcoin by selling goods or services, then (2) exchanges the Bitcoin for a fiat-denominated instrument that is then (3) used to buy goods and services, Bitcoin and fiat both serve as media of exchange. By contrast, if the Bitcoin is neither acquired in sales nor spent on goods, but instead is acquired by currency exchange (fiat for Bitcoin), or by mining, only to be later exchanged for fiat, then BTC serves as an investment vehicle but not as a medium of exchange.

BitPay is not the only retail BTC payment processor. Cryptobuyer, based in Panama, has provided a similar service in Latin America since 2015. Its retail clients reportedly number 40,000 businesses (Frost 2020). Bitrefill.com, which focuses on selling fiat-denominated gift cards and phone card refills for cryptocurrency, reports (Bitrefill 2022) doing "several times" the transactions volume of BitPay.

Decentralized sales of goods and services directly for Bitcoin are, in the nature of the case, difficult to measure. The small-business software firm Skynova (2021) reported that a surprising 32 percent of respondents in its survey of 183 US small-business owners and 401 executives said that they currently accept payment in one or more cryptocurrencies (most commonly BTC [Bitcoin], BCH [Bitcoin Cash], or ETH [Ether]). What portion of their sales are made in crypto was not reported. Overstock. com was one of the first prominent online sellers to accept Bitcoin, but according to a *NY Times* reporter (Bernstein 2021) "Bitcoin isn't a very big source of Overstock's revenue." Of almost $2 billion in revenue during the first three quarters of 2021, cryptocurrency accounted for $30,000 to $50,000.

BTCPay Server, a provider of software enabling merchants to sell goods and services directly for Bitcoin, lists 130 businesses offering goods and services (excluding organizations seeking donations) in its January 2022 directory of participants (directory.btcpayserver.org). Coinpayments.net is a competing service that enables merchant sales and automated end-of-day exchanges of crypto revenues into fiat. Transaction volumes using these two services are known only to the merchants, however.

In November 2020, the popular fiat payment service PayPal added an option for its account-holders to buy, hold, and sell claims to four

---

[21] Granted, some individuals buy gift cards not as a step toward buying goods, but rather as a step in money laundering.

cryptoassets (Bitcoin, Ether, Litecoin, and Bitcoin Cash) on its plat-form.[22] In November 2021, it added "Checkout with Crypto." The "Checkout with Crypto" feature, its FAQ page[23] explains, enables US customers "to utilize their cryptocurrency holdings to pay for select online purchases with millions of online businesses." Pay indirectly, that is: "customers using Checkout with Crypto can now choose to check out safely and easily by converting cryptocurrency holdings to fiat currency at checkout, with certainty of value and no additional transaction fees." Here the phrase "no additional transaction fees" means no transaction fees beyond PayPal's ordinary fee for crypto purchases or sales, which slides between 1.5 percent for transactions above $1000, 2.3 percent for $25–100, and a flat 50 cents for $1–24.99.[24] In addition there is an exchange-rate spread below the current market bid price for Bitcoin, which reportedly (Newberry 2021) runs about 0.5 percent.

When a PayPal customer checks out with Bitcoin, then, the accepting merchant receives dollars (much as in a BitPay-mediated transaction). Paypal buys and offloads the customer's Bitcoin (either sells it or adds it to the balances of other customers who are concurrently buying PayPal Bitcoin balances). The charge for using the checkout service, as for the buying and holding service, includes the buy/sell transaction fees plus the exchange-rate spread. Note that the service does not allow a customer to add BTC acquired elsewhere to PayPal account balances directly. PayPal crypto balances can only be acquired by purchasing them with dollars on site. It is a "walled garden." The checkout service makes Bitcoin or other crypto balances at PayPal a closer substitute for a dollar check-ing account, although the total fees (minimum 4 percent) for parking transactions balances in a PayPal Bitcoin account (going USD-BTC-USD) will discourage using crypto balances for buying daily coffee or even pay-ing monthly rent. Thus far no data on the volume of "Checkout with Crypto" purchases is available, but the service bears watching as an indi-cator of medium-of-exchange use of cryptocurrencies.

A second layer for Bitcoin-denominated payments, Lightning Network, first launched in 2018. Parties open a channel on the network to make BTC transactions (in both directions) off the blockchain, which enables transactions that are cheap enough to be used for small-value

---

[22] PayPal competitor Cash App similarly enables buying, selling, and holding Bitcoin, with the additional feature of allowing the transfer of BTC to a third-party wallet.

[23] www.paypal.com/us/smarthelp/article/how-to-use-crypto-at-checkout-faq4477.

[24] www.paypal.com/us/smarthelp/article/how-to-use-crypto-at-checkout-faq4477; www .paypal.com/us/webapps/mpp/paypal-fees.

transactions. When participants close a channel, net changes in BTC positions are made on the blockchain. The value of funds currently committed to open channels was running about $96 million, or 0.02 percent of all BTC, in October 2022, according to 1ml.com/statistics. Studies by Arcane Research indicate that the payment volume actually sent on the Lightning Network in February 2022 was about 800,000 transactions, worth in total only about $20 million (LeClair and Rule 2022).

The core constituency for transactions use of Bitcoin are not ordinary shoppers in developed economies, but people who want to make private and censorship-resistant payments or donations. Bitcoin provides greater privacy by enabling users to route transactions outside today's regulated banking rails, where "Know Your Customer" and "Anti-Money-Laundering" rules require banks to report certain kinds of account activity to the authorities, and where authorities sometimes block payments to or from disfavored individuals or groups. Successfully routing Bitcoin around government censorship, however, requires peer-to-peer transfers. In February 2022 the government of the province of Ontario obtained a court order restraining Canadian banks and other intermediaries from disbursing dollars donated via a crowdfunding site to two groups supporting truckers who were protesting – in an illegal fashion, the government said – in Ottawa. In response, protest organizers "touted the cryptocurrency Bitcoin as another way to generate funds for protesters and avoid other potential fundraising shutdowns" (Taylor 2022). Canadian Bitcoin exchanges, however, would not disburse the crowdsourced funds for fear of risking a similar court order. The effort to support the truckers with Bitcoin failed because the centralized exchanges were a choke point (Koning 2022).

Bitcoin also allows people to protect their savings from exchange controls and account confiscations. For example, during a 2013 banking crisis in Cyprus, buying Bitcoin offered account-holders a way to escape from government limit on international bank transfers and from a proposed government plan to expropriate 6.75 percent of all bank balances (Bustillos 2013).

However, the way Bitcoin's distributed ledger system shares sender and recipient addresses and size information about every transaction provides less privacy than would a design sharing less information. Bitcoin ownership is not anonymous, only pseudonymous, and pseudonyms have sometimes been pierced when owners have been insufficiently cautious. This limitation has inspired a number of "privacy coin" projects that reveal less information. The best-known up-and-running projects are Monero and Zcash. It also inspired Tornado Cash, a service that provides privacy by hiding the link between a sender and a recipient of the cryptocurrency Ether. In August 2022 the United States Treasury sanctioned Tornado Cash on allegations of facilitating money laundering. The legality of the Treasury's action has been challenged (Wright 2022).

Bitcoin's niche medium-of-exchange role is small in comparison to – and as J. P. Koning (2019) has argued, is kept small by – its popularity as a speculative investment and its resultant purchasing-power volatility. Ordinary transactors prefer a more stable-valued medium of exchange, and Bitcoin investors don't want to miss a possible run-up in price by spending their tokens. As a result, "the promise of mainstream bitcoin payments" remains unfulfilled. Bitcoin's "game-based engine" limits Bitcoin payments to "the niche role that they currently occupy." Bitcoin investor-celebrity Tyler Winklevoss, who with his brother paid for a $500,000 Virgin Galactic space jaunt in 2014 by selling Bitcoin that would have grown into millions of dollars' worth had they kept it, has summarized the lesson he learned (Bernstein 2021): "Spend cash, invest in Bitcoin. Cash is trash."

In addition, Koning (2020) notes, fees for transfers on the Bitcoin blockchain are higher than fees (often zero) for ordinary dollar transfers between bank accounts. Those who place a high value on censorship-resistance are willing to pay blockchain fees for certain transactions, but most transactors today do not show a willingness to pay those fees for privacy in everyday transactions. The Lightning Network has lowered the price for Bitcoin-denominated transfers, but fees and inconvenience and purchasing-power risk remain. In addition to network transaction fees, a payment that the sender first converts from dollars to BTC, and that the recipient then converts back, incurs foreign-currency exchange fees twice.

The censorship-resistance of BTC payments comes from Bitcoin's pseudonymity (the blockchain identifies UTXO owners only by Bitcoin addresses) and from its payment network operating entirely outside of central banks. As John Cochrane (2017) has noted, putting speculative investment motives aside, "there is a perfectly rational demand for bitcoin as it is an excellent way to avoid both the beneficial and destructive attempts of governments to control economic activity and to grab wealth."

Avoiding government censorship or control raises the question of whether Bitcoin is especially attractive to people engaged in criminal transactions.[25] Studies by the firm Chainalysis (2022) have estimated that illicit use of cryptocurrencies is small, less than 1 percent of all crypto transactions volume in three of the last five years, and only 0.15 percent in 2021. This figure includes much-publicized ransomware attacks demanding payment in Bitcoin, financial scams, and thefts.

A feature of Bitcoin that discourages its use for illicit activity is that the Bitcoin blockchain provides a permanent public record of every transaction. Although the addresses are pseudonymous, Chainalysis and other forensic firms claim to be able to associate specific addresses with illegal activity.

5.7 INVESTMENT DEMAND FOR BITCOIN

In practice, while Bitcoin's value and trading volume have certainly grown dramatically since its early days, the growth has overwhelmingly been driven by people buying it as an investment or speculative asset, rather than by people accepting it as a medium of exchange. Observing the speculation, some economists have argued that the demand for Bitcoin rests largely on a "greater fool theory." Bitcoin being an asset that pays no dividends and has no redemption value, investors can realize a positive pecuniary return only by selling it at a higher price to someone else, a "greater fool." As Robert McCauley (2021) puts it, "Bitcoin is bought not as an income-earning asset but rather as a zero-coupon perpetual. ... The only way a holder of bitcoin can cash out is by a sale to someone else." Focusing on the greater-fool aspect of Bitcoin as an investment, while downplaying its actual and potential use as a medium of exchange, critics have applied a number of pejorative labels to Bitcoin, including:

- "pyramid scheme" (Grym 2021a, 2021b)
- "Ponzi scheme" (Stankiewicz 2021)
- "fundamental value of zero" (Hanke 2021), and
- "digital chain letter" (Koning 2019).

Let's consider each of these labels in turn.

A *pyramid scheme* is an organization that recruits individuals who pay to join, promising them a share of the money paid by later joiners whom they recruit. Aleksi Grym (2021b) asserted: "That's literally how bitcoin works." But that isn't *literally* how Bitcoin works. There is no

---

[25] From a non-paternalistic economics perspective, transactions that facilitate mutual gains from trade with no third-party harms are welfare-improving even if illegal ("victimless crimes").

organization that Bitcoin investors must pay to join. There are no incentive payments to individuals who recruit additional investors. There is a payoff from additional Bitcoin investors only in the sense that existing coins appreciate with additional demand. (In Bitcoin Twitter parlance, "number go up.") A charitable interpretation is that Grym simply meant to characterize Bitcoin investments as resting on a greater fool theory.

A *Ponzi scheme*, as run by Charles Ponzi or Bernie Madoff, is a fraudulent intermediary that attracts clients' funds with promises of steady above-market returns. Early clients are paid using funds received from later-joining clients. The scheme collapses when attempts to withdraw reveal that liabilities exceed assets. This kind of arrangement is also not *literally* how Bitcoin works. There is no Mr. Ponzi taking in money and pocketing the proceeds. There are no promises by Bitcoin to pay above-market returns. Bitcoin units are assets to the holders but nobody's liabilities. At most there is a rough similarity in the feature that high returns to early investors rely on growth in the pool of investors, that is, on greater fools.

The problem with relying on greater fools, of course, is that in a finite population the day must come when you run out of greater fools. Bitcoin's price cannot, for example, double each year forever because its market capitalization cannot exceed total global wealth. If there is *no* demand for Bitcoin other than by investors who expect it to keep outperforming other assets, an evident end to rapid appreciation will dampen demand and make the price crash. For Bitcoin to escape this scenario, there must be demand to hold it as a medium of exchange or a reasonable expectation of such demand in the foreseeable future.

Its price being supported neither by expected dividends nor by shared ownership of productive assets (like stock shares in a firm that pays no dividends), some critics versed in finance terminology assert that Bitcoin has *a fundamental value of zero*.[26] Any positive price, in excess of fundamental value, is correspondingly described as a "bubble." Economist Steve Hanke (2021), for example, has tweeted that "although we know Bitcoin's price, it's [sic] value is unknown & is probably ZERO." Here it should be noted that "probably zero" is not the same as "surely zero." If an asset's fundamental value is zero with less than 100 percent probability, then its expected value is positive. For example, Hal Finney (2009b) once offered on bitcoin-list "an amusing thought experiment" in

---

[26] To quote a standard definition: "In finance, the fundamental value of a security or derivative contract refers to the expected risk-adjusted present value of all cash flows or, more generally, all associated entitlements or obligations."

which Bitcoin replaces every fiat currency in the world (a scenario now known as "hyperbitcoinization"), which would give the stock of Bitcoin the value of all existing fiat currencies today combined. He estimated a value of $10 million per Bitcoin in that event, given its quantity limit of 21 million coins. (One can quibble with Finney's number, but it serves here merely as an illustration.) If we assign Bitcoin (to pick an arbitrary number) a 2 percent probability of reaching such a status (and a 98 percent chance of going to zero), then .02 × $10,000,000 = $200,000 is the expected future value per coin, and its fundamental value today would be $200,000 discounted back to the present at an appropriate discount rate. (Needless to say, the probability of a one-time historical event is not a measurable frequency but a subjectively assigned value.)

An analyst who personally assigns a zero probability to hyperbitcoinization may be tempted to claim that Bitcoin has a zero fundamental value. But such a claim overlooks two things. First, what matters is the *market's* (the marginal Bitcoin holder's) assignment of the probability, not the analyst's. Second, *some* part of Bitcoin's current market value plausibly derives from a demand to hold it as a niche censorship-resistant medium of exchange.[27]

Any would-be non-commodity money, fiat or crypto, has a zero price as a potential equilibrium value. Each person's demand to hold it as a medium of exchange depends on the belief that other people will accept it as medium of exchange. As economist David Andolfatto (2008, p. 1) has put it, "an asset may be valued not just for its intrinsic worth, but also for its expected ability to serve as a medium of exchange. In turn, this expectation may not rely entirely on the fact that the object in question is backed in some manner; rather, it may rely on a self-fulfilling expectation that others may believe the same thing." Such beliefs are self-reinforcing among a group of people when they converge on non-commodity B as a promising medium of exchange, and support a positive value for B. But if beliefs converge instead on potential medium C, then the equilibrium value of B is zero. (Here "non-commodity" means that it has no use other than as a medium of exchange.) If each individual expects *everyone else* to refuse Venezuelan bolivars, then each individual's best trading strategy is to refuse them. When all refuse, the bolivar's market value is zero. If *everyone* holding Bitcoin in hopes of its becoming a dominant global money were to switch their hopes to some alternative coin because they now consider that coin more likely to succeed, and likewise everyone switches to preferring

---

[27] See Luther (2019) for a simple model of a potential money's valuation that incorporates both medium-of-exchange value, subject to network effects, and non-monetary value.

alternative coins for current censorship-resistant payments, Bitcoin's market value would fall to zero. As Berentsen and Schär (2018, p. 9) write:

From monetary theory, we know that currencies with no intrinsic value have many equilibrium prices. One of them is always zero. If all market participants expect that Bitcoin will have no value in the future, then no one is willing to pay anything for it today.

Which is to say: Zero is a potential equilibrium value for Bitcoin *in exactly the same way* that it is a potential equilibrium value for any fiat currency.

J. P. Koning (2019) describes Bitcoin investment as "a new sort of financial betting game. It is a digital, global, highly-secure, and fairer version of the old-fashioned chain letter." A typical *chain letter* asks the recipient to send a sum of money to the person at the top of a list, then to send multiple copies of the same letter to others, modified to add his or her name to the bottom of the list and deleting the name at the top. If for example $10 is the amount to be sent, there are four names on the list, five copies are to be sent, and no subsequent recipient "breaks the chain," the sender will receive back ($10) × 5^4 = $6250. A chain letter is a kind of decentralized pyramid scheme whose initiator is obscure. Bitcoin is obviously not a literal chain letter, but is similar insofar as both are investments whose success relies on "greater fools."

Koning considers Bitcoin investment a "betting game" because "the current wave of buyers must guess when (or if) a subsequent wave of buyers will emerge .... If they guess right, the early birds win at the expense of the late ones." Because the guesses change with "fickle" crowd psychology, the price of Bitcoin "will always be jittery." This is not to say that Bitcoin is a social evil: "there is a demand as-such for financial games and bets," and "[c]ompared to many of the fly-by-night games out there, bitcoin provides a fair and trustworthy option."

Koning here overstates his case. While some Bitcoin buyers may be as cynical (or as naïve) as chain-letter participants, others are not. The typical chain letter encourages recipients not to "break the chain" to keep the cash rewards coming, but the letter has no social-change or economic reform agenda. A vocal share of Bitcoin investors, by contrast, promote Bitcoin on social media as a world-changer, a privacy-preserving, oppression-fighting, self-governing future global medium of exchange. Those who place a positive probability on Bitcoin becoming a worldwide common medium of exchange are not relying on "greater fools" to make their investment pay off. They see Bitcoin as having a fundamental value rooted in future payment network use.

5.8 THE SUPPLY OF BITCOIN

Nakamoto's source code contains a Bitcoin generation algorithm that governs the number of new Bitcoin units to be released with each block added to the chain. Initially the reward was BTC 50 per block, while now (and until March 2024) it is BTC 6.25. The reward per block has been cut in half three times, roughly every fourth year, events called "halvenings." The algorithm keeps the number of blocks produced per time period (6 per hour) close to constant. The expansion rate of Bitcoin has accordingly, and right on schedule, dropped since mining began, both absolutely (in new BTC per year) and even more in proportional growth (new BTC per existing BTC) per year. Figure 5.1 shows the declining expansion rate (in proportional growth rate terms) and the path of total Bitcoin in existence. As it shows by extrapolating into the future, the number of BTC released will never exceed 21 million. Nakamoto's chosen numerical parameters were arbitrary, but they govern only the nominal and not the real quantity (market cap) of Bitcoin. For any given real demand to hold Bitcoin, half as many BTC in circulation would mean twice the purchasing power per coin, leaving the market cap unchanged. Similarly, measuring carpet by the square meter rather by the square foot doesn't affect the real floor area that a given carpet covers.

The Bitcoin algorithm issues the newly released coins as block rewards, payments to nodes that win the race to mine particular blocks by being first to solve a proof-of-work problem.

When the price of Bitcoin is high, the real reward for mining blocks is high, which attracts more miners to the competition. Expenditures on electricity and equipment rise to eliminate any excess of expected reward over marginal cost. Thus the Bitcoin mining industry's electricity and other expenditures adjust at the margin to the expected market price, as determined by the intersection of demand and pre-programmed supply. A higher price of Bitcoin attracts more competition to receive the given block reward, bringing about an increase in the resources expended on mining. At a lower price, the resource expenditure is lower.[28]

The metaphorical description of people who run Bitcoin validation nodes as "miners" has given rise to the common misconception that "mining" activity increases the stock of Bitcoin in circulation just as gold mining increases the stock of above-ground gold. Recall that NLS offered to buy and sell Bitcoin at the average electricity cost per mined Bitcoin,

---

[28] On this profit-dissipation dynamic, and on contrasts between proof-of-work and alternative proof-of-stake validation systems, see Carter and Nuzzi (2021).

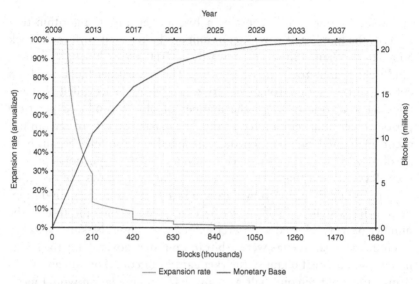

FIGURE 5.1 Nominal quantity of Bitcoin and its proportional expansion rate over time

which might suggest that production cost can proxy for the competitive equilibrium price of Bitcoin. That *would* be true if the supply curve for Bitcoin were flat. The cost of production determines the equilibrium price of any good where there are constant returns to production scale – a flat market supply curve at that price – so that the scale of demand determines quantity but not price. But that is not at all how Bitcoin supply works. The quantity of Bitcoin in existence on any date is governed entirely by the release schedule in the source code (minus any lost coins), *not at all by the volume of expenditures on mining.*

Because the market price of Bitcoin varies with the demand to hold it, both in the short and in the long run, and because supply is pre-determined, price does not follow the electricity cost of mining.[29] NewLibertyStandard (2010b) clearly understood that the equilibrium price of Bitcoin depends on demand, rightly declaring: "The value of a bitcoin is not based on the cost to produce a bitcoin but rather on whatever people are willing to pay for it."

Nakamoto's choice to pre-commit Bitcoin to a fixed quantity path may be understood as a way to assure holders of an irredeemable medium

---

[29] Statements to the effect that "Bitcoin is backed by the electricity used to mine it" or "Bitcoin is stored energy" express misunderstandings.

that its value would not be diluted in the future by surprise expansion in its quantity. Traditional private money, in the form of gold coins or banknotes, assured holders of their value by being naturally costly to produce, or by being redeemable for a scarce reserve money like gold or silver. Under the gold standard, a banknote was worth $20 when the bank of issue was credibly committed to pay a $20 gold coin for it. Redeemability is a buy-back guarantee. Leading stablecoins like Tether and USDC operate on a redeemability model. But because a buy-back guarantee requires a central pool of reserves to serve as a redemption fund, it is not an option for a decentralized or distributed system. The other two options are to be naturally costly to produce, or to have a quantitatively limited issuance.

The economist Ronald Coase (1972) analyzed the assurance problem in the general setting of a firm selling a durable good priced well above marginal cost.[30] Potential buyers will be reluctant to buy today if they worry that the firm will later sell at a lower price, which they know it can profitably do. To get more customers to pay $200 for a lithographic art print when the marginal paper-and-ink cost of producing another copy is $5, for example, an artist may want to convince them that she will not produce and sell unlimited copies for $100 after they buy. To credibly commit herself, the artist produces the print in a numbered edition with a stated maximum ("this print is #45/200"). The numbering provides an enforceable quantity commitment that she will issue no more than a fixed number of prints. Nakamoto creatively introduced this strategy to the field of digital assets. The limit on the number of Bitcoin units in the market is not guaranteed by any enforceable promise (there is no Bitcoin-issuing firm to enforce it on), but rather by a limit *programmed into* the Bitcoin system's open-source code and continuously verifiable on the system's publicly observable blockchain. Most later cryptocurrencies employ the same basic idea of a programmed quantity commitment verified through a public ledger.

Despite recognizing, many years before the introduction of Bitcoin, that a quantity commitment device could in principle solve the Coasean assurance problem for a free-market irredeemable money (White 1989), I did not foresee that the device could or would in practice be used to successfully launch a medium of exchange. But while Bitcoin exhibits niche use as a medium of exchange, it is not yet a *commonly accepted* medium of exchange. It has even lost one niche where

[30] This paragraph draws on White (2015).

it *was* the leading medium of exchange, namely in markets for other cryptoassets. Bitcoin's use in buying and selling "altcoins" – whose combined market cap now exceeds that of Bitcoin – has receded in recent years. That role has been taken over by Tether and other dollar-denominated stablecoins.

Thus a narrower prediction – that a quantity commitment is not a suitable way to create a *commonly accepted* medium of exchange – has not yet been falsified. The case for such a prediction is that a fixed quantity path in the face of volatile speculative demand creates so much purchasing-power volatility as to discourage all but a niche use as a transaction medium. This case will be further discussed in Chapter 6.

5.9 THE SUPPLY MEETS THE DEMAND FOR BITCOIN

The principal source of demand to hold Bitcoin today is speculation on its future value. A second source is use of BTC as a censorship-resistant transaction medium. For both uses, the demand to hold a certain real value in BTC at a point in time implies that the demand curve is a rectangular hyperbola in purchasing power / quantity space, like the stock monetary demand curve for gold seen in Chapter 2 or for fiat money seen in Chapter 4. At a higher price, proportionally fewer units need to be held to satisfy the demand for holding a certain real value. We combine such a demand curve with a vertical supply curve to illustrate in Figure 5.2 the determination of the purchasing power or market price of Bitcoin on a given day. The figure's snapshot of demand and supply doesn't capture movements in speculative demand, to be sure. In Figure 5.3 we see the impact of movement in the demand curve. Because the supply curve is vertical, the impact of demand shifts is entirely on price and not at all on quantity. In this respect purchasing-power volatility is baked into Bitcoin's design.

Measures of the volatility of Bitcoin's dollar price show it to be 3.5 to 9 times greater than the volatility of foreign fiat currencies, gold, or even the S&P 500 index (World Gold Council 2018, chart 2). According to the Bitcoin Volatility Index[31], the annual average of the thirty-day volatility of the BTC/USD price has averaged around 4.5 percent over the past four years (2018–21), while comparable figures for the price of gold average around 1.2 percent, and other major fiat currencies 0.5 percent and 1.0 percent. Bitcoin's price volatility is not due only to upward

---

[31] www.buybitcoinworldwide.com/volatility-index/.

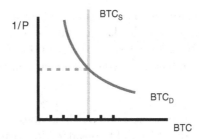

FIGURE 5.2 Supply and demand for Bitcoin determine the market-clearing price

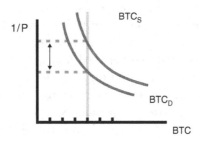

FIGURE 5.3 Variations in BTC demand cause variations in purchasing power, with no response in quantity supplied

movements. Bitcoin's price reached $41,900 on 8 January 2021 and happened to reach the same price one year later. In between, however, it went as low as $30,000 and as high as $67,500.

To consider the properties of Bitcoin *as a potential monetary standard*, we can treat the demand curve as representing an economy where Bitcoin speculative demand has faded away, and Bitcoin has become the commonly accepted medium of exchange. In such an economy, Bitcoin's release schedule plays the role of a monetary policy governed by a strict quantity rule. Unlike the "k percent" rule for ongoing annual money growth proposed by Milton Friedman (1960), where k is initially calibrated to the economy's real growth rate of output in the hope of producing zero inflation on average, Bitcoin's release schedule sets its expansion rate on a declining path toward zero. The scheduled expansion rate is around 1.8 percent per year for 2020–24, after which it will be cut in half for the next four years.

Purchasing-power volatility is baked into Bitcoin's vertical supply curve. If Bitcoin were only demanded as a medium of exchange and not at all as a speculative investment, then the volatility of the demand curve, and thus of purchasing power, would be lower than it is today. But because increased investment holding and not medium-of-exchange holding has been primarily responsible for the increase of Bitcoin's market capitalization over the last decade, it is not surprising that (contrary to predictions of a few years ago) no reduction in the volatility of Bitcoin's purchasing power has been seen with growth in its market cap.

Wei Dai (2013), whose design for b-money was intended to have a flat supply curve, was an early critic of Nakamoto's choice of a vertical supply curve. He wrote: "I would consider Bitcoin to have failed with regard to its monetary policy (because the policy causes high price volatility which imposes a heavy cost on its users, who have to either take undesirable risks or engage in costly hedging in order to use the currency)." A vertical supply curve means that changes in money demand induce no changes in quantity supplied, but instead cause unmitigated changes in purchasing power. On the other hand, in favor of Bitcoin's strict quantity commitment, it can be noted that the path of the stock of BTC is completely free from surprising exogenous changes, unlike the path of the stock of monetary gold under a gold standard (there were some surprising upward shifts in annual output, like the California gold rush) or the stock of fiat base money under a fiat standard (there has been unprecedented "quantitative easing" and other surprising changes in the rate of money growth). We will return to the choice between flat and vertical long-run supply curves in Chapter 6.

5.10 WHO BEARS THE COST OF OPERATING THE BITCOIN NETWORK?

Who bears the electricity and other costs of Bitcoin mining? Electricity and computer hardware bills are paid by miners. But miners need to cover their costs to stay in business, so they must receive compensation. Transactors pay fees to miners for including their transactions quickly in blocks (in effect, transactors pay to move toward the front of the processing queue), covering some of the cost.[32] In early 2022, miner fees per Bitcoin transaction mostly ran in the range of $1.20 to $2.70.[33] But fees are currently only a very small part of the cost-covering revenues to miners. The lion's share of revenue comes from block rewards. For example, a very lucky solo miner with a relatively

---

[32] The system brings to mind Steven Wright's one-liner: "I was arrested today for scalping low numbers at the deli. Sold number 3 for 28 bucks."

[33] https://ycharts.com/indicators/bitcoin_average_transaction_fee.

low-powered machine successfully mined a block on 11 January 2022 that earned a block reward of 6.25 BTC (then worth about $265,600) together with a fee reward of 0.10461270 BTC (then worth about $4,436).[34] More than 98 percent of his reward came in the form of newly released Bitcoin.

Who pays for block rewards? Bitcoin holders do. The payment is hidden, but nonetheless real. By contrast to a world in which block rewards are zero, and so miners receive only fees, block rewards expand the pool of BTC in circulation, diluting the purchasing power of each existing BTC unit (holding real demand constant). We can illustrate the dilution effect by shifting the supply curve rightward, as shown in Figure 5.4. Keeping real demand for Bitcoin constant means holding Bitcoin's market cap constant. With a constant market cap for BTC, dividing by a larger number of BTC units implies that the price per BTC unit is lower in an inverse proportion. For example, a 5 percent increase in circulating supply implies nearly a 5 percent drop in the price, or more precisely a 4.76 percent drop, given that 100/105 = 0.9524. Bitcoin's release schedule calls for the supply curve to shift rightward at a diminishing rate over time, and eventually to stop shifting, so that the costs of the network will in the long run be paid entirely by those who pay transaction fees.

Block rewards are a kind of non-coercive seigniorage: The burden is borne only by BTC holders, who have voluntarily opted in. Its size is completely pre-announced, and so presumably its effect is fully priced in. The burden is well hidden in that increases in the price of Bitcoin, at least until 2021, have far outweighed and obscured the dilution effect.

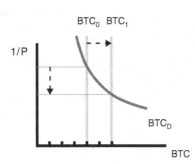

FIGURE 5.4 As the quantity of BTC grows, shifting the supply curve rightward, the price per unit falls proportionally, other things equal

[34] See Namcios (2022) and www.btc.com/btc/block/718124.

5.11 IS BITCOIN SOCIALLY WASTEFUL?

Building a bridge is costly: It takes labor and capital that have alternative uses. Does it follow that building it is a waste? No. Does it follow that building it is worth doing? No again. Waste occurs when the cost incurred exceeds the benefit attained. Cost greater than zero does not imply cost greater than benefit. Nor does it imply that the cost must have been worth incurring: A mistake might have been made. A bridge to nowhere is wasteful. To know whether a particular bridge is worth building we need to compare benefit to cost.

The same considerations apply to Bitcoin. It is a *non sequitur* to leap to the conclusion, without considering its benefits, that because "the Bitcoin network comes with a large energy hunger due to its reliance on proof-of-work" it therefore "wastes power" (Bindseil, Papsdorf, and Schaaf 2022, p. 4). It is still an error if stated in a comparative fashion like: "Bitcoin is wasteful because the proof-of-work method of processing transactions uses more energy per transaction than alternative methods like proof-of-stake or like the status quo banking system. All the extra energy spent by Bitcoin is wasted." To avoid rushing prematurely to judgment we need to consider the marginal benefits, the value of the additional system security and other features that can be attributed to the proof-of-work protocol. To say that the proof-of-work method is wasteful simply because it uses more energy is to suppose that it provides zero benefits (no privacy, no security, no greater credibility of the quantity limit) over a payment system run by shareholders, such that Nakamoto's innovation was pointless.

Rather than deferring to third-party judgments about the balance of benefits and costs, we should first ask: Whose evaluation of costs and benefits matters? None of us has access to a god-like perspective. What economists can observe is market prices and transaction quantities. A free-enterprise economy leaves judgments about whether the benefits of an activity exceed its costs to people who actually bear the costs. In the case of Bitcoin, as explained earlier, the electricity bills for proof of work are ultimately paid by Bitcoin users, just as costs of production for bread and milk are covered by buyers of bread and milk. The default presumption of standard Paretian welfare economics is that under the force of competition the market for a private good like Bitcoin (or any other cryptoasset) tends toward efficient operation. To rebut that presumption, a benevolent would-be increaser of net social benefits needs to meet a burden of proof before restricting mutually beneficial trades. Evidence is needed to show that Bitcoin production is harming non-users in ways that violate their property rights or, as economists (e.g. Bindseil, Papsdorf, and Schaaf 2022, p. 2) put it, that Bitcoin imposes significant negative externalities.

The fact that the Bitcoin network uses electricity does not provide the requisite evidence. Hospitals use electricity, as do school buses and airplanes. Virtually every industry uses electricity to produce its output. Bitcoin is not exceptional in that regard. It is true that Bitcoin's demand for electricity contributes somewhat to total demand and thereby to determining the price of electricity. The greater is Bitcoin's electricity use, the higher is the price of electricity. But that is equally true for every other electricity-using industry. The spillover effect of additional electricity demand on the price of electricity is, in technical economic terms, merely a *pecuniary* externality (transmitted through the price system) and not a *technological* externality (transmitted outside the price system, like pollution). Raising the price of electricity is not a source of inefficiency. Prices changes are necessary for the market to regain efficiency in the face of supply or demand shifts. It does not interfere with anyone's use and enjoyment of his property. It is not the kind of negative externality we should worry about.

An understandable concern about electricity use, from any industry, is that additional electricity generation generates significant negative externalities in the form of additional carbon dioxide and other emissions. *If* it were known what the economic costs of marginal carbon emissions are, one standard ("Pigovian") remedy would be to impose an appropriately sized tax on emissions, thereby "internalizing the externality" by bringing the cost to bear on energy producers.[35] An alternative ("Coasean") remedy would be to cap carbon dioxide emissions and allow trading of emission permits. But note that the case for a tax or a cap on emission is not a case for banning any particular electricity-using activity. To allow the economy produce the highest-valued mix of outputs, we must allow producers who have the highest-valued uses for electricity (that is, produce the outputs per dollar's-worth of electricity for which consumers are willing to pay the most) to bid kilowatt-hours away from others.

Some Bitcoin proponents emphasize that Bitcoin mining operations are able to locate wherever electricity can be produced at least cost (natural gas fields where excess gas would otherwise be burned off, remote

---

[35] For the argument that correct price tags for technological externalities are inherently unknowable, because (lacking excludability) individual consumers cannot reveal their willingness to pay for remediation, see White (2012, p. 353).

hydroelectric plants). While this ability reduces the cost of Bitcoin's total electricity consumption compared to the counterfactual of using only high-cost electricity, it does not eliminate the cost or turn it into a benefit. Other Bitcoin proponents applaud the fact that the Bitcoin mining industry consumes a higher proportion of renewable or sustainable energy than other industries. But that energy could have been used elsewhere. When Bitcoin mining stimulates investment in new electricity generating facilities, building them remains a costly use of resources and not a benefit, even if the new facilities burn no fossil fuel and emit no carbon. Still other proponents note that Bitcoin miners can help to smooth the demand for electricity from the grid by contractually agreeing up front with the electricity provider that they will turn off their operations at times of peak electricity demand. This too means that Bitcoin mining is less costly than otherwise, not that it isn't costly.

On the other side, critics who declare that Bitcoin is "worthless," despite users' willingness to pay for it, signal that they disrespect consumers' valuations, and arbitrarily invoke their own personal valuations – just as they would if they declared that hospitals, school buses, or airplanes are worthless. Sometimes the invocation of the critic's personal preferences is clear, as for example when a critic says that "Bitcoin is merely a gambling game, so there are no social benefits to offset its costs, only transfers." Absent fraud, people who freely choose to gamble at casinos or participate in lotteries benefit from the choice in the sense that they chose gambling over other forms of entertainment. Of course, most Bitcoin investors don't think that the odds of coming out ahead are stacked against them the way the odds in casino games and lotteries are, but the contrary. Their risk-taking attitude is more like that of an investor who thinks a particular stock is likely to outperform the market. Thus Vijay Boyapati (2018), author of "The Bullish Case for Bitcoin," calls investing in Bitcoin an "asymmetric bet." They think that there's at least a good chance that the purchasing power of Bitcoin will continue to rise as the medium-of-exchange use of Bitcoin spreads, perhaps to the point of hyperbitcoinization. They may be overestimating the likelihood of that outcome (my own view is that the volatility of Bitcoin's purchasing power makes its widespread use as a medium of exchange very unlikely), but only time will tell.

At the pessimistic extreme, Bindseil, Papsdorf, and Schaaf (2022, p. 2) forecast that the use and the price of Bitcoin will collapse, and that as a result "the net welfare effects of Bitcoin over its life cycle will have been significantly negative." Their forecast clearly clashes with the forecasts of Bitcoin holders, not to mention the forecasts of venture capitalists and entrepreneurs who are investing large sums in ancillary products to facilitate Bitcoin use. None of us yet knows what the future transaction use and price will be. Meanwhile, the Efficient Markets Hypothesis suggests that the best point estimate of the discounted future price of Bitcoin is the current price.

5.12 CRYPTOCURRENCY MARKETS ARE AN ONGOING DISCOVERY PROCESS

On a historical scale, Bitcoin and other cryptocurrencies have existed only very briefly. The market has hardly settled into a long-run equilibrium. The warning that Nick Szabo (2011) issued soon after Bitcoin's launch remains relevant: "There remain many open questions and arguable points about these kinds of technologies and currencies, many of which can only be settled by actually fielding them and seeing how they work in practice, both in economic and security terms." Gwern (2011) has noted that among early objections to the Bitcoin program were the views that it was "bizarre" to have a fixed quantity path, and "inelegant" to have a mining system that gave "such a blatant bribe to early adopters."

As already noted, Wei Dai (2013) regretted Bitcoin's "deficient monetary policy and associated price volatility." He worried that, because of this feature, "it can't grow to very large scales, and by taking over the cryptocurrency niche, it has precluded a future where a cryptocurrency does grow to very large scales." The counter-argument can be made that the fixed quantity path, together with other choices, helped to attract a support community, a critical mass of investors that has enabled Bitcoin take off and even prosper as an investment asset. But as for growing into a commonly accepted medium of exchange, Dai has a point.

To compete with Bitcoin, later cryptoassets have tried to improve on its design. They have promised greater transaction speed (Litecoin and most others), greater security against potential collusion ("51-percent attacks") by miners, greater user anonymity (privacy coins), and greater utility as smart-contract and defi platforms (Ethereum, Solana, and others). Achieving a critical mass of users is presumably more difficult for latecomers than it has been for Bitcoin. And yet today, even while Bitcoin's market cap has grown remarkably, alternative coins have captured more than half of total crypto market capitalization.[36]

---

[36] Before 2017, Bitcoin consistently accounted for more than 80 percent of total crypto market capitalization, as reported by Coinmarketcap.com. By late 2021 its share had fallen to the range of 40 to 45 percent.

A relatively recent development has been the spread of fiat or BTC-denominated "stablecoins," crypto tokens whose value is pegged to the US dollar or another fiat currency. Like Bitcoin they provide a way to route payments around central bank settlement systems. But like DigiCash, dollar-denominated stablecoins do not offer an alternative to fiat standards, only a new type of dollar-denominated payment instrument. Because the US dollar has a much more stable purchasing power than Bitcoin, dollar stablecoins have grown in popularity as crypto media of exchange. They have displaced Bitcoin from its previous role as the common medium for buying other cryptoassets. Recently BitPay reported (Nagarajan 2022) that the stablecoins have grown to 13 percent of the retail crypto payments it processes, at the expense of Bitcoin's share (down to 65 percent). Again, Bitcoin's relative volatility is an obstacle to its achieving greater use as a medium of exchange.

6

Comparing and Contrasting Gold and Bitcoin Standards

When commentators compare Bitcoin to gold, they usually aim to rank them as alternative portfolio assets. For example, "Bitcoin is increasingly set to replace gold as a hedge against uncertainty," writes a *Cointelegraph* reporter (Valenzuela 2017). In this chapter, by contrast, we consider how a monetary system based on Bitcoin compares to a monetary system based on gold. In what important respects are a Bitcoin standard and a gold standard similar? In what important respects are they different?[1]

Bitcoin is similar to a gold standard in at least two ways. (1) Both Bitcoin and gold are stateless, so either can provide an international reserve money that is not controlled by any national central bank or finance ministry. (2) Both provide a base money that is reliably limited in quantity. Bitcoin's programmed rather than natural scarcity is the basis for George Selgin's (2015) characterization of Bitcoin as a "synthetic commodity money." Both Bitcoin and gold are unlike a fiat money that a central bank can issue in any quantity that it likes, as if out of thin air.

Bitcoin and gold are obviously different in other ways. Gold is a tangible physical commodity; bitcoin is a purely digital asset. This difference is not important for an individual's experience in paying them out. Ownership of (or a claim to) either asset can be transferred online, or at a point-of-sale by phone app or chip card. The "front ends" of the payments can look the same. The "back ends" are different. Gold payments can go from peer to peer without involvement of any trusted third party only when a physical coin or bar is handed over. Gold-redeemable

---

[1] The present section is based on White (2018a). Ammous (2018) also compares and contrasts gold and Bitcoin.

banknotes or checks, or online gold payments, require a bank or other trusted vault-keeping intermediary. Bitcoin payments operate on a distributed ledger and can go electronically from peer to peer without the help of a financial institution, even though in practice many Bitcoin holders use the custodial services of exchanges like Coinbase or Binance.

6.1 CONTRASTING SUPPLY MECHANISMS CREATE DIFFERENCES IN PURCHASING-POWER VOLATILITY

The most important difference between Bitcoin and gold as monetary standards lies in their contrasting supply mechanisms, which give them very different degrees of purchasing power stability.[2] As spelled out in Chapter 2, even in the short run (without any change in the rate of mining output) the supply curve for monetary gold is not vertical. A nontransitory increase in monetary demand for gold will bring an increase in the quantity of gold supplied, via some conversion of non-monetary into monetary gold stocks, which dampens movements in the purchasing power of money by contrast to the zero response of the quantity of Bitcoin. An incipient rise in the purchasing power of gold incentivizes owners of non-monetary gold items (jewelry and candlesticks) to melt some of them down and monetize them (assuming open mints) in response to the rising opportunity cost of holding them.

Even when there is no significant change in the purchasing power of gold, the stock of gold above ground is slowly augmented each year by gold mines around the world. This is somewhat similar to the programmed growth in the stock of Bitcoin before 2140. A crucial difference – to be elaborated in the following text – is that the annual rate of gold production is not predetermined but responds to, *and stabilizes*, the purchasing power of gold. The rate of Bitcoin creation, by contrast, is entirely programmed. It does not respond to or act to stabilize Bitcoin's purchasing power.

When rising money demand begins to raise the purchasing power of gold rise above its marginal cost of production, the profit motive pushes owners of existing mines to increase annual output, and incentivizes prospectors to find and open new mines, until the purchasing

---

[2] In saying this, we assume that the demand for a base money does not depend importantly on its material or immaterial nature. Quantity demanded will of course depend on the realized volatility of a money's purchasing power, but differences in volatility come from differences in supply mechanisms.

power of gold returns to trend. Call this the *induced variation* in the rate of production of gold. Induced variation makes the purchasing power of gold mean-reverting over the long run, a pattern clearly evident in the historical record of the gold standard (see Figures 3.1 and 3.2). The self-correcting process has produced a near-zero secular rate of inflation in gold standard countries. There is no guarantee that the marginal cost of gold production remains constant forever, of course. Recent developments like environmental restrictions on mine expansions and new mine openings appear to be increasing the marginal cost of mining gold over time, which implies a rising purchasing power of gold over time.

A rise in the purchasing power of BTC due to increased demand, by contrast, does not provoke any change in the quantity of BTC in the short run or in the long run. The quantity to be released is pre-determined by the source code. The supply curve for BTC is always vertical.

We can illustrate the contrast between supply mechanisms by putting the supply and demand diagrams from Chapters 2 and 5 side by side in Figures 6.1 and 6.2. In the Bitcoin diagram, we assume full monetization of Bitcoin, and in the gold diagram, we assume full monetization of gold.

Because the BTC supply curve is vertical, while the short-run supply curve for monetary gold is not, a given shift in money demand, up or down, brings more variation in the purchasing power of bitcoin than in the purchasing power of gold.

In the long run, the BTC supply curve is still vertical. Bitcoin "mining" activity increases with an increase in price, but not the quantity produced (as governed by the programmed release schedule). The long-run monetary gold supply curve, which takes into account the induced variation in gold production and the accumulation of greater mining volume until the price returns to the long-run marginal cost of production, is nearly flat. As a result, the short-run rise in the purchasing power of gold is nearly reversed in long run (perhaps twenty to thirty years) by increased mine output. Bitcoin's purchasing power remains volatile, while gold's is mean-reverting.

Long-run purchasing-power stabilization by induced supply is reinforced and sped up by the expectations of the public that this is how the system works in response to demand shocks. If financial markets expect mean-reversion in the purchasing power of gold, speculation will dampen even short-run swings in the ppg. When gold's purchasing power falls below trend, but is expected to appreciate and return to trend, the smart move is to hold more now. Conversely, because Bitcoin's purchasing

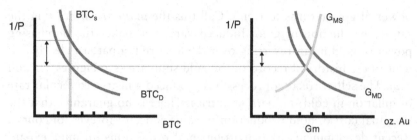

FIGURE 6.1 In response to a given shift in the demand for money, the purchasing power of Bitcoin under a Bitcoin standard varies more in the short run than the purchasing power of gold under a gold standard

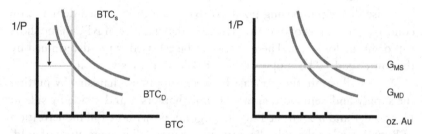

FIGURE 6.2 In response to a given shift in the demand for money, the purchasing power of Bitcoin under a Bitcoin standard varies *much* more in the long run than the purchasing power of gold under a gold standard

power has no mean-reverting tendency, but is something like a random walk, there are no expectations of reversion to dampen volatility.[3]

Historically, under the classical gold standard, gradual changes in the world stock of monetary gold came about every year from normal mining. Uninduced gold strikes like the California gold rush brought about changes in the *expansion rate* (not immediately the level) of the stock. Even in the most impactful case, the California and Australian gold rushes in the decade after 1849, the changes in the expansion rate were smaller than changes in the postwar expansion rates of fiat monies. The California and Australian gold rushes together, according to Rockoff's figures, created only 6.39 percent annual growth in the world stock of gold during the decade 1849–1859, resulting in less than 1.5 percent annual inflation in gold-standard countries over that decade. By comparison, the average monetary gold stock expansion rate over 1807–1919 inclusive was about 2.3 percent. As noted in Chapter 2, the growth of

[3] I am indebted to Cameron Harwick for this observation.

monetary gold stocks over longer periods tended to match the rate of growth of real output, and not accidentally rose with faster real output growth after 1870.

As often as not, the changes in gold stock growth rates were equilibrating, speeding the return of the purchasing power of gold to trend from above trend or below trend. As Hugh Rockoff (1984) noted, some important gold strikes (like the Klondike in the 1890s) and some important technical breakthroughs (like the cyanide process of 1887) were induced by the high purchasing power of gold at the time, which gave added incentive for prospecting and research. They provide examples of the greater elasticity (ppg responsiveness) of the monetary gold stock in the long run than in the short run.

Because its quantity is pre-programmed, the stock of BTC is completely free from supply shocks, unlike that of monetary gold in the nineteenth century. The potential for major gold strikes in the twenty-first century is small, given that the globe has now been geologically mapped nearly exhaustively. Profitable gold mining of asteroids is unlikely in the next fifty years, given its enormous expense.

When economist John Cochrane (2017) writes that Bitcoin is "an electronic version of gold, and the price variation should be a warning to economists who long for a return to gold," he errs by neglecting the contrast between the long-run mean-reverting character of the purchasing power of gold, due to induced variation in mining, and the absence of that feature from Bitcoin. He also neglects the dampening of short-run volatility from the fact that the short-run supply curve of monetary gold, unlike Bitcoin, is not vertical. The perfectly inelastic supply mechanism that produces purchasing-power volatility in Bitcoin is not informative about the long-run behavior of the purchasing power of gold under a gold standard with very elastic long-run gold supply.

With respect to the goal of providing a money with stable purchasing power, we can contrast the supply mechanisms of bitcoin, gold, and fiat standards in the following way. A Bitcoin standard has the advantage that the Bitcoin supply curve does not shift, but the disadvantage that the supply curve is vertical in both the short run and the long run, implying unstable purchasing power in the face of money demand variations. A gold standard has the advantage that the global stock supply curve for monetary gold is non-vertical in the short run and nearly horizontal in the long run, providing responses in the quantity that stabilize the purchasing power of gold, but the disadvantage that the supply curve can occasionally shift. A fiat standard has the *potential* advantage that its supply can be deliberately managed to stabilize the price level both in the short run and in the long run, but the disadvantage that has seldom been managed that way in practice, due to the incentives that accompany government control over the quantity of money.

6.2 WILL BITCOIN'S PURCHASING-POWER VOLATILITY BE NO GREATER THAN GOLD'S UNDER FULL MONETIZATION?

Bitcoin advocates sometimes argue that Bitcoin's purchasing-power volatility is a transitory phenomenon that will disappear with the full monetization of Bitcoin. The above figures, which assume full monetization, show that this argument is incorrect, at least when judging purchasing-power volatility by comparison to a gold standard. Vijay Boyapati (2018) has written:

> When Bitcoin achieves the market capitalization of gold, it will display a similar level of volatility. As Bitcoin surpasses the market capitalization of gold, its volatility will decrease to a level that will make it suitable as a widely used medium of exchange.

In fact, as its market capitalization has grown over the years, Bitcoin's volatility has not declined. And there is no reason to think that volatility would decline merely on account of higher market capitalization. Higher market capitalization does not change the perfect unresponsiveness of the quantity of Bitcoin to changes in its purchasing power. Nor does it change the volatility of demand to hold Bitcoin as an investment asset. Only if fickle investment demand is supplanted by stable transaction demand can we expect a decline in the volatility of Bitcoin demand and thereby in the volatility of purchasing power.

It is defensible, then to argue that Bitcoin's purchasing power would become less volatile if the demand to hold Bitcoin as a medium of exchange were to grow relative to demand to hold it as an investment. Transactions demand for money is more stable than speculative demand for a financial asset, so demand curve shifts would be smaller. In the limit, in a hyperbitcoinized scenario where Bitcoin is the world's money (and no longer a speculative asset), the demand for Bitcoin would presumably be as stable as the demand for gold was when gold was the world's money (and not yet demonetized into a speculative asset). This makes sense as an other-things-equal proposition about equal stability of *demand*. Purchasing-power stability equal to that of gold does not follow, however, because the supply curve for monetary gold is less vertical than the supply curve for Bitcoin. As illustrated in Figure 6.1, gold's purchasing power variation is less in response to any given money demand shock.

As a result of the long-run price-elasticity of gold supply combined with the rarity of large supply shocks, the purchasing power of gold under the classical gold standard was reasonably predictable over 10+ year horizons. It was more predictable to make a concrete comparison than the purchasing power of the post–Second World War fiat dollar has been (Selgin, Lastrapes, and White 2012). We do not have any historical track record of a Bitcoin standard for comparison, but demonetized gold has been much less volatile in purchasing power than not-yet-monetized Bitcoin. As emphasized, Bitcoin lacks any stabilizing response of supply to a rise or fall in purchasing power due to demand shocks. There is no mean-reversion to be expected in the purchasing power of BTC. Even supposing that Bitcoin becomes money, its purchasing power would remain subject to greater short-run instability and to greater drift over time. It would be harder to predict at any horizon.

6.3 LEGAL OBSTACLES TO MONETIZATION OF BITCOIN AND GOLD

Why aren't Bitcoin and gold used more widely as media of exchange today? We can divide the obstacles they face into market challenges (discussed in Section 6.4), and legal and tax challenges (discussed in this section).

According to a report by the Library of Congress (2021, p. 3), cryptocurrency use is outright banned by the governments of nine nations (including China, where Bitcoin mining was banned in 2021) and "implicitly banned" by forty-two. Examples of "implicit bans" are rules against financial institutions serving crypto businesses and prohibitions of domestic crypto exchanges. Taxes and "Know Your Customer/Anti Money Laundering" (KYC/AML) restrictions are applied to cryptocurrencies in 109 nations. The second and third numbers have significantly increased since 2018. Governments may be unable to detect and punish people who quietly purchase and sell Bitcoin peer-to-peer, not using public exchanges, and even people who quietly mine Bitcoin, as reports from China show (Sigalos 2021). But outright and implicit bans that make it impossible for exchanges and other services to advertise openly that they sell Bitcoin, or for businesses to advertise openly that they accept it in payment, can succeed in minimizing transaction use by driving Bitcoin use underground.

Gold mining is a heavily regulated business everywhere, with licensing requirements, environmental and safety rules, and tax or royalty obligations. Legal restrictions against the use of gold (or claims to gold) as a medium of exchange are mostly of the implicit kind. Hand-to-hand transactions with physical gold coins being inconvenient for most purposes and impossible for online business, the widespread use of gold as a medium of exchange historically rested on and today requires the use of conveniently transferable bank or warehouse claims denominated in gold. Gold-based banking is implicitly barred by bank licensing requirements. Gold money warehousing with transferable claims is theoretically legal in the United States, but faces KYC/AML reporting and money-transmitter licensing requirements, as the proprietor of E-Gold found out the hard way when shut down by the US Treasury (White 2014).

In the United States, Bitcoin (and other cryptoassets) and gold holdings are subject to capital gains taxes. Both are treated as non-cash capital assets, like stock shares. All purchases and sales are to be reported to the Internal Revenue Service (IRS) on Form 8949. Using BTC or gold as a transaction medium thus carries two burdens: The financial burden of the capital gains tax, and the paperwork burden of recording the price and quantity of each acquisition (which counts as an asset purchase) and each spend (which counts as an asset sale) and figuring the capital gain realized with each spend. For Bitcoin held with an intermediary like PayPal or Coinbase, the intermediary will track transactions and compute the customer's capital gain or loss each year. For Bitcoin held in a self-hosted wallet, the individual bears the burden of recording and reporting. Commercial tax software is available to help calculate the tax burden, but only after the acquisition and spend data are entered. These taxes discourage US taxpayers from using BTC or gold rather than the US dollar as a transaction medium.

IRS rules treat foreign fiat currencies more favorably than Bitcoin for ordinary transaction purposes. Although gains are taxed as income rather than capital gains, which usually means a higher tax rate, the IRS excludes personal foreign currency transactions of under $200 from income or capital gains taxation and its recording and reporting burdens (American Institute of CPAs 2018). To relieve taxpayers from a paperwork burden that generates little revenue, the American Institute of Certified Public Accountants reasonably recommends that for personal transactions "[t]he same exclusion should apply to virtual currencies even though they are considered property rather than foreign currency."

For anti-money-laundering purposes, Bitcoin is regulated like currency. Crypto exchanges must know their account-holders, just as banks must, and crypto exchanges must gather ID information from anyone who sells crypto for US dollars in any amount.[4] Buried in the Infrastructure Investment and Jobs Act passed in November 2021 are provisions that, Martha Belcher (2022) finds, place cryptocurrency use under even more surveillance than cash or bank account use. Any party who receives $10,000 worth of crypto must report the transaction and the identity of the spender to the IRS on form 8300, a provision that previously applied only to dollar currency transactions. In the case of crypto, Belcher notes, further information is revealed: "If the government knows the identity associated with a cryptocurrency wallet, then it knows the identity behind all transactions for that wallet, even when those transactions are far below $10,000."

Both gold payment businesses and Bitcoin exchange businesses are currently subject to KYC restrictions (George 2022). Account-holders may not be anonymous or pseudonymous, but must furnish government-approved ID. The government may ask to see the list of account-holders and any holder's account activity. Either type of payment business is potentially censorable – as fiat payment rails that run through central banks already are – by a government that requires the blacklisting of customers it disfavors.

Bitcoin transfers are *less* subject to censorship than fiat bank transfers are when BTC is transferred peer-to-peer pseudonymously, using "unhosted" wallets rather than by using an exchange or custodial intermediary that is legally forced to know its customers.[5] But the same is true of stablecoin transfers. Myanmar's opposition National Unity Government announced in December 2021 that it would begin accepting international donations in Tether USD to escape payment censorship by the military junta that controls the central bank. As a news report (Nikkei Asia 2022) noted: "Tether offers Myanmar citizens the advantage of being able to make transactions or remit money without having to worry about being monitored or obstructed by the authorities." Transfers of a

---

[4] Note that crypto "exchanges" do a lot more than act as venues for buyers and sellers to meet. They also custody crypto holdings, in effect taking deposits, on which they often pay interest. They make loans. Their deposit-transfer services relieve crypto depositors of the inconvenience of peer-to-peer coin transfers. I am indebted to Nic Carter for emphasizing this point.

[5] On privacy and legal issues surrounded custodial versus self-hosted wallets, see Pocher (2021).

gold stablecoin like Tether Gold or Pax Gold (PAXG) (discussed in the following text) are likewise less subject to censorship than interbank fiat transfers that run through central bank gateways.

It is true that, because gold stablecoins are basically account claims to vaulted gold, transfers require the issuer to debit one account balance and credit another, and the issuer can be required to impose KYC rules on account-holders in order to interact with regulated banks. Gold stablecoins can be transferred wallet-to-wallet just as Bitcoin can, but the wallets do not hold keys to pseudonymous addresses on a distributed ledger. Rather they hold claims to gold in the name of identified account-holders on a single vault ledger. In that sense, they are not as resistant as Bitcoin to censorship in the form of blacklisting of disfavored account-holders by a government that has power over the ledger-keeper. In the Myanmar case, however, the ruling junta has no power to censor stablecoin transfers. They proceed outside the central bank that the junta controls. Transfers of gold stablecoins can do the same.

Non-intermediated and ungated transfers include crypto swaps on decentralized currency exchanges or DEXs, where software automatically matches traders peer-to-peer.[6] The US financial regulatory authorities are not happy with financial activity outside their supervision. Attempts to impose supervision exhibit a cat-and-mouse dynamic. The firm ShapeShift operated a non-custodial crypto exchange in 2014–2018, meaning that it held no customer funds but only acted as a market-maker, and did not require identification from its users. Under "duress" from regulators, ShapeShift instituted KYC rules in 2018. When the rules drove away 95 percent of its customers, the firm responded by discontinuing its market-making role, instead connecting its customers to multiple DEXs, and dropping KYC (Foxley 2021). Trade on Uniswap, the largest DEX, grew so remarkably in 2020 and 2021 that its volume now rivals that of the largest centralized exchanges like Coinbase. In September 2021, the Securities and Exchange Commission launched an investigation into Uniswap (Osipovich 2021; Michaels and Osipovich 2021). Activity on a DEX, it should be noted, is limited to swaps of one cryptoasset for another, and unlike Coinbase or another centralized exchange does not allow dollar payouts to bank accounts. It does allow

[6] An alternative strategy for avoiding KYC is to use an exchange domiciled in a jurisdiction where KYC restrictions are minimal. One such jurisdiction was Seychelles, but the US government has successfully pressured the Seychelles government to institute US-grade KYC (Alison 2020).

exchange for dollar-pegged stablecoins. DEXs and decentralized finance in general, then, facilitate investment in cryptoassets rather than their use in buying goods and services.

6.4 MARKET OBSTACLES TO MONETIZATION OF BITCOIN AND GOLD

Some Bitcoin proponents suggest that its monetization is inevitable. One version of the argument posits a positive feedback loop: As Bitcoin's price keeps rising, it eventually becomes the world's asset with the greatest trading volume, which gives it the smallest bid-ask spread of all assets, which stabilizes its value. But even supposing that Bitcoin's price keeps rising (which is not at all inevitable, as 2021 and 2022 have shown), a smaller bid-ask spread does not imply a more stable purchasing power in the presence of volatile demand.

Some claim that monetization is underway, despite a lack of evidence for growing use of Bitcoin as a medium of exchange. Bitcoin has certainly risen in value since its start, but rising market value as an asset is neither the same nor a pathway to monetization, which means growing commonness as a medium of exchange. An ever-rising value for Tesla shares, and an ever-thicker market for them, do not imply that Tesla shares are becoming a common medium of exchange. When it is said that a growing number of people are "adopting" Bitcoin, it is important to recognize that "adopting" in the sense of opening an account or a wallet to hold Bitcoin is not the same as accepting or using Bitcoin as a medium of exchange.

There are several market obstacles to the monetization of Bitcoin or gold starting from where we are today. The first is a *network effect* that works in favor of the incumbent money. A money is more beneficial to each transactor the larger is the network of potential trading partners who will accept it. Other things equal, people prefer to be paid in the medium that they can spend most widely. Transactors are more willing to accept a medium of exchange that is more widely accepted by others, which in turn reinforces its wide acceptance. Any alternative medium of exchange – gold, Bitcoin, foreign currency – faces an uphill battle in achieving critical mass against an incumbent money.

Local network effects can be and are overcome when an alternative medium is sufficiently better than the incumbent common medium along some other dimension like purchasing-power stability. Latin America has seen many cases of popular dollarization, a spontaneous switch to the US dollar as the most commonly accepted medium of exchange, when the local peso or bolivar becomes highly inflationary. Under high inflation, the inconvenience and risk of being early to switch to an alternative currency becomes smaller than the certain loss of value from not switching.

Network effects mean, however, that in the choice among alternative currencies, not only their relative inflation rates but also their relative network sizes matter. It is noteworthy that residents of Latin America adopt the US dollar, rather than the Swiss Franc, even though the Swiss Franc has a better track record than the dollar for low and steady inflation. Business firms in the United States are major dollar-accepting trading partners for Latin American firms. The Swiss Franc has little acceptance in local or international trade for Latin American firms, despite its superior inflation history.

Compared to the dollar, Bitcoin and gold share the twin disadvantages of smaller transaction networks and greater purchasing-power volatility. Very high inflation in Venezuela has accordingly brought about widespread dollarization of payments (despite its initial illegality), while the uptick in Bitcoin acceptance by shops (as discussed in the Introduction) has been more limited, and the emergence of monetary gold circulation has been confined to the gold mining region of southeastern Venezuela (Vasquez and Fieser 2021).

In Myanmar, after a military coup in February 2021, people scrambled to get US dollars and gold, bidding up their prices in local currency (Reed 2021). I can find no reports of increased use of Bitcoin.

The dominance of the US dollar over Bitcoin and gold in Venezuela and other high-inflation countries suggests that if the dollar's inflation rate remains in low single digits, the dollar is unlikely to lose much ground to Bitcoin or gold in popularity as an everyday medium of exchange. Due to the network advantage of a status-quo currency, it would be unlikely even on a level legal playing field.

Vitalik Buterin, co-founder of Ethereum, addressed the likelihood of hyperbitcoinization in a powerpoint slide entitled "Cryptocurrency: A Reality Check."[7] Most money-users, he noted, are "decently served by the modern financial system (if in the 1st world)." They also "dislike price volatility." From these premises, he predicted that "BTC will never become a substantially used unit-of-account." My analysis in this chapter is similar except that my prediction is that BTC is unlikely to become a commonly used *medium of exchange* for the same reason, namely that its

[7] https://imgur.com/kIYAy5F

purchasing-power risk and transaction costs make it unattractive to use as a medium of exchange. Since the unit of account normally adheres to the commonly accepted medium of exchange (White 1984a), it follows that BTC is also unlikely to become a common unit of account.

The country of El Salvador provides an opportunity to test our prediction. El Salvador has been officially dollarized since 2001: The local currency (previously pegged to the US dollar) was retired, and the US dollar became the currency for everyday pricing and payments, and the official currency for taxes and court judgments. Federal Reserve notes circulate. In June 2021, the Salvadoran government passed a new law, effective in September, to make Bitcoin a "legal tender" in payment of debts and taxes, and to eliminate capital gains taxes on Bitcoin holdings. Most controversially, the law initially required merchants with internet connectivity to accept payment in Bitcoin, with the option to immediately sell it to the government at the market exchange rate. A later modification, after public protest, made acceptance optional. The government introduced its own Bitcoin wallet, called Chivo, and pre-loaded it with $30 worth of Bitcoin to jumpstart its adoption and use.

Our analysis predicts that the Salvadoran public would not find Bitcoin more attractive than the established US dollar as a medium of exchange even on a legally level playing field, due to Bitcoin's more volatile purchasing power, its higher transaction costs, and the incumbency advantage of the dollar. In practice, the government initiative, despite giving Bitcoin legal privileges and reducing transaction fees, did not achieve a critical mass of Bitcoin users and did not falsify our prediction. Two months into the experiment, former central bank president Óscar Cabrera observed that "the population continues to reject the use of bitcoin as legal tender." Citizens of modest means downloaded the Chivo wallet "only to use the 30 dollars to buy goods and services" and "not to enter the world of bitcoin, invest and see what happens because their economic conditions do not allow it" (La Prensa Grafica 2021). Widespread transaction use of BTC did not occur. Remittances of Bitcoin into El Salvador actually diminished relative to dollar remittances (Urquilla 2021).

6.5 BITCOIN AND GOLD HEAD-TO-HEAD

Whether money-users remain "decently served" by fiat monies depends, of course, on whether their inflation rates remain in low single digits, which depends on central bank policies. Even first-world fiat central banks have produced double-digit inflation rates before. If the day arrives when the US dollar and all other major fiat currencies degrade into high inflation, money-users would *then* pivot to face a choice between Bitcoin and gold. Which would they consider the better money?

Some Bitcoin proponents, like blogger Sven Schnieders (2020), suggest that gold is at a disadvantage partly because they anachronistically suppose that monetary gold payment means physically handing over coins and bullion. Since the introduction of the electric telegraph, gold payment mostly means electronically transferring claims to vaulted gold. Today gold-denominated transfers even take place on blockchains.

It is true that gold vaults must be secured against theft, but this is equally true of Bitcoin wallets. As vaulted gold holdings increase in value, it is true that, "incentives for theft also increase, pushing up the cost of secure custody." But this again is equally true of Bitcoin holdings. As the value of Bitcoin holdings rise, incentives for theft rise, pushing the cost of cybersecurity higher. In neither case does it follow that the cost of security rises as a percentage of the value held. Gold warehouses typically charge a flat percentage storage fee.

Schnieders notes that transporting physical gold is costly, requiring guards and armored trucks. This helps explain why, with the development of modern silver- and gold-based banking beginning in the twelfth century, large payments transitioned from being made in bags of silver and gold coins toward being made by check and giro transfers between bank accounts. Interbank settlements became transfers of the ownership of the gold banks kept in clearinghouse association vaults. Today account-balance transfer is quick and nearly costless online, for gold accounts just as well as for fiat or crypto accounts. Ownership is transferred while the gold remains untouched in the vault.

It was once a problem that whenever transacting in gold coin or bullion, the gold had to "be both verified for its authenticity and denominated in such quantities as to suit both the buyer and seller." This again is a reason why people began to transact normally with claims to vaulted gold, rather than by handing over coins or bullion. Receiving payment in gold-redeemable banknotes or checks issued by reputable banks eliminated a need to verify the authenticity of gold coins or bars that remained in bank vaults. Banks authenticated gold coins when taking them in or paying them out.[8] When banks could rely on reputable mints – private

---

[8] Many banks and finance companies in India today offer loans collateralized by bullion or 22 karat gold jewelry left on deposit. Such firms are already experienced in gold appraisal. The largest gold-collateralized lender in the southern Indian state of Kerala, Muthoot

or public – that reliably certified the purity and weight of the coins they issued, the costs of verification were minimal. (Before the end of debasement as common practice by state monopoly mints, by contrast, bankers had to spend much time and effort weighing and scrutinizing coins.) We conclude that authenticity verification is not a significant burden under a gold standard with modern banking.

While it is true that thick gold bars require more costly verification than coins, there was and is little call for large payments by physical transfers of coins or bars, even in international trade. Bars from non-reputable refiners or of uncertain provenance may need to have their cores sampled to assure their genuineness, but for that very reason, vaults offering transferable claims to be settled in physical gold will shun such bars. The London Bullion Markets Association sets strict provenance standards for "Good Delivery" bars.

In high-inflation developing countries where many people hold their savings in physical gold rather than in banks, physical gold depositories that offer gold-denominated account transfers as well as storage services could be a stepping stone to banking services as they were historically, were such services legal. Gold payment phone apps are just as feasible as fiat payment phone apps.

Gold today has two main advantages over Bitcoin as a potential medium of exchange. (1) Its purchasing-power volatility is lower, as already emphasized. (2) Its established base of owners is larger. Gold held in quasi-monetary forms (excluding jewelry and industrial inventories) is presently about six times the value of Bitcoin held. During May 2022, while Bitcoin's market cap ranged between $500 billion and $600 billion, private plus central bank holdings of gold in quasi-monetary forms totaled about $4.7 trillion.[9] Those quasi-monetary holdings make up 39 percent of above-ground gold. Adding the bullion value of gold jewelry raises the value figure for privately held gold above $10 trillion.

Finance, held a reported Rs. 542 billion (Rs. 54,214.9 crore) in gold loans on its balance sheet at the end of 2021 (Dutta 2022). At the regulatory maximum loan-to-gold ratio of 75 percent, and the 31 December 2021 Rupee-US Dollar exchange rate, this implies that it held more than $9.5 billion worth of gold.

[9] The World Gold Council (2021) in February 2021 estimated that 44,384 tonnes of gold were privately held as bars, coins, and ETFs, and another 34,211 tonnes were held by central banks, for a total of 78,595 tonnes held in quasi-monetary form. Converting to troy ounces (32,150.7 troy oz. per tonne) gives a figure of 2.526 billion troy ounces. At the May 2022 price of $1850 per troy ounce, we have a value above $4.6 trillion. Adding 1.8 percent for expected 2021 growth in the stock from gold mining brings the figure to approximately $4.7 trillion.

Bitcoin has two main advantages over gold today as a potential medium of exchange: (1) The Bitcoin blockchain has established its reliability for making payments, whereas online gold payment systems are newer; and (2) Bitcoin can be self-custodied and transferred peer-to-peer without the need for a trusted third party, whereas vaulted gold of course relies on the trustworthiness of the vault-keepers. Because of the second feature, Bitcoin can be custodied in ways that are more resistant to third-party failure and to government intervention.

Self-custody is inconvenient, however, as evidenced by the fact that most Bitcoin holders do not practice self-custody. Chainalysis (2020) has estimated that in 2020 hosted wallets (including accounts at exchanges) held 60 percent of the non-lost Bitcoin stock, with that percentage steadily rising year by year, indicating that most owners value the convenience of a custodial account over the security of self-custody. Hosted wallets dominate Bitcoin flows even more. Some 40 percent of flows moved directly between two custodial wallets, with another 43 percent moving to or from a custodial wallet, leaving only 17 percent of flows moving between self-custodied wallets. Most users of Bitcoin, like users of custodied gold, therefore face sovereign risk: A government that wants to suppress Bitcoin transfers can raise their cost for the vast majority of users by shutting down custodial services, or remove their privacy by imposing surveillance of custodial wallets.

When it comes to user fees, Bitcoin avoids the storage costs of vaulted gold. But because access to the Bitcoin blockchain is priced per transaction, regardless of the value to be transferred, the fees are currently lower for gold payment services in retail-sized transactions, such as the proverbial purchase of a cup of coffee, than on the Bitcoin blockchain. Second-layer payment services for Bitcoin eliminate this advantage to gold.

Before Bitcoin, the firm E-gold provided online gold payments by transfer of gold account balances, until it ran afoul of money transmitter laws (despite gold no longer being money) and was shut down by the US Treasury (White 2014). Since 2009, a number of businesses have proposed to provide speedy and secure online gold payments while complying with applicable regulations. Several have come and gone. None has caught on in a big way relative to Bitcoin or US dollar stablecoins. They come in two main varieties: gold stablecoins in the form of exchange-traded tokens and gold warehouse accounts with transferable but non-exchange-traded tokens.

In December 2022, according to Etherscan[10], seven gold-pegged sta-blecoins with known market caps were available as ERC-20 tokens on the Ethereum platform. The top two were Paxos Gold (PAXG), with a market cap of about $485 million, followed closely by Tether Gold, with a market cap of about $390 million. Here is how the Tether Gold website (gold.tether.to) describes its contractual structure:

Each XAUt represents ownership of one troy fine ounce of physical gold on a specific gold bar. Therefore, holders will obtain undivided ownership rights to gold on the specified gold bar(s). The allocated gold is identifiable with a unique serial number, purity and weight. At any time, XAUt holders can check the details of the gold bars associated with their address through the Look-up web-site. ... The holder's physical gold can be delivered to a location of their choice in Switzerland.[11]

As an ERC-20 token, Tether Gold (like the other gold stablecoins) "can be traded or moved easily at any time, anywhere in the world" for the price of Ethereum transaction fees.

Somewhat curiously, Tether Gold and PAXG do not charge explicit fees to cover the costs of physical gold storage. Assuming that they really do store the allocated gold bars they claim to hold, the cost of storage must be covered by the buy-in and cash-out (token creation and destruc-tion) fees of up to 1 percent (less in bulk) that they do charge. These in-and-out fees discourage the use of gold stablecoins for transactions in a world where gold is not yet re-monetized and therefore few goods-sellers want to keep the gold stablecoins they are paid.

Smaller gold stablecoin projects, lagging far behind in market cap, were Cache Gold at $5.8 million, and four others smaller still. In total, less than $800 million was held in gold stablecoins with reported mar-ket caps. Twenty-nine other listed gold tokens had no reported market caps, apparently just because their token quantities in circulation are not reported, even though many have trading volumes and prices continu-ously reported on exchanges.

A number of firms, not issuing tokens traded on exchanges, offer redeemable and transferable warehouse claims to gold that are held by customers in digital wallets. Where Tether Gold (gold.tether.to/legal/feeschedule) has a minimum purchase of 50 troy ounces to establish an

---

[10] etherscan.io/tokens.
[11] The contractual rights of an owner of Tether USD, and the portfolio assets held to redeem it, by contrast, are both very fuzzy.

account, and a minimum of 430 ounces to redeem for a physical bar, these services have much smaller minimums and will redeem for coins or small biscuits. A recent directory (Clark 2021) included eleven firms that promise to enable peer-to-peer transfers and thereby gold payments for goods and services: G-Coin, GoldGo, Kinesis, Lode AUX, Meld Gold, OLegacy Token, OroPocket, Quintric iQuint, ACU Gold, AgAu Gold Token, and DaVinci Gold. There seems to be no data available on the size of their gold stocks held or on their volume of transfers.

Two additional services, absent from the above list, are Glint (glint-pay.com) and Coro (coro.global). In early 2022 both advertised a 0.5 percent fee on the value of each transaction, plus monthly storage fees. Glint charged the lower storage fee, 0.02 percent per month (0.243 percent per year). For comparison's sake, average Bitcoin transaction fees were mostly in the range of $1.50 to $2.00 per transaction during January 2022, which was substantially lower than in prior years.[12] If these represent the only fees, then Glint and Bitcoin payments are equally costly ($17.50 per month) when $1125 in transaction balances are held on average, $300 is the average transaction size, and ten transactions are made per month. Glint becomes cheaper if average balances or transaction sizes are lower, while Bitcoin becomes cheaper if they are larger. This suggests that the advantage goes to Glint for everyday transactions. It should be noted, however, that where Bitcoin payments can be sent via the Lightning Network (which notably does not introduce a trusted third party), small transactions become cheaper by avoiding the need to pay blockchain access fees with each transaction. In early 2022, the service Cash App began offering zero fees on Bitcoin payments to merchants who accept Lightning Network (Perez 2022). It should likewise be noted that the PAXG stablecoin charges a mere 0.02 percent for transfers from one address to another on the Ethereum blockchain.[13]

6.6 COSTS OF A GOLD STANDARD COMPARED TO COSTS OF A BITCOIN STANDARD

Neither a gold standard nor a Bitcoin standard has a systemic aggregate resource cost advantage over the other. Free entry into gold mining and into Bitcoin mining implies that the value of the marginal unit of either

[12] https://glintpay.com/en_us/faqs/what-are-the-glint-fees-limits/, https://ycharts.com/indicators/bitcoin_average_transaction_fee
[13] https://help.paxos.com/hc/en-us/articles/360041903832-PAX-Gold-Fees

money will be matched by its marginal mining cost. $1000 worth of mining costs will be incurred to produce an additional $1000 worth of gold coins or an expected $1000 in Bitcoin rewards plus blockchain fees.

Do the resource costs of gold and Bitcoin mean that a fiat standard supplies money at lower cost, enlarging the overall social gain from money? It does not follow. In practice, as argued in Chapter 2, fiat standards have imposed the deadweight costs associated with higher inflation. Fiat seigniorage profit is not a free lunch to the public. In addition, the logic of the profit motive in the political arena suggests that political competition to capture control over seigniorage revenue will lead to campaigning and lobbying expenditures that dissipate the revenue. The "public choice" logic of the case has been spelled out by Geoffrey Brennan and James Buchanan (1981). Brennan and Buchanan look for a solution in "a constitution to discipline government" in money creation. They unfortunately give little attention to possible constitutional designs that would safeguard the public from the inflationary tax on cash balances by separating money and state, entirely removing money creation from government.

6.7 IS LONG-RUN FIXITY IN THE STOCK OF BITCOIN A PROBLEM?

The number of BTC in circulation was programmed to expand at around 2.0 percent in 2022, but the expansion rate is programmed to fall progressively in the future and to reach zero in 2140.[14] At that point, assuming for the sake of argument that the demand to hold BTC is entirely monetary and grows at the same rate as real GDP, Bitcoin would exhibit mild secular growth in its purchasing power, or equivalently we would see deflation in BTC-denominated prices of goods and services (Weber 2016). Deflation follows from the dynamic equation of exchange discussed in Chapter 4: In an economy where the money stock grows more slowly than real output, absent technological changes that continuously raise the velocity of money, the price level must fall. The US economy's real GDP has grown at a geometric average rate of 2.1 percent over the most recent ten years. With 2.1 percent per year growth in real output, and constant velocity, a constant stock of money (as Bitcoin will eventually have) implies deflation at 2.1 percent per year.

---

[14] Bitcoin Wiki, https://en.bitcoin.it/wiki/Controlled_supply

Because the deflation would be foreseen, it *might* not be a problem for the economy. Price and wage expectations would adjust. It might even improve the economy's efficiency, for reasons Milton Friedman (1969) spelled out in his case for achieving an "optimum quantity of money" via deflation. But it might not. Friedman's case rests on deflation reducing the incentive and thereby the costs agents incur to economize on money balances, by eliminating the difference between the yield on money and the yield on equally safe (very-short-term Treasury) bonds. The right rate of deflation brings the nominal very-short-term risk-free bond yield (equal to the real yield minus deflation) down to the zero nominal yield on money. If the equilibrium real interest rate is less than 2 percent, a 2.1 deflation rate would overdo it, pushing equilibrium nominal bond yields into negative territory, where they cannot go when cash pays a zero nominal yield. Put another way, a 2.1 percent risk-free real return to holding money is likely too high for intertemporal equilibrium when plausible estimates of the "natural rate of interest" put it below 2 percent for very-short-term bonds.[15] For example, if the equilibrium real interest rate is 1 percent on risk-free one-year bonds, the bond market cannot reach that equilibrium – nobody will buy one-year bonds yielding 1 percent real (negative 1.1 percent nominal) – when money's yield is 2.1 percent real (0 percent nominal). The "zero lower bound" on nominal rates means that 2.1 percent deflation interferes with efficient intertemporal allocation when equilibrium real rates are lower.

6.8 THE QUESTION OF "BACKING"

In common vernacular, to "back" an effort or a project means to support it in some way. In technical monetary theory, the term is used more narrowly. This has led to much confusion about "backing" for currencies. A form of money is "backed" in the technical sense if there is a pool of reserves held to redeem it. For example, gold coins are held as reserves for gold-redeemable banknotes, and gold bullion for gold stablecoins. US dollar assets are held as reserves for a dollar stablecoin or for a peso issued by a currency board with an exchange rate fixed to the US dollar.[16] In

---

[15] In aggregate intertemporal production models, the economy's *marginal* return on investment (or marginal rate of intertemporal transformation) equals the natural rate of interest in equilibrium (Hirshleifer 1970). But diminishing returns to investment mean that the economy's *average* growth rate is above the marginal return on investment.

[16] A borderline case is a fiat money with a binding price-level or nominal income target, with liquid central bank assets available for open market sales serving as reserves.

this technical sense Bitcoin is not backed. Neither is a fiat money with a floating exchange rate. Nor are gold coins backed. They are all "outside" or "base" monies. For a currency to be unbacked in the technical sense is not to say that its purchasing power is not supported in some other way.

We can interpret statements about currency "backing" that do not refer to reserves and redemption arrangements as using the term in the vernacular sense of "providing support." They are beside the point for explaining the purchasing power of the currency if they do not identify a mechanism that limits supply or enhances demand. For example, to say that Bitcoin is backed by a blockchain ledger, or by mathematics, or by software, is at best a very incomplete account of its market value. A connection to supply or demand must be added.

6.9 CONCLUSION: LET POTENTIAL MONIES COMPETE

It is tempting to say that all that is needed for better money to emerge is only what is generally needed for better goods and services to emerge: freedom for market experimentation and consumer selection. Public policy could allow that freedom simply by removing restrictions on entry and exit. "Let a thousand currencies bloom, but do not artificially preserve any of them." This is good advice, there being no warrant for protecting incumbent fiat standards against alternative standards. But we should be aware that parallel monetary standards will have a hard time blooming even with free entry except where the inflation rate of the incumbent fiat rises well into double digits. Incumbent fiat monies are somewhat protected by network effects, the strong tendency to stay with the most common currency, so long as central banks keep inflation rates reasonably low.

That fiat standards currently rule the roost hardly makes discussion of gold and Bitcoin as alternative standards irrelevant. There is an intellectual value in understanding them for the reason that the contrast provides a deeper understanding of fiat money regimes. There is also a long-run policy value. Wider discussion of the implications of alternative monetary standards should make the concept of switching to a better money more familiar and harder to dismiss out of hand. Recall that in the early 1960s, when Milton Friedman promoted discussion of flexible exchange rates, the idea was considered beyond the pale. A Johnson administration Treasury official, Frederick Deming, later commented (as quoted by Odell 1982, p. 142):

There was absolutely no acceptance of flexibility of exchange rates on the part of any responsible officials I knew. And there was not really much acceptance in the academic community. There was almost a total lack of support for them in the banking community. Now you had a few mavericks. But I can't recall any serious discussion on this; we didn't look at it all that seriously.

Nevertheless, Friedman and others persisted. When crisis visited the Bretton Woods system of fixed exchange rates in 1971, an alternative was ready on the shelf. If an inflation crisis visits today's system of floating fiat monies – something certainly not to be wished for – it cannot hurt to have alternatives on the shelf. There is some US dollar inflation rate high enough to make it individually and socially prudent to switch to an alternative monetary standard, no matter how unlikely such an inflation rate may currently seem. In the same way, high inflation crises in local currencies have led to popular dollarization in Latin American countries, sometimes followed by official dollarization.

Of course, a crisis is not the only conceivable way to make a transition to a better money. Before a crisis arrives, a date can be set after which the US dollar is to be redefined as – and redeemed for – so many grams of pure gold or so many satoshis (fractions of one Bitcoin). A smooth transition of this sort, back to the gold standard, followed the irredeemable greenback standard of the US Civil War.

We see analogs to these two transitional paths when we observe how two Latin American countries have made the transition to using the US dollar (White 2012). In Ecuador in 1998–2000, a parallel unofficial US dollar system emerged after the annual inflation rate in the local currency rose from low to high double digits, then to triple digits. The private sector of the economy was already heavily dollarized when the government finally pulled the plug on the heavily depreciated local currency unit in 2000 and the dollarization became official. In El Salvador in 2001, the government chose to permanently lock in the dollar value of the currency – by switching from a dollar-pegged exchange rate to outright adoption of the US dollar – while inflation was low and the local currency still dominant. In a nutshell, when the official switch to the better money came in Ecuador, it was an act of necessity in the midst of a near-hyperinflation crisis. In El Salvador it was an act of foresight, to rule out such a crisis.

In countries that today have fiat monies with single-digit inflation rates, adoption of a gold or a Bitcoin standard before an inflationary crisis seems very unlikely. Nakamoto's second reason for wanting to switch was to preserve privacy. But a switch for that reason requires that Bitcoin and gold stablecoins retain their privacy advantages. It remains to be seen whether they can avoid incorporation into the KYC financial panopticons that national governments seem determined to build.

References

Abrams, Burton A., and James L. Butkiewicz. 2012. "The Political Business Cycle: New Evidence from the Nixon Tapes," *Journal of Money, Credit and Banking* 44 (March–April), pp. 385–99.

Adams, Edgar H. 1913. *Private Gold Coinage of California*. Brooklyn: Edgar H. Adams.

Alchian, Armen A. and Benjamin Klein. 1973. "On a Correct Measure of Inflation'," *Journal of Money, Credit and Banking* 5 (February), pp. 173–91.

Alison, Ian. 2020. "Seychelles, Longtime Home of BitMEX, Is Bending to US Pressure on KYC," CoinDesk (17 December), www.coindesk.com/policy/2020/12/17/seychelles-longtime-home-of-bitmex-is-bending-to-us-pressure-on-kyc/.

American Institute of CPAs. 2018. "Comment Letter on Notice 2014–21 Virtual Currency," https://us.aicpa.org/content/dam/aicpa/advocacy/tax/downloadable-documents/20180530-aicpa-comment-letter-on-notice-2014-21-virtual-currency.pdf.

Ammous, Saifedean. 2018. *The Bitcoin Standard*. New York: Wiley.

Anderson, Richard G. 2003. "Some Tables of Historical U.S. Currency and Monetary Aggregates Data," St. Louis Federal Reserve Bank Working Paper 2003-006A (April), http://research.stlouisfed.org/wp/2003/2003-006.pdf.

Andolfatto, David. 2008. "A Model of Fiat Money," unpublished ms. http://citeseerx.ist.psu.edu/viewdoc/summary?doi=10.1.1.547.3150.

Armas, Mayela. 2022. "Venezuela's Inflation Hit 686.4% in 2021 – Central Bank," Reuters.com (8 January), www.reuters.com/world/americas/venezuelas-inflation-hit-6864-2021-central-bank-2022-01-08/.

Atkeson, Andrew, and Patrick J. Kehoe. 2004. "Deflation and Depression: Is there an Empirical Link?" *The American Economic Review* 94 (2), pp. 99–103.

Babelon, Ernest. 1897. *Les Origines de la Monnaie Considérées au Point de Vue Économique et Historique*. Paris: Librairie de Firmin-Didot et Cie.

Back, Adam. 2002. "Hashcash – A Denial of Service Counter-Measure," www.hashcash.org/papers/hashcash.pdf.

Bagehot, Walter. 1873. *Lombard Street: A Description of the Money Market*. London: Henry S. King.

Barnett II, William, and Walter E. Block. 2009. "Time Deposits, Dimensions, and Fraud," *Journal of Business Ethics* 88 (September), pp. 711–16.

Barro, Robert J. 1979. "Money and the Price Level Under the Gold Standard," *Economic Journal* 89 (March), pp. 13–33.

Barro, Robert J. 1983. "United States Inflation and the Choice of Monetary Standard," in R. E. Hall, ed., *Inflation: Causes and Effects*, pp. 99–110. Chicago: University of Chicago Press.

Barry, Dave. 2006. *Dave Barry's Money Secrets*. New York: Three Rivers Press.

Bastiat, Frédéric. 1996. *Economic Sophisms*, ed. and trans. Arthur Goddard, intro. by Henry Hazlitt. Irvington-on-Hudson, NY: Foundation for Economic Education. https://oll.libertyfund.org/titles/276#Bastiat_0182_624.

Bates, Leslie Snyder. 2010. *Why Gold?: The One Sure Cure for Inflation and Economic Tyranny*. Bloomington, IN: AuthorHouse.

Bayoumi, Tamim, and Joseph Gagnon. 1996. "Taxation and Inflation: A New Explanation for Capital Flows," *Journal of Monetary Economics* 38 (October), pp. 303–30.

Beckerman, Paul. 2001. "Dollarization and Semi-Dollarization in Ecuador," World Bank Policy Research Working Paper 2643 (July).

Belcher, Martha. 2022. "Tucked Inside Biden Infrastructure Bill: Unconstitutional Crypto Surveillance," *Coin Desk* (25 January), www.coindesk.com/layer2/privacyweek/2022/01/25/tucked-inside-biden-infrastructure-bill-unconstitutional-crypto-surveillance/.

Berentsen, Aleksander, Mariana Rojas Breu, and Shouyong Shi. 2012. "Liquidity, Innovation and Growth," *Journal of Monetary Economics* 59 (December), pp. 721–37.

Berentsen, Aleksander, and Fabian Schär. 2018. "A Short Introduction to the World of Cryptocurrencies," *Federal Reserve Bank of St. Louis Review* (Q1), pp. 1–16. https://files.stlouisfed.org/files/htdocs/publications/review/2018/01/10/a-short-introduction-to-the-world-of-cryptocurrencies.pdf.

Bernanke, Ben S. 2010. "Rebalancing the Global Recovery" (19 November), www.federalreserve.gov/newsevents/speech/bernanke20101119a.htm.

Bernholz, Peter. 2003. *Monetary Regimes and Inflation*. Cheltenham, UK: Edward Elgar.

Bernholz, Peter. 2014. *Monetary Regimes, Stability, Politics and Inflation in History*. Cheltenham, UK: Edward Elgar.

Bernstein, Jacob. 2021. "What Can You Actually Buy with Bitcoin," *New York Times* (3 February), www.nytimes.com/2021/02/03/style/what-can-you-actually-buy-with-bitcoin.html.

Bhatia, Nik. 2021. *Layered Money: From Gold and Dollars to Bitcoin and Central Bank Digital Currencies*. Self-published.

Binder, Carola. 2021. "Political Pressure on Central Banks," *Journal of Money, Credit, and Banking* 53 (June), pp. 715–44.

Bindseil, Ulrich, Patrick Papsdorf, and Jürgen Schaaf. 2022. "The Encrypted Threat: Bitcoin's Social Cost and Regulatory Responses," SUERF Policy Note, Issue no 262 (January), www.suerf.org/policynotes/38771/the-encrypted-threat-bitcoins-social-cost-and-regulatory-responses.

Bitrefill. 2022. https://twitter.com/bitrefill/status/1480907751731650563.

Boettke, Peter J., Alexander William Salter, and Daniel J. Smith. 2021. *Money and the Rule of Law: Generality and Predictability in Monetary Institutions*. New York: Cambridge University Press.

Bordo, Michael D. 2007. "Gold Standard," in David R. Henderson ed., *The Concise Encyclopedia of Economics*, pp. 222–24. Indianapolis: Liberty Fund. www.econlib.org/library/Enc/GoldStandard.html.

Bordo, Michael D., Ehsan U. Choudhri, and Anna J. Schwartz. 2002. "Was Expansionary Monetary Policy Feasible during the Great Contraction? An Examination of the Gold Standard Constraint," *Explorations in Economic History* 39 (January), pp. 1–28.

Bordo, Michael David, and Richard Wayne Ellson. 1985. "A Model of the Classical Gold Standard with Depletion," *Journal of Monetary Economics* 16, pp. 109–20.

Bordo, Michael D., John Landon-Lane, and Angela Redish. 2010. "Deflation, Productivity Shocks and Gold: Evidence from the 1880–1914 Period, " *Open Economies Review* 21 (September), pp. 515–46.

Boyapati, Vijay. 2018. "The Bullish Case for Bitcoin," Medium (2 March). https://vijayboyapati.medium.com/the-bullish-case-for-bitcoin-6ecc8bdecc1.

Boyd, John H., Ross Levine, and Bruce D. Smith. 2001. "The Impact of Inflation on Financial Sector Performance," *Journal of Monetary Economics* 47 (April 2001), pp. 221–48.

Boyer-Xambeau, Marie-Therese, Ghislain Deleplace, and Lucien Gillard. 1994. *Private Money and Public Currencies: The 16th Century Challenge*. Armonk, NY: M. E. Sharpe.

Brennan, Geoffrey, and James M. Buchanan. 1981. *Monopoly in Money and Inflation: The Case for a Constitution to Discipline Government*. London: Institute of Economic Affairs.

Briones, Ignacio, and Hugh Rockoff. 2005. "Do Economists Reach a Conclusion on Free-Banking Episodes?," *Econ Journal Watch* 2 (August), pp. 279–324. https://econjwatch.org/articles/do-economists-reach-a-conclusion-on-free-banking-episodes.

British Museum. n.d. "The Origins of Coinage," www.britishmuseum.org/explore/themes/money/the_origins_of_coinage.aspx.

Burns, Arthur R. 1965. *Money and Monetary Policy in Early Times*. New York: Augustus M. Kelley.

Bustillos, Maria. 2013. "The Bitcoin Boom," *The New Yorker* (1 April), www.newyorker.com/tech/annals-of-technology/the-bitcoin-boom.

Butler, Alexander, Xiang Gao, and Cihan Uzmanoglu. 2021. "Maturity Clienteles and Corporate Bond Maturities," SSRN working paper (27 September), https://papers.ssrn.com/sol3/papers.cfm?abstract_id=3315551.

Cachanosky, Nicholas. 2022. "What Can the US Learn from Argentina's Inflation?," American Institute for Economic Research *Sound Money* blog (24 February), www.aier.org/article/what-can-the-us-learn-from-argentinas-inflation/.

Carter, Nic, and Lucas Nuzzi. 2021. "Bitcoin's Proof of Work Is Well Worth Its Fees," *Bitcoin Magazine* (22 December), https://bitcoinmagazine.com/business/the-value-of-bitcoin-proof-of-work.

Cassel, Gustav. 1920. "Further Observations on the World's Monetary Problem," *Economic Journal* 30 (March), pp. 39–45.

Cecchetti, Stephen, and Kermit Schoenholtz. 2016. "Why a Gold Standard Is a Very Bad Idea." Money and Banking blog (19 December). www.moneyandbanking.com/commentary/2016/12/14/why-a-gold-standard-is-a-very-bad-idea.

Chainalysis. 2020. "60% of Bitcoin Is Held Long Term as Digital Gold. What About the Rest?," https://blog.chainalysis.com/reports/bitcoin-market-data-exchanges-trading/.

Chainalysis. 2022. "Crypto Crime Trends for 2022: Illicit Transaction Activity Reaches All-Time High in Value, All-Time Low in Share of All Cryptocurrency Activity," blog.chainalysis.com/reports/2022-crypto-crime-report-introduction/.

Chinn, Menzie. 2019. "What Would It Take to Implement Cain's Gold Standard, Interest-rate-wise?." Econobrowser blog (7 April), http://econbrowser.com/archives/2019/04/what-would-it-take-to-implement-cains-gold-standard-interest-rate-wise.

Cipolla, Carlo. M. 1956. *Money, Prices, and Civilization in the Mediterranean World: Fifth to Seventeenth Century*. Princeton: Princeton University Press.

Clark, James. 2021. "A Complete Guide to Gold-Backed Cryptocurrency," Goldscape.net (14 November), www.goldscape.net/gold-blog/gold-backed-cryptocurrency/.

Click, Reid W. 1998. "Seigniorage in a Cross-Section of Countries," *Journal of Money, Credit, and Banking* 30 (May), pp. 154–71.

Coase, R. H. 1972. "Durability and Monopoly," *Journal of Law and Economics* 15 (April), pp. 143–47.

Coase, R. H. 1974. "The Lighthouse in Economics," *Journal of Law and Economics* 17 (October), pp. 357–76.

Cochrane, John. 2017. "Bitcoin and Bubbles," *The Grumpy Economist* blog (30 November), https://johnhcochrane.blogspot.com/2017/11/bitcoin-and-bubbles.html.

Collins, Andrew, and John Walsh. 2014. "Fractional Reserve Banking in the Roman Republic and Empire," *Ancient Society* 44 (January), pp. 179–212.

Conant, Charles A. 1905. *The Principles of Money and Banking*, vol. 1. New York: Harper and Brothers.

Cowen, Tyler. 2011. "What Exactly Is the Argument against Gold?," *Marginal Revolution* blog (29 December), https://marginalrevolution.com/marginalrevolution/2011/12/what-exactly-is-the-argument-against-gold.html.

Cowen, Tyler. 2012. "A Short Note on the Gold Standard," *Marginal Revolution* blog (3 September), https://marginalrevolution.com/marginalrevolution/2012/09/a-short-note-on-the-gold-standard.html.

Crabbe, Leland. 1989. "The International Gold Standard and U.S. Monetary Policy from World War I to the New Deal," *Federal Reserve Bulletin* (June), pp. 423–40.

Cutsinger, Bryan P., and Joshua S. Ingber. 2019. "Seigniorage in the Civil War South," *Explorations in Economic History* 72 (April), pp. 74–92.

Dai, Wei. 1998. *b-money*. www.weidai.com/bmoney.txt.

Dai, Wei. 2011. [Blog comment] (25 February). www.lesswrong.com/posts/ ijr8rsyvJci2edxot/making-money-with-bitcoin?commentId=hbEu9ue9eymNza F2J.

Dai, Wei. 2013. [Blog comment] (20 April). www.lesswrong.com/posts/ P9jggxRZTMJcjnaPw/bitcoins-are-not-digital-greenbacks?commentId=3XvTr oRzb23NphHQDc#MwJE7tFnJZdu56Qbz.

Darby, Michael R. 1984. "Some Pleasant Monetarist Arithmetic," *Federal Reserve Bank of Minneapolis Quarterly Review* 8 (Spring), pp. 15–20.

Davanzati, Bernardo. 1696 [1588]. *A Discourse on Coins*, trans. John Toland. London: Printed by J.D. for Awnsham and John Churchil. https://avalon.law .yale.edu/16th_century/coins.asp.

de Mariana, Juan. 2018 [1605]. *On the Coinage [De Moneta]*, ed. Eric Clifford Graf, trans. Hazzard Bagg. Guatemala City: Universidad Francisco Marroquin.

De Roover, Raymond. 1963. "The Organization of Trade," in M. M. Postan, E. E. Rich, and E. Miller, eds., *The Cambridge Economic History of Europe*, vol. III, pp. 42–118. London: Cambridge University Press.

Diamond, Douglas W., and Philip J. Dybvig. 1983. "Bank Runs, Deposit Insurance, and Liquidity," *Journal of Political Economy* 91 (June), pp. 401–19.

Dowd, Kevin, ed. 1992. *The Experience of Free Banking*. London: Routledge.

Dowd, Kevin. 1996. *Competition and Finance: A Reinterpretation of Financial and Monetary Economics*. London: Palgrave Macmillan.

Dowd, Kevin. 2014. *New Private Monies: A Bit-Part Player?* London: Institute of Economic Affairs.

Dutta, Bhaskar. 2022. "Muthoot Finance skids 5% on flattish rise in Q3 profit, broader market selloff," *Economic Times* (14 February), https:// economictimes.indiatimes.com/markets/stocks/news/muthoot-finance-skids-5-on-flattish-rise-in-q3-profit-broader-market-selloff/articleshow/89559 167.cms.

Edie, Lionel D. 1932. "The Future of the Gold Standard," in Quincy Wright, ed., *Gold and Monetary Stabilization*, pp. 111–30. Chicago: University of Chicago Press.

Eichengreen, Barry. 1992. *Golden Fetters: The Gold Standard and the Great Depression, 1919–1939*. New York: Oxford University Press.

Eichengreen, Barry. 2011. "A Critique of Pure Gold," *The National Interest* (September–October), http://nationalinterest.org/article/critique-puregold-5741.

Eifler, Mark A. 2016. *The California Gold Rush: The Stampede that Changed the World*. New York: Routledge.

Ellsworth, Brian. 2021. "As Venezuela's Economy Regresses, Crypto Fills the Gaps," *Reuters.com* (22 June), www.reuters.com/technology/ venezuelas-economy-regresses-crypto-fills-gaps-2021-06-22/.

Exter, John. 1972. "Currencies Today Are IOU-Nothings," *American Institute for Economic Research Economic Education Bulletin* 12 (June), pp. 1–3.

Fekete, Antal E. 2002. "The Real Bills Doctrine of Adam Smith Lecture 13 (Concluding Lecture): The Unadulterated Gold Standard," https://professorfekete .com/articles/AEFMonEcon101Lecture13.pdf.

Fetter, Frank Whitson. 1950. "Legal Tender during the English and Irish Bank Restrictions," *Journal of Political Economy* 58 (June), pp. 241–53.

Fettig, David. 1993. "Shadowing the Shadows: The Shadow Open Market Committee Has Persistently, and Faithfully, Trailed Its Federal Reserve Namesake for 20 Years," Federal Reserve Bank of Minneapolis *The Region* (June), www.minneapolisfed.org/article/1993/shadowing-the-shadows.

Finney, Hal. 1993. "Protecting Privacy with Electronic Cash," *Extropy* #10 (Winter/Spring), pp. 8–14. https://github.com/Extropians/Extropy/blob/master/ext10_1.pdf.

Finney, Hal. 1996. "Digital Checking," *Extropy* 16 (Q1), p. 7. https://github.com/Extropians/Extropy/blob/master/Extropy-16.pdf.

Finney, Hal. 2004. "Reusable Proofs of Work," https://nakamotoinstitute.org/finney/rpow/index.html.

Finney, Hal. 2008a. www.mail-archive.com/cryptography@metzdowd.com/msg09975.html.

Finney, Hal. 2008b. www.mail-archive.com/cryptography@metzdowd.com/msg09996.html.

Finney, Hal. 2009a. https://twitter.com/halfin/status/1110302988.

Finney, Hal. 2009b. http://diswww.mit.edu/bloom-picayune/crypto/142207.

Finney, Hal. 2010. "Re: Bitcoin Bank," https://bitcointalk.org/index.php?topic=2500.msg34211#msg34211.

Finney, Hal. 2013. "Bitcoin and Me," https://bitcointalk.org/index.php?topic=155054.0.

Flandreau, Marc. 1995. "Coin Memories: Estimates of the French Metallic Currency, 1840–1878," *Journal of European Economic History* 24 (2), pp. 271–310.

Forbes, Steve, and Elizabeth Ames. 2014. *Money: How the Destruction of the Dollar Threatens the Global Economy—And What We Can Do about It.* New York: McGraw-Hill.

Foxley, William. 2021. "ShapeShift Is Going Full Defi to Lose KYC Rules," *CoinDesk* (6 January), www.coindesk.com/business/2021/01/06/shapeshift-is-going-full-defi-to-lose-kyc-rules/.

Friedman, Milton. 1951. "Commodity-Reserve Currency," *Journal of Political Economy* 59 (June), pp. 203–32.

Friedman, Milton. 1960. *A Program for Monetary Stability.* New York: Fordham University Press.

Friedman, Milton. 1969. "The Optimum Quantity of Money," in *The Optimum Quantity of Money and Other Essays*, pp. 1–50. Chicago: Aldine.

Friedman, Milton. 1970. *The Counter-Revolution in Monetary Theory.* London: Institute of Economic Affairs.

Friedman, Milton. 1976. "Has Gold Lost Its Monetary Role?" in Meyer Feldberg, Kate Jowell, and Stephen Mulholland, eds., *Milton Friedman in South Africa*, pp 33–41. Cape Town and Johannesburg: Graduate School of Business of the University of Cape Town and The Sunday Times.

Friedman, Milton. 1986. "The Resource Cost of Irredeemable Paper Money," *Journal of Political Economy* 94 (June), pp. 642–47.

Friedman, Milton. 1987. "Review of Rational Expectations and Inflation by Thomas J. Sargent," *Journal of Political Economy* 95 (February), pp. 218–21.

Friedman, Milton. 1992. *Money Mischief: Episodes in Monetary History*. New York: Harcourt Brace Jovanovich.

Friedman, Milton, and Anna J. Schwartz. 1986. "Has Government Any Role in Money?," *Journal of Monetary Economics* 17 (January), pp. 37–42.

Frost, Liam. 2020. "Pizza Hut Now Accepts Bitcoin, Ethereum, in Venezuela," *Decrypt* (30 November), https://decrypt.co/49885/pizza-hut-now-accepts-bitcoin-ethereum-in-venezuela.

Garside, M. 2019. "Average Gold Price from 1900 to 2019," Statista website (25 January), www.statista.com/statistics/268027/change-in-gold-price-since-1990/.

George, Benedict. 2022. "What Is KYC and Why Does It Matter for Crypto?," *CoinDesk* (19 January), www.coindesk.com/learn/what-is-kyc-and-why-does-it-matter-for-crypto/.

Gerlach, Stefan, and Peter Kugler. 2018. "Money Demand Under Free Banking: Switzerland 1851–1906," *Swiss Journal of Economics and Statistics* 154 (March), pp. 1–8.

Gladstein, Alex. 2020. https://mobile.twitter.com/gladstein/status/1340836877595594752.

Gladstein, Alex. 2022. *Check Your Financial Privilege: Inside the Global Bitcoin Revolution*. Nashville: BTC Media.

Gibson, Heather D., Stephen G. Hall, and George S. Tavlas. 2014. "Fundamentally Wrong: Market Pricing of Sovereigns and the Greek Financial Crisis," *Journal of Macroeconomics* 39 (March), pp. 405–19.

Gilder, George. 2015. *The 21st Century Case for Gold: A New Information Theory of Money*. Arlington, VA: American Principles Project. americanprinciplesproject.org/wp-content/uploads/2020/12/Gilder-21-Century-Gold.pdf.

Glasner, David. 1992. "The Real-Bills Doctrine in the Light of the Law of Reflux," *History of Political Economy* 24 (Winter), pp. 867–94.

Goodhart, Charles A. E. 1998. "The Two Concepts of Money: Implications for the Analysis of Optimal Currency Areas," *European Journal of Political Economy* 14 (August), pp. 407–32.

Goodhart, Charles. 2001. "What Weight Should Be Given to Asset Prices in the Measurement of Inflation?," *Economic Journal* 111 (June), pp. F335–F356.

Gorton, Gary. 1999. "Pricing Free Bank Notes," *Journal of Monetary Economics* 44 (August), pp. 33–64.

Graeber, David. 2011a. *Debt: The First 5,000 Years*. Brooklyn: Melville House.

Graeber, David. 2011b. "What Is Debt? An Interview with Economic Anthropologist David Graeber," *Naked Capitalism* blog (26 August), www.nakedcapitalism.com/2011/08/what-is-debt-%E2%80%93-an-interview-with-economic-anthropologist-david-graeber.html.

Greaves, Percy. 1978. "Introduction" to Ludwig von Mises, *On the Manipulation of Money and Credit*, ed. Percy Greaves. Dobbs Ferry, NY: Free Market Books.

Greenspan, Alan. 1967. "Gold and Economic Freedom," in Ayn Rand, *Capitalism: The Unknown Ideal*, pp. 101–7. New York: Signet.

Grierson, Philip, and Mark Blackburn. 1986. *Medieval European Coinage. Vol. 1: The Early Middle Ages.* Cambridge: Cambridge University Press.

Grigg, Ian. 2005. "Triple Entry Accounting," www.gwern.net/docs/www/iang .org/fb21fd49c2283e494890e756c8beff2cd9098bcf.html.

Grym, Aleksi. 2021a. twitter.com/aleksigrym/status/1475781732620283906.

Grym, Aleksi. 2021b. twitter.com/aleksigrym/status/1475468323806666758.

Guttmann, Robert, ed. 2016. *Reforming Money and Finance: Toward a New Monetary Regime,* 2nd ed. New York: Routledge.

Gwern. 2011. "Bitcoin Is Worse Is Better," www.gwern.net/Bitcoin-is-Worse-is- Better.

Gwern. 2014. "2014 Jed McCaleb MtGox Interview," www.gwern.net/docs/ bitcoin/2014-mccaleb.

Gwern. 2017. "Wei Dai/Satoshi Nakamoto 2009 Bitcoin emails," www.gwern .net/docs/bitcoin/2008-nakamoto.

Hall, George J., and Thomas J. Sargent. 2019. "Complications for the United States from International Credits: 1913–40," in Era Dabla-Norris, ed., *Debt and Entanglements between the Wars,* pp. 1–58. Washington, DC: International Monetary Fund.

Hamilton, James D. 2012a. "Return to the Gold Standard," *Econbrowser* blog (1 September), http://econbrowser.com/archives/2012/09/return_to_the_g.

Hamilton, James D. 2012b. "The Gold Standard and Economic Growth," *Econbrowser* blog (5 September), http://econbrowser.com/archives/2012/09/ the_gold_standa_1.

Hanes, Christopher. 2020. "How the Bank of England Influenced British Interest Rates in the Classical Gold Standard Era," SUNY Binghamton working paper (November).

Hanke, Steve. 2021. https://twitter.com/steve_hanke/status/14748167146343 71074.

Harari, Yuval Noah. 2015. *Sapiens: A Brief History of Humankind.* New York: Harper.

Hayek, F. A. 1976. *The Denationalisation of Money.* London: Institute of Economic Affairs.

Hayek, F. A. 1999 [1937]. "*Monetary Nationalism and International Stability,*" in Stephen Kresge, ed., *Good Money, Part II,* pp. 37–99. The Collected Works of F. A. Hayek, vol. 6. Chicago: University of Chicago Press.

Hayek, F. A. 2012 [1931]. "*Prices and Production,*" in Hansjoerg Klausinger, ed., *Business Cycles, Part I,* pp. 169–284. The Collected Works of F. A. Hayek, vol. 7. Chicago: University of Chicago Press.

Hernandez, Carlos. 2019. "Bitcoin Has Saved My Family," *New York Times* (23 February), www.nytimes.com/2019/02/23/opinion/sunday/venezuela-bitcoin- inflation-cryptocurrencies.html.

Hetzel, Robert L. 2002. "German Monetary History in the First Half of the Twentieth Century," *Federal Reserve Bank of Richmond Economic Quarterly* 88 (Winter), pp. 1–35.

Heymann, Daniel, and Axel Leijonhufvud. 1995. *High Inflation.* New York: Oxford University Press.

Hicks, John R. 1935. "A Suggestion for Simplifying the Theory of Money," *Economica* N.S. 2 (February), pp. 1–19.

Hirshleifer, J. 1970. *Investment, Interest and Capital*. Englewood Cliffs, NJ: Prentice-Hall.

Hogan, Thomas L., and Lawrence H. White. 2021. "Hayek, Cassel, and the Origins of the Great Depression," *Journal of Economic Behavior and Organization* 181 (January), pp. 241–51.

Horwitz, Steven. 2003. "The Costs of Inflation Revisited," *Review of Austrian Economics* 16 (March), pp. 77–95.

Hsieh, Chang-Tai, and Christina D. Romer. 2006. "Was the Federal Reserve Constrained by the Gold Standard during the Great Depression? Evidence from the 1932 Open Market Purchase Program," *Journal of Economic History* 66 (March), pp. 140–76.

Huerta de Soto, Jesus. 1995. "A Critical Analysis of Central Banks and Fractional Reserve Free Banking from the Austrian Perspective," *Review of Austrian Economics* 8 (September), pp. 25–38.

Huerta de Soto, Jesus. 2009. *Money, Credit, and Economic Cycles*. Auburn, AL: Ludwig von Mises Institute.

Hume, David. 1752. "Of the Balance of Trade," in Eugene F. Miller, ed., Reprinted in Hume, *Essays Moral, Political, Literary*, pp. 308–26. Indianapolis: Liberty Fund, 1987.

Hummel, Jeffrey Rogers. 2010. "Wreck the Currency or Default on the Debt? Jeffrey Rogers Hummel Anticipates U.S. Sovereign Default," interview with Lawrence H. White, *Econ Journal Watch Audio Podcast* (6 July), https://econjwatch.org/podcast/save-the-currency-or-default-on-the-debt-jeffrey-rogers-hummel-anticipates-us-sovereign-default.

Humphrey, Thomas M., and Richard H. Timberlake. 2019. *Gold, the Real Bills Doctrine, and the Fed*. Washington, DC: Cato Institute.

Hurtado, Albert L. 2006. *John Sutter: A Life on the North American Frontier*. Norman: University of Oklahoma Press.

IGM Forum. 2012. "Gold Standard" (12 January), www.igmchicago.org/surveys/gold-standard/.

Irwin, Douglas A. 2012. "The French Gold Sink and the Great Deflation of 1929–32," *Cato Papers on Public Policy* Working Paper 2. www.dartmouth.edu/~dirwin/French%20Gold%20Sink.pdf.

Irwin, Douglas A. 2014. "Who Anticipated the Great Depression? Gustav Cassel versus Keynes and Hayek on the Interwar Gold Standard," *Journal of Money, Credit and Banking* 46 (1), pp. 199–227.

James, Harold. 2018. "The Bitcoin Threat," *Project Syndicate* blog (2 February), www.project-syndicate.org/commentary/bitcoin-threat-to-political-stability-by-harold-james-2018-02.

Jefferson, Thomas. 1790. "Plan for Establishing Uniformity in the Coinage, Weights, and Measures of the United States," https://avalon.law.yale.edu/18th_century/jeffplan.asp.

Johnston, Louis, and Samuel H. Williamson. 2014a. "The Annual Consumer Price Index for the United States, 1774–2013," MeasuringWorth website, www.measuringworth.com/uscpi/.

Johnston, Louis, and Samuel H. Williamson. 2014b. "What Was the U.S. GDP Then?," MeasuringWorth website, www.measuringworth.org/usgdp/.

Kagin, Donald. 1981. *Private Gold Coins and Patterns of the United States*. New York: Arco Publishing.

Karaman, K. Kıvanç, Sevket Pamuk, and Seçil Yıldırım-Karaman. 2018. "Money and Monetary Stability in Europe, 1300–1914," Vox EU / CEPR Policy Portal (24 February), https://voxeu.org/article/money-and-monetary-stability-europe-1300-1914.

Keeley, Michael C., and Frederick T. Furlong. 1986. "Bank Regulation and the Public Interest," *Federal Reserve Bank of San Francisco Economic Review* 2 (Spring), pp. 55–71.

Kelleher, Richard, Fitzwilliam Museum, and Barrie Cook. n.d. "Medieval Coins—An Introduction," web document. [London:] British Museum. www.moneyandmedals.org.uk/download/i/mark_dl/u/4008551411/4603172348/Introduction%20to%20later%20medieval%20coins.pdf.

Kirzner, Israel. 1992. "Knowledge Problems and their Solutions: Some Relevant Distinctions," in Kirzner, ed., *The Meaning of Market Process: Essays in the Development of Modern Austrian Economics*, pp. 163–79. London: Routledge.

Kiyotaki, Nobuhiro, Ricardo Lagos, and Randall Wright. 2016. "Introduction to the symposium issue on money and liquidity." *Journal of Economic Theory* 164 (July), pp. 1–9.

Kiyotaki, Nobuhiro, and Randall Wright. 1991. "A Contribution to the Pure Theory of Money," *Journal of Economic Theory* (April), pp. 215–35.

Klein, Benjamin. 1974. "The Competitive Supply of Money," *Journal of Money, Credit and Banking* 6 (November), pp. 423–53.

Klein, Ezra. 2012. "The GOP Has Picked the Wrong Time to Rediscover Gold," *Washington Post* (24 August). www.washingtonpost.com/news/wonk/wp/2012/08/24/the-gop-has-picked-the-wrong-time-to-rediscover-gold/.

Knapp, George Friedrich. 1973. *The State Theory of Money*. Clifton, NY: Augustus M. Kelley. First published 1924.

Koning. 2019. "Bitcoin, 11-years in," *Moneyness* blog (2 November), http://jpkoning.blogspot.com/2019/11/bitcoin-11-years-in.html.

Koning, John Paul. 2020. https://twitter.com/jp_koning/status/1264231977487683584.

Koning, John Paul. 2022. "Bitcoin Failed as a Tool for Funding the Ottawa Protestors, and That's a Good Thing for Canada," *Moneyness* blog (18 February), http://jpkoning.blogspot.com/2022/02/bitcoin-failed-as-tool-for-funding.html.

Kotlikoff, Laurence H. 2010. *Jimmy Stewart Is Dead: Ending the World's Ongoing Financial Plague with Limited Purpose Banking*. Hoboken, NJ: Wiley.

Kroll, John H. 2011. "The Monetary Use of Weighed Bullion in Archaic Greece," in W. V. Harris, ed., *The Monetary Systems of the Greeks and Romans*, pp. 12–37. Oxford: Oxford University Press.

Krugman, Paul. 2019. "Goldbugs for Trump," *New York Times* (13 July). www.nytimes.com/2019/07/13/opinion/goldbugs-for-trump.html.

La Prensa Grafica. 2021. "Uso de bitcóin cumple 2 meses en El Salvador entre polémicas y 'ganancias'" (5 November), www.laprensagrafica.com/elsalvador/Uso-de-bitcoin-cumple-2-meses-en-El-Salvador-entre-polemicas-y-ganancias-20211105-0038.html.

Lagos, Ricardo, Guillaume Rocheteau, and Randall Wright. 2016. "Liquidity: A New Monetarist Perspective," *Journal of Economic Literature* 55 (June), pp. 371–44.

Laidler, David W. 1984. "Misconceptions about the Real-Bills Doctrine: A Comment on Sargent and Wallace," *Journal of Political Economy* 92 (February), pp. 149–55.

LeClair, Dylan, and Sam Rule. 2022. "The State of Lightning Network Adoption," *Bitcoin Magazine* (10 June), https://bitcoinmagazine.com/business/the-state-of-lightning-network-adoption.

Lee, Lawrence, and Richard Frajola. 2008. "Gold Coinage of Colorado during the Territorial Period," Richard Frajola website, www.rfrajola.com/MayerGold/MayerGold.htm.

Leijonhufvud, Axel. 1981. "The Costs and Consequences of Inflation," in *Leijonhufvud, Information and Coordination*, pp. 227–69. New York: Oxford University Press.

Library of Congress. 2021. *Regulation of Cryptocurrency Around the World: November 2021 Update*, https://tile.loc.gov/storage-services/service/ll/llglrd/2021687419/2021687419.pdf.

Locke, John. 1692. *Some Considerations of the Consequences of the Lowering of Interest and Raising the Value of Money*.

Luther, William J. 2019. "Getting Off the Ground: The Case of Bitcoin," *Journal of Institutional Economics* 15 (April), pp. 189–205.

Luther, William J., and Nikhil Sridhar. 2021. "On the Origin of Cryptocurrencies," AIER Sound Money Project Working Paper 2022-02, papers.ssrn.com/sol3/papers.cfm?abstract_id=3976424.

Luther, William J., and Lawrence H. White. 2016. "Positively Valued Fiat Money after the Sovereign Disappears: The Case of Somalia," *Review of Behavioral Economics* 3 (3–4), pp. 311–34.

Maddison, Angus. 2007. *Contours of the World Economy 1-2030 AD: Essays in Macro-Economic History*. Oxford: Oxford University Press.

Malmi, Martti. 2014. https://twitter.com/marttimalmi/status/423455561703624704.

Marshall, Monty G. and Keith Jaggers. 2008. "Polity IV Country Report 2008: Somalia," Center for International Development and Conflict Management, University of Maryland. Archived at https://web.archive.org/web/20110725015539/www.systemicpeace.org/polity/Somalia2008.pdf.

May, Timothy C. 1992. "The Crypto Anarchist Manifesto," https://activism.net/cypherpunk/crypto-anarchy.html.

Mayhew, Nicholas. 2000. *Sterling: The History of a Currency*. New York: Wiley.

Mazumder, Sandeep, and John H. Wood. 2013. "The Great Deflation of 1929–33: It (Almost) Had to Happen," *Economic History Review* 66 (February), pp. 156–77.

McCauley, Robert. 2021. "Why Bitcoin Is Worse than a Madoff-style Ponzi Scheme," *FT Alphaville* blog (22 December), www.ft.com/content/83a14261-598d-4601-87fc-5dde528b33d0.

McCloskey, Donald N., and J. Richard Zecher. 1984. "The Success of Purchasing Power Parity: Historical Evidence and Its Implications for Macroeconomics," in Michael D. Bordo and Anna J. Schwartz, eds., *A Retrospective on the Classical Gold Standard, 1821–1931*, pp. 121–70. Chicago: University of Chicago Press.

McCormack, Peter. 2019. "Nick Szabo on Cypherpunks, Money and Bitcoin," *What Bitcoin Did podcast*, www.whatbitcoindid.com/podcast/nick-szabo-on-cypherpunks-money-and-bitcoin.

McCracken, Michael W., and Aaron Amburgey. 2021. "Inflation Expectations and the Fed's New Monetary Framework," Federal Reserve Bank of St. Louis *On the Economy Blog* (8 July). www.stlouisfed.org/on-the-economy/2021/july/inflation-expectations-fed-new-monetary-framework.

McCulloch, J. Huston. 2014. "Misesian Insights for Modern Economics," *Quarterly Journal of Austrian Economics* 17 (Spring), pp. 3–18.

McElroy, Wendy. 2020. *The Satoshi Revolution: A Revolution of Rising Expectations.* https://news.btctest.net/wp-content/uploads/2020/02/the-satoshi-revolution-final.pdf.

Meissner, Christopher. 2005. "A New World Order: Explaining the International Diffusion of the Gold Standard, 1870–1913," *Journal of International Economics* 66 (July), pp. 385–406.

Menger, [C]arl. 1892. "On the Origin of Money," *Economic Journal* 2 (June), pp. 239–55.

Menger, Carl. 2002. "Money," in Michael Latzer and Stefan W. Schmitz, eds., *Carl Menger and the Evolution of Payments Systems: From Barter to Electronic Money*, pp. 25–107. Cheltenham, UK and Northampton, MA: Edward Elgar. First published 1909.

Michaels, Dave, and Andrew Ackerman. 2021. "Bitcoin Fraud Concerns Draw Scrutiny from Regulators," *Wall St. Journal* (6 July), www.wsj.com/articles/bitcoin-draws-more-scrutiny-from-regulators-worried-about-fraud-11625576400.

Michaels, Dave, and Alexander Osipovich. 2021. "Regulators Investigate Crypto-Exchange Developer Uniswap Labs," *Wall St. Journal* (3 September), www.wsj.com/articles/regulators-investigate-crypto-exchange-developer-uniswap-labs-11630666800.

Mises, Ludwig von. "Stabilization of the Monetary Unit – From the Standpoint of Theory," in Mises, *On the Manipulation of Money and Credit*, ed. Percy Greaves, pp. 1–51. Dobbs Ferry, NY: Free Market Books.

Mises, Ludwig von. 1980 [1912]. *The Theory of Money and Credit.* Indianapolis: Liberty Fund.

Mises, Ludwig von. 2007. *Human Action: A Treatise on Economics*, in 4 vols., ed. Bettina Bien Greaves. Indianapolis: Liberty Fund.

Moody, Clark. 2020. "Ten Years of Bitcoin Market Data," Clark Moody Bitcoin blog, https://bitcoin.clarkmoody.com/posts/ten-years-bitcoin-market-data.

Motomura, Akira. 1994. "The Best and Worst of Currencies: Seigniorage and Currency Policy in Spain, 1597–1650," *Journal of Economic History* 54 (March), pp. 104–27.

Mubarak, Jamil A. 1997. "The 'Hidden Hand' Behind the Resilience of the Stateless Economy of Somalia," *World Development* 25 (December), pp. 2027–41.

Mueller, Reinhold C. 1997. *The Venetian Money Market: Banks, Panics, and the Public Debt, 1200–1500*. Baltimore: John Hopkins University Press.

Mukherjee, B. N. 2012. "Money and Social Changes in India (up to c. AD 1200)," in S. Z. H. Jafri, ed., *Recording the Progress of Indian History: Symposia Papers of the Indian History Congress*, pp. 411–32. Delhi: Primus Books.

Mundell, Robert. 1999. "A Reconsideration of the Twentieth Century." www.nobelprize.org/uploads/2018/06/mundell-lecture.pdf.

Nagarajan, Shalini. 2022. "Bitcoin Is Losing Its Dominance over Other Cryptocurrencies in Payments to Merchants, Crypto Processor BitPay Says," *Markets Insider* (17 January), https://markets.businessinsider.com/news/currencies/bitcoin-crypto-payments-merchants-dominance-losing-bitpay-ether-stablecoins-transactions-2022-1.

Nakamoto, Satoshi. 2008a. "Bitcoin: A Peer-to-Peer Electronic Cash System." https://bitcoin.org/bitcoin.pdf.

Nakamoto, Satoshi. 2008b. "Bitcoin P2P e-cash paper" (31 October), satoshi.nakamotoinstitute.org/emails/cryptography/1/

Nakamoto, Satoshi. 2008b. "Bitcoin P2P e-cash paper" (17 November), satoshi.nakamotoinstitute.org/emails/cryptography/15/

Nakamoto, Satoshi. 2009a. "Bitcoin v0.1 released," www.metzdowd.com/pipermail/cryptography/2009-January/014994.html.

Nakamoto, Satoshi. 2009b. "Bitcoin Open Source Implementation of P2P Currency" (9 February), http://p2pfoundation.ning.com/forum/topics/bitcoin-open-source.

Nakamoto, Satoshi. 2009c. "Re: Questions About Bitcoin," bitcointalk.org/index.php?topic=13.msg46#msg46.

Nakamoto, Satoshi. 2010. "Re: They Want to Delete the Wikipedia Article" (20 July). https://bitcointalk.org/index.php?topic=342.msg4508#msg4508.

Namcios. "Solo Bitcoin Miner with Only 120 TH Finds Valid Block," *Bitcoin Magazine* (11 January), bitcoinmagazine.com/markets/solo-bitcoin-miner-finds-valid-block.

Narayan, Arvind, and Jeremy Clark. 2017. "Bitcoin's Academic Pedigree," *ACM Queue* 15 (July–August), pp. 20–49. https://dl.acm.org/doi/10.1145/3134434.3136559.

Newberry, Emma. 2021. "Coinbase vs. PayPal: Which Crypto Exchange Is Right for You?," *The Ascent blog* (30 November), www.fool.com/the-ascent/cryptocurrency/coinbase-vs-paypal/.

NewLibertyStandard. 2009. https://web.archive.org/web/20091229132610/https://newlibertystandard.wetpaint.com/page/Exchange+Rate.

NewLibertyStandard. 2010a. "Re: New Exchange Service: 'BTC 2 PSC'," https://bitcointalk.org/index.php?topic=15.msg111#msg111.

NewLibertyStandard. 2010b. "Re: New Exchange (Bitcoin Market)," https://bitcointalk.org/index.php?topic=20.msg662#msg662.

Nikkei Asia. 2022. "Myanmar's Pro-democracy Forces Resist with Cryptocurrency: Tether Emerges as Potential Savior for People Seeking Freedom over Their Assets" (16 January), https://asia.nikkei.com/Spotlight/Cryptocurrencies/Myanmar-s-pro-democracy-forces-resist-with-cryptocurrency.

Noyes, Alfred Dana. 1910. *History of the National-bank Currency*. Washington, DC: Government Printing Office.

Odell, John S. 1982. *U.S. International Monetary Policy: Markets, Power, and Ideas as Sources of Change*. Princeton, NJ: Princeton University Press.

O'Donoghue, Jim, Louise Goulding, and Grahame Allen. 2004. "Consumer Price Inflation since 1750," *UK Office of National Statistics Economic Trends* 604 (March), pp. 38–46.

Onion. 2016. "U.S. Economy Grinds to Halt as Nation Realizes Money Just a Symbolic, Mutually Shared Illusion" (16 February), www.theonion.com/u-s-economy-grinds-to-halt-as-nation-realizes-money-ju-1819571322.

Oresme, Nicholas. 2000 [1355]. "*De Moneta*," trans. Charles Johnson, in Lawrence H. White, ed., *The History of Gold and Silver* (3 vols.), vol. 1, pp. 1–36. London: Pickering and Chatto.

Osipovich, Alexander. 2021. "Upstart Peer-to-Peer Crypto Exchanges Take Aim at Coinbase," *Wall St. Journal* (24 May), www.wsj.com/articles/upstart-peer-to-peer-crypto-exchanges-take-aim-at-coinbase-11621848601.

Ostroy, Joseph M., and Starr, Ross M. 1990. "The Transactions Role of Money," in Benjamin M. Friedman and Frank H. Hahn, eds., *Handbook of Monetary Economics*, vol. 1. Amsterdam: North-Holland.

Palyi, Mechior. 1936. "Liquidity. Minneapolis: Minnesota Bankers Association." Online at https://babel.hathitrust.org/cgi/pt?id=wu.89101073567.

Patinkin, Don. 1965. *Money, Interest, and Prices*, 2nd. ed. New York: Harper & Row.

Perez, Sarah. 2022. "Block's Cash App Adopts Lightning Network for Free Bitcoin Payments," Tech Crunch (18 January), https://techcrunch.com/2022/01/18/blocks-cash-app-adopts-lightning-network-for-free-bitcoin-payments/.

Pirenne, Henri. 1925. *Medieval Cities and the Revival of Trade*. Princeton: Princeton University Press.

Pitta, Julie. 1999. "Requiem for a Bright Idea," *Forbes* (1 November), www.forbes.com/forbes/1999/1101/6411390a.html?sh=622828b3715f.

Pocher, Nadia. 2021. "Self-hosted Wallets: The Elephant in the Room?," KU Leuven Centre for IT & IP Law blog (11 March), www.law.kuleuven.be/citip/blog/self-hosted-wallets/.

Popper, Nathaniel. 2015. "The Shy College Student Who Helped Build Bitcoin into a Global Phenomenon," *The Verge* (10 June), www.theverge.com/2015/6/10/8751933/the-shy-college-student-who-helped-build-bitcoin-into-a-global.

Powell, James. 2005. *The History of the Canadian Dollar*. Ottawa: Bank of Canada.

Qureshi, Haseeb. 2019. "The Cypherpunks," https://nakamoto.com/the-cypherpunks/

Quinn, Stephen. 1997. "Goldsmith-Banking: Mutual Acceptance and Interbanker Clearing in Restoration London," *Explorations in Economic History* 34 (October), pp. 411–32.

rcm___. 2022. https://twitter.com/rcm___/status/1492861918419329025.

Reed, John. 2021. "Cash Shortage Threatens a Banking Crisis in Myanmar," *Financial Times* (30 May), www.ft.com/content/7632c1b0-4581-434f-86d6-bdceaff8e947.

Rolnick, Arthur J., and Warren E. Weber. 1997. "Money, Inflation, and Output under Alternative Monetary Standards," *Journal of Political Economy* 105 (December), pp. 1308–21.

Rockoff, Hugh. 1984. "Some Evidence on the Real Price of Gold, Its Costs of Production, and Commodity Prices," in Michael D. Bordon and Anna J. Schwartz, eds., *A Retrospective on the Classical Gold Standard, 1821–1931*, pp. 613–44. Chicago: University of Chicago Press.

Rothbard, Murray N. 1962. "The Case for a 100 Percent Gold Dollar," in Leland B. Yeager, ed., *In Search of a Monetary Constitution*, pp. 94–136. Cambridge, MA: Harvard University Press.

Rothbard, Murray N. 1985. "The Case for a Genuine Gold Dollar," in Llewellyn H. Rockwell, Jr., ed., *The Gold Standard: An Austrian Perspective*, pp. 1–17. Lexington, MA: D.C. Heath.

Rothbard, Murray N. 1990. *What Has Government Done to Our Money?*, Auburn, AL: Ludwig von Mises Institute. www.mises.org/rothbard/rothmoney.pdf.

Rousseau, Peter L., and Paul Wachtel. 2001. "Inflation, Financial Development and Growth," in T. Negishi, R. V. Ramachandran, and K. Mino, eds., *Economic Theory, Dynamics and Markets*, pp. 309–24. Boston: Springer.

Rueff, Jacques. 1972. *The Monetary Sin of the West*. New York: Macmillan.

Sargent, Thomas J. 1982. "The Ends of Four Big Inflations," in Robert E. Hall, ed., *Inflation: Causes and Effects*, pp. 41–98. Chicago: University of Chicago Press.

Sargent, Thomas J. 2011. "Where to Draw Lines: Stability Versus Efficiency," *Economica* 78 (April), pp. 197–214.

Sargent, Thomas J., and François R. Velde. 2003. *The Big Problem of Small Change*. Princeton: Princeton University Press.

Sargent, Thomas J., and Neil Wallace. 1981. "Some Unpleasant Monetarist Arithmetic," *Federal Reserve Bank of Minneapolis Quarterly Review* 5 (Fall), pp. 1–17.

Sargent, Thomas J., and Neil Wallace. 1982. "The Real Bills Doctrine versus the Quantity Theory: A Reconsideration," *Journal of Political Economy* 90 (December), pp. 1212–36.

Schabas, Margaret, and Carl Wennerlind. 2020. *A Philosopher's Economist: Hume and the Rise of Capitalism*. Chicago: University of Chicago Press.

Schaps, David M. 2006. "The Invention of Coinage in Lydia, in India, and in China," working paper presented at XIV International Economic History Congress, Helsinki, www.slideshare.net/dokka/the-invention-of-coinage-in-lydia-in-india-and-in-china.

Schär, Fabian, and Aleksander Berentsen. 2020. *Bitcoin, Blockchain, and Cryptoassets: A Comprehensive Introduction*. Cambridge, MA: MIT Press.

Schneider, Howard, and Anthony Faiola. 2011. "Jump in European Borrowing Costs Adds to Debt Crisis," *Washington Post* (16 November 2011), p. A17.

Schneiders, Sven. 2020. "The End of Gold: The Reason Why Bitcoin Is Much Better Money," *Unfashionable* blog (17 July), https://unfashionable.substack.com/p/the-end-of-gold.

Schuler, Kurt. 1992. "The World History of Free Banking: An Overview," in Kevin Dowd, ed., *The Experience of Free Banking*, pp. 4–47. London: Routledge.

Schumpeter, Joseph. 1954. *History of Economic Analysis*. New York: Oxford University Press.

Selgin, George A. 1988. *The Theory of Free Banking*. Totowa, NJ: Rowman and Littlefield.

Selgin, George A. 1989. "The Analytical Framework of the Real-Bills Doctrine." *Journal of Institutional and Theoretical Economics (JITE) / Zeitschrift Für Die Gesamte Staatswissenschaft* 145 (September), pp. 489–507.

Selgin, George. 1994a. "Are Banking Crises a Free-Market Phenomenon?," *Critical Review* 8 (September), pp. 59–608.

Selgin, George. 1994b. "On Ensuring the Acceptability of a New Fiat Money," *Journal of Money, Credit and Banking* 26 (November), pp. 808–26.

Selgin, George. 2008. *Good Money: Birmingham Button Makers, the Royal Mint, and the Beginnings of Modern Coinage, 1775–1821: Private Enterprise and Popular Coinage*. Ann Arbor: University of Michigan Press.

Selgin, George. 2012. "Those Dishonest Goldsmiths," *Financial History Review* 19 (December), pp. 269–88.

Selgin, George. 2013. "The Rise and Fall of the Gold Standard in the United States," Cato Institute Policy Analysis no. 729 (20 June).

Selgin, George. 2015. "Synthetic Commodity Money," *Journal of Financial Stability* 17 (April), pp. 92–99.

Selgin, George. 2016. "The Myth of the Myth of Barter," *Alt-M* blog (15 March), www.alt-m.org/2016/03/15/myth-myth-barter/.

Selgin, George. 2021. "The Fable of the Cats," *Alt-M* blog (6 July), www.alt-m.org/2021/07/06/the-fable-of-the-cats/.

Selgin, George, William D. Lastrapes, and Lawrence H. White. 2012. "Has the Fed Been a Failure?" *Journal of Macroeconomics* 34 (September), pp. 569–96.

Selgin, George A., and Lawrence H. White. 1994. "How Would the Invisible Hand Handle Money?" *Journal of Economic Literature* 32 (December), pp. 1718–49.

Selgin, George A., and Lawrence H. White. 1996. "In Defense of Fiduciary Media," *Review of Austrian Economics* 9 (September 1996), pp. 83–107.

Selgin, George A., and Lawrence H. White. 1999. "A Fiscal Theory of Government's Role in Money," *Economic Inquiry* 37 (January), pp. 154–65.

Selgin, George, and Lawrence H. White. 2005. "Credible Currency: A Constitutional Perspective," *Constitutional Political Economy* 16 (March 2005): 71–83.

Sidgwick, Henry. 1883. *Principles of Political Economy*. London: Macmillan.

Sigalos, MacKenzie. 2021. "Inside China's Underground Crypto Mining Operation, Where People Are Risking It All to Make Bitcoin," CNBC.com (18 December), www.cnbc.com/2021/12/18/chinas-underground-bitcoin-miners-.html.

Simons, Henry C. 1934. *A Positive Program for Laissez-Faire: Some Proposals for a Liberal Economic Policy*. Public Policy Pamphlet No. 15, ed. Harry D. Gideonse. Chicago: University of Chicago Press.

Skidelsky, Robert. 2018. *Money and Government: The Past and Future of Economics*. New Haven: Yale University Press.

Skynova. 2021. "Accepting Bitcoin Payments." www.skynova.com/blog/accepting-bitcoin.

Smiley, Gene. 1975. "Interest Rate Movement in the United States, 1888–1913," *Journal of Economic History* 35 (September), pp. 591–620.

Smith, Adam. 1982 [1776]. *An Inquiry into the Nature and Causes of the Wealth of Nations*. eds. R. H. Campbell and A. S. Skinner. Indianapolis: Liberty Fund.

Smith, Vera C. 1936. *The Rationale of Central Banking*. London: P. S. King.

Sobrado, Boaz. 2021. "We All Need to Stop Seeing Only the Dark Side of Crypto," *Wired* (19 December), www.wired.com/story/crypto-remittances-cuba/.

Spufford, Peter. 1988. *Money and Its Use in Medieval Europe*. Cambridge: Cambridge University Press.

Stankiewicz, Kevin. 2021. "'Black Swan' Author Calls Bitcoin a 'Gimmick' and a 'Game,' Says It Resembles a Ponzi Scheme," CNBC.com (23 April), www.cnbc.com/2021/04/23/bitcoin-a-gimmick-and-resembles-a-ponzi-scheme-black-swan-author-.html.

Statista. 2022. "Number of Blockchain Wallet Users Worldwide from November 2011 to January 9, 2022," www.statista.com/statistics/647374/worldwide-blockchain-wallet-users/.

Sumner, Scott. 2021. *The Money Illusion: Market Monetarism, the Great Recession, and the Future of Monetary Policy*. Chicago: University of Chicago Press.

Szabo, Nick. 1999. "Intrapolynomial Cryptography," https://web.archive.org/web/20011217091748/http://szabo.best.vwh.net/intrapoly.html.

Szabo, Nick. 2002. "Shelling Out." https://nakamotoinstitute.org/shelling-out/.

Szabo, Nick. 2005. "Bit Gold." *Unenumerated* blog, http://unenumerated.blogspot.com/2005/12/bit-gold.html.

Szabo, Nick. 2011. "Bitcoin, what took ye so long?" *Unenumerated* blog (28 May), https://unenumerated.blogspot.com/2011/05/bitcoin-what-took-ye-so-long.html.

Szabo, Nick. 2017. "Money, Blockchains, and Social Scalability," *Unenumerated* blog (9 February) https://unenumerated.blogspot.com/2017/02/money-block-chains-and-social-scalability.html.

Szabo, Nick. 2019a. https://twitter.com/NickSzabo4/status/1165334657170165761.

Szabo, Nick. 2019b. https://twitter.com/NickSzabo4/status/1154788102986092545.

Szabo, Nick. 2019c. https://twitter.com/nickszabo4/status/1154798946369146880.

Tamny, John. 2010. "Gold Standard for Inflation," *Orange County Register* (1 February). www.ocregister.com/2010/02/01/john-tamny-gold-standard-for-inflation/.

Tamny, John. 2019a. "Blaming Gold for the 1930s Is Like Kim Jong-un Blaming the Foot for His Height," *Real Clear Markets* blog (11 April). www.realclearmarkets.com/articles/2019/04/11/economists_trashing_the_gold_standard_is_like_kim_jong-un_trashing_the_foot_103690.html.

Tamny, John. 2019b. "Your Move Gold Critics: Please Explain What Money Is," *Real Clear Markets* blog (9 April). www.realclearmarkets.com/articles/2019/04/09/your_move_gold_critics_please_explain_what_money_is_103688.html.

Taylor, Alan. 2002. *American Colonies: The Settling of North America*. New York: Penguin.

Taylor, John B. 2019. *Reform of the International Monetary System: Why and How?* Cambridge: MIT Press.

Taylor, Stephanie. 2022. "Ontario Freezes Funds from GiveSendGo Trucker Convoy Fundraiser," *Global News* (10 February), https://globalnews.ca/news/8610512/givesendgo-fundraiser-trucker-convoy-frozen/.

Thornton, Henry. 1802. *An Enquiry into the Nature and Effects of the Paper Credit of Great Britain*. London: J. Hatchard.

Timberlake, Richard H. 2008. "The Federal Reserve's Role in the Great Contraction and the Subprime Crisis," *Cato Journal* 28 (Spring/Summer), pp. 303–12.

Urquilla, Katlen. 2021. "Solo $44.6 millones de remesas llegó por billeteras de criptomonedas a El Salvador," elsalvador.com, www.elsalvador.com/noticias/negocios/el-salvador-bitcoin-remesas-familiares-bcr-chivo-wallet/910438/2021/.

Valenzuela, Joël. 2017. "As Bitcoin Becomes New Gold, Ex Fed Chairman Calls for Return to Gold Standard," *Cointelegraph* (22 February), https://cointelegraph.com/news/as-bitcoin-becomes-new-gold-ex-fed-chairman-calls-for-return-to-gold-standard.

van der Crabben, Jan. 2011. "Coinage," *Ancient History Encyclopedia* website, www.ancient.eu/coinage/.

Van Wirdum, Aaron. 2018. "The Genesis Files: With Bit Gold, Szabo Was Inches away from Inventing Bitcoin," *Bitcoin Magazine* (12 July), https://bitcoinmagazine.com/culture/genesis-files-bit-gold-szabo-was-inches-away-inventing-bitcoin.

Vasquez, Alex, and Ezra Fieser. 2021. "In Venezuela, People Break Off Flakes of Gold to Pay for Meals and Haircuts," *Bloomberg News* (20 October), www.bloomberg.com/news/articles/2021-10-20/venezuelans-break-off-flakes-of-gold-to-pay-for-meals-haircuts.

Walras, Léon. 1954. *Elements of Pure Economics*, trans. by William Jaffé. London: Allen & Unwin.

Watson, Michael V. Spindzor. 2022. "Menger vs. Chartalism on the Origins of Money: Theory and History," Ph.D. dissertation, George Mason University.

Weber, Warren. 2016. "A Bitcoin Standard: Lessons from the Gold Standard," Bank of Canada Staff Working Paper 2016–14 (March). www.bankofcanada.ca/wp-content/uploads/2016/03/swp2016-14.pdf.

Whaples, Robert. 2008. "California Gold Rush," *EH.Net Encyclopedia*, ed. Robert Whaples (16 March), at http://eh.net/encyclopedia/california-gold-rush/.

White, Lawrence H. 1984a. "Competitive Payment Systems and the Unit of Account," *American Economic Review* 74 (September), pp. 699–712.

White, Lawrence H. 1984b. *Free Banking in Britain: Theory, Experience, and Debate*. Cambridge: Cambridge University Press.

White, Lawrence H. 1986. "A Subjectivist Perspective on the Definition and Identification of Money," in Israel M. Kirzner, ed., *Subjectivism, Intelligibility, and Economic Understanding: Essays in Honor of Ludwig M. Lachmann on his Eightieth Birthday*, pp. 301–14. New York: New York University Press.

White, Lawrence H. 1989. "What Kinds of Monetary Institutions Would a Free Market Deliver?," *Cato Journal* 9 (Fall), pp. 367–91.

White, Lawrence H. 1995. "Thoughts on the Economics of Digital Currency," *Extropy* #15 (Q2-3), pp. 16–19. https://github.com/Extropians/Extropy/blob/master/ext15.pdf.

White, Lawrence H. 1999. *The Theory of Monetary Institutions*. Oxford: Basil Blackwell.

White, Lawrence H. 2000. "Introduction," to White, ed., *The History of Gold and Silver*, vol. 1, pp. vii–xxxiii. London: Pickering and Chatto.

White, Lawrence H. 2002. "Does a Superior Monetary Standard Spontaneously Emerge?," *Journal des Economistes et des Etudes Humaines* 12 (June/September 2002), pp. 269–81.

White, Lawrence H. 2003. "Accounting for Fractional-Reserve Banknotes and Deposits – or, What's Twenty Quid to the Bloody Midland Bank," *The Independent Review* 7 (Winter), pp. 425–43.

White, Lawrence H. 2005. "The Federal Reserve System's Influence on Research in Monetary Economics," *Econ Journal Watch* 2 (August), pp. 325–54. https://econjwatch.org/articles/the-federal-reserve-system-s-influence-on-research-in-monetary-economics.

White, Lawrence H. 2008. "Is the Gold Standard Still the Gold Standard among Monetary Systems?," Cato Institute Briefing Paper No. 100 (8 February). www.cato.org/publications/briefing-paper/is-gold-standard-still-gold-standard-among-monetary-systems.

White, Lawrence H. 2012. *The Clash of Economic Ideas*. Cambridge: Cambridge University Press.

White, Lawrence H. 2013. "Recent Arguments against the Gold Standard," *Cato Institute Policy Analysis* 728 (20 June). www.cato.org/publications/policy-analysis/recent-arguments-against-gold-standard.

White, Lawrence H. 2014. "The Troubling Suppression of Competition from Alternative Monies: The Cases of the Liberty Dollar and E-gold," *Cato Journal* 34 (Spring/Summer), pp. 281–301.

White, Lawrence H. 2015. "The Merits and Feasibility of a Commodity Standard," *Journal of Financial Stability* 17 (April), pp. 59–64.

White, Lawrence H. 2016. "Needed: A Federal Reserve Exit from Preferential Credit Allocation," *Cato Journal* 36 (Spring/Summer), pp. 353–65.

White, Lawrence H. 2018a. "How a Bitcoin System Is Like and Unlike a Gold Standard," *Alt-M* blog (11 January), www.alt-m.org/2018/01/11/how-a-bitcoin-system-is-like-and-unlike-a-gold-standard/.

White, Lawrence H. 2018b. "Bitcoin: More Trustworthy than some Academic Critics," *Alt-M* blog (22 February), www.alt-m.org/2018/02/22/bitcoin-more-trustworthy-than-some-academic-critics/.

White, Lawrence H. 2018. "The Output Gap, the Federal Budget Deficit, and the Threat of Debt Monetization," *Alt-M* blog (15 May), www.alt-m.org/2018/05/15/the-output-gap-the-federal-budget-deficit-and-the-threat-of-debt-monetization/.

White, Lawrence H. 2018c. "Why the State Theory of Money Doesn't Explain the Coinage of Precious Metals," *Alt-M* blog (24 August), www.alt-m.org/2017/08/24/why-the-state-theory-of-money-doesnt-explain-the-coinage-of-precious-metals/.

White, Lawrence H. 2019a. "A Gold Standard Does Not Require Interest-Rate Targeting," *Alt-M* blog (18 April), www.alt-m.org/2019/04/18/a-gold-standard-does-not-require-interest-rate-targeting/.

White, Lawrence H. 2019b. "The Resource Costs of Fiat Money Are Now Higher Than Those of a Gold Standard," *Alt-M* blog (17 December), www.alt-m.org/2019/12/17/the-resource-costs-of-fiat-money-are-now-higher-than-those-of-a-gold-standard/.

White, Lawrence H. 2021. "The End of Bretton Woods, Jacques Rueff, and 'The Monetary Sin of the West'," *Alt-M* blog, www.alt-m.org/2021/08/10/the-end-of-bretton-woods-jacques-rueff-and-the-monetary-sin-of-the-west/.

White, Lawrence H. 2022. "The Private Mint in Economics: Evidence from the American Gold Rushes," *Economic History Review* 75 (February), pp. 3–21.

White, Lawrence H., Viktor J. Vanberg, and Ekkehard A. Köhler, eds. 2015. *Renewing the Search for a Monetary Constitution*. Washington, DC: Cato Institute.

Williams, F. M. 1922. "International Price Indexes. The French Index Number," *Federal Reserve Bulletin* 8 (August), pp. 922–29.

World Gold Council. 2018. "Cryptocurrencies Are No Substitute for Gold," *GoldHub* blog (25 January), www.gold.org/goldhub/research/cryptocurrencies-are-no-substitute-gold.

World Gold Council. 2019. "Above Ground Stocks" (31 January), at www.gold.org/goldhub/data/above-ground-stocks.

World Gold Council. 2021. "Above Ground Stocks," Gold Hub data site, www.gold.org/goldhub/data/above-ground-stocks.

Wray, L. Randall. 2000. "Modern Money," in John Smithin, ed., *What Is Money?*, pp. 43–66. London: Routledge.

Wray, L. Randall. 2004. "The Credit Money and State Money Approaches," Levy Economics Institute of Bard College working paper 32 (April), at https://pdfs.semanticscholar.org/5a43/df7322cd84df5062de2d668eb6f076bec16e.pdf.

Wray, L. Randall. 2009. "Money and the Public Purpose: The Modern Money Theory Approach," Multiplier Effect: The Levy Institute Blog (27 October), at https://multiplier-effect.org/money-and-the-public-purpose-the-modern-money-theory-approach/.

Wray, L. Randall. 2014. "From the State Theory of Money to Modern Money Theory: An Alternative to Economic Orthodoxy," Levy Economics Institute of Bard College working paper 792 (March).

Wright, Robert. 2008. "Origins of Commercial Banking in the United States, 1781–1830," *EH.Net Encyclopedia*, ed. Robert Whaples (26 March), http://eh.net/encyclopedia/origins-of-commercial-banking-in-the-united-states-1781-1830/.

Wright, Turner. 2022. "Coin Center Files Lawsuit against US Treasury over Tornado Cash Sanctions," *Cointelegraph* (12 October), https://cointelegraph.com/news/coin-center-files-lawsuit-against-us-treasury-over-tornado-cash-sanctions.

Yeager, Leland B. 1966. *International Monetary Relations: Theory, History, and Policy*. New York: Harper & Row.

Yeager, Leland B. 1984. "The Image of the Gold Standard," in Michael D. Bordo and Anna J. Schwartz, eds., *A Retrospective on the Classical Gold Standard, 1821–1931*, pp. 651–69. Chicago: University of Chicago Press.

Index

Printed in the United States
by Baker & Taylor Publisher Services